Online Offending Behaviour and Child Victimization

Online Offending Behaviour and Child Victimization

New Findings and Policy

Edited by

Stephen Webster
Research Psychologist, Policy Research Centre, National Centre for Social Research, UK

Julia Davidson
Professor of Criminology, Middlesex University, UK; Co-Director, Centre for Abuse and Trauma Studies, UK; Adjunct Professor, Faculty of Law, Queensland University of Technology, Australia

Antonia Bifulco
Professor of Psychology and Head of the Department of Psychology, Middlesex University, UK; Co-Director of the Centre for Abuse and Trauma Studies, UK

palgrave
macmillan

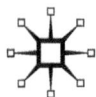

First published 2015 by
PALGRAVE MACMILLAN

Palgrave Macmillan in the UK is an imprint of Macmillan Publishers Limited,
registered in England, company number 785998, of Houndmills, Basingstoke,
Hampshire RG21 6XS.

Palgrave Macmillan in the US is a division of St Martin's Press LLC,
175 Fifth Avenue, New York, NY 10010.

Palgrave Macmillan is the global academic imprint of the above companies
and has companies and representatives throughout the world.

Palgrave® and Macmillan® are registered trademarks in the United States,
the United Kingdom, Europe and other countries.

ISBN 978–1–137–36509–5

This book is printed on paper suitable for recycling and made from fully
managed and sustained forest sources. Logging, pulping and manufacturing
processes are expected to conform to the environmental regulations of the
country of origin.

A catalogue record for this book is available from the British Library.

A catalog record for this book is available from the Library of Congress.

In memory of Stefano Ciulla and Vincent Bifulco

Contents

Tables and Figures

Tables

Figures

Preface and Acknowledgements

When we wrote our research proposal in 2008 to the European Commission Safer Internet Plus Programme, a core aim of the European Online Grooming Project was for the work to have applied operational value to support frontline child protection efforts. Since 2011, the project team has tackled that goal by travelling around the globe presenting findings to law-enforcement officers, social workers, teachers, students, academics and policymakers. We remain very grateful for the feedback that these expert audiences have given, which has helped refine our thinking in this sensitive area of work. More recently, we were delighted to hear that our work has helped shape online grooming legislation in Belgium and Italy, has informed sexual offences policy in England and Wales (2013) and was quoted by Interpol investigators as an example of good practice.

The motivation for writing this book was to set the project findings in the context of recent research in this area. We have therefore gone back to our original dataset and reports and present here some additional analysis of our data about the role of online networks and technology in the sexual abuse of children and young people. However, it seems clear to us that online technology is developing at a pace which high-quality research struggles to match. Therefore, we cannot assume this book will be definitive about online abuse and grooming at the time of press. When this book is in circulation, the nature and extent of online risks to children and young people may have developed further. We would encourage further testing of and challenges to all the findings presented here to ensure the evidence base on which critical policy and practice decisions are made is as robust as possible. We would also add that within the scope of this book, it has not been possible for us to cover every theory and piece of evidence about online abuse, and so apologize for any omissions that readers may identify.

Finally, we would like to acknowledge the support and encouragement of Harriet Barker at Palgrave Macmillan, and Evangelia Markidou and Margareta Traung from the European Commission Safer Internet Plus Programme. We are indebted to the outstanding contribution made by our colleagues on the European Online Grooming Project research team: Petter Gottschalk, Vincenzo Caretti, Thierry Pham, Julie Grove-Hills, Caroline Turley, Charlotte Tompkins, Stefano Ciulla, Vanessa

Milazzo, Adriano Schimmenti and Giuseppe Craparo. Of course, we would also like to thank and acknowledge all the participants from the European Online Grooming Project who spoke so openly to us about some of their challenging experiences of life online. We dedicate this book to our colleagues in online law enforcement, offender management and child protection for their inspirational work in keeping children and young people safe.

Stephen Webster, Julia Davidson and Antonia Bifulco

Contributors

Stephen Webster, CPsychol AFBPsS, is a research psychologist at the National Centre for Social Research. He has been directing and conducting research into sexual offending in the United Kingdom and internationally for 16 years and has published extensively in the area.

Julia Davidson, PhD, is Professor of Criminology at Middlesex University Law School and is Co-Director of the Centre for Abuse and Trauma Studies. She is one of the United Kingdom's foremost experts on child sexual abuse and online offending. She plays an active role in key national committees such as the UK Council for Child Internet Safety (Chair of the Evidence Group) and provides expert advice to international organizations such as UNICEF, ECPAT, the US Sentencing Commission and the UN ITU. She has directed a large amount of research spanning 25 years in the criminal justice area and is known for her work with child sexual offenders and young victims of abuse.

Antonia Bifulco, PhD, is Professor of Lifespan Psychology and Head of Department of Psychology at Middlesex University. She is Co-Director of the Centre for Abuse and Trauma Studies. Her 35-year research career has been focused on impacts of childhood neglect and abuse on lifetime psychological disorder and attachment difficulties. She is known for her development of interviews to assess childhood maltreatment and lifetime psychosocial risk factors, which are now used in research internationally and increasingly in practice contexts. She is involved in projects looking at childhood maltreatment, including sexual abuse, in both offender and victim groups.

Vincenzo Caretti is a psychoanalyst, clinical psychologist and Professor of Dynamic Psychology at the Department of Human Science, LUMSA University of Rome, Italy.

Petter Gottschalk is Professor in the Department of Leadership and Organizational Management at BI Norwegian Business School in Oslo, Norway, where he teaches courses on white-collar crime detection and prevention. He did his master's degrees in Germany and the United States, and his doctoral degree in the United Kingdom. He has been managing director of several companies, including ABB Datacables and the Norwegian Computing Centre.

Julie Grove-Hills is a research associate in the Department of Criminology and Sociology at Middlesex University Law School, United Kingdom. For the last five years, she has worked with Professor Davidson and Professor Bifulco at the Centre for Abuse and Trauma Studies.

Thierry Pham is a psychologist and Professor of Forensic Psychology, UMons, Belgium. He is also Director of the Centre de Recherche en Défense Sociale, Tournai.

Adriano Schimmenti is Professor of Dynamic and Clinical Psychology at UKE – Kore Univeristy of Enna, Italy. He is also the Vice-Director of the SIPDC – the Italian Society of Psychological Assessment.

1
The Context of Online Abuse: Policy and Legislation

Julia Davidson and Petter Gottschalk

Introduction

In less than two decades, the internet has moved from being a communications channel used by an elite few to an everyday tool used in our homes, schools, workplaces and on our travels. It enables people to search for information, perform routine tasks and communicate with others at any time of day or night. The technological aspects of the internet are developing at the same high speed as the increase in the number of users globally. The internet provides a social context for us to meet with others and to exchange information on a scale we would never have thought possible in the past. The World Wide Web is a system with universally accepted standards for storing, retrieving, formatting, changing and displaying information in a networked environment. Information is stored and displayed as electronic pages that can contain numbers, text, pictures, graphics, sound and video. These web pages can be linked electronically to other web pages, independent of where they are located, and web pages can be viewed by any type of computer. This chapter sets out the legislation and policy that can help to conceptualize the diverse forms of online sexual abuse described in subsequent chapters. It begins by looking at prevalence data about young people online before providing a brief summary of what we know about the rate of sexual offending online. The chapter then examines legislation and policy at the European and global level, before exploring the role of industry in combating child sexual abuse online.

Young people online

Information technology (IT) now forms a core part of the formal education system in many countries, ensuring that each new generation of young internet users is more adept than the last. Recent comparative work (Livingstone, Haddon, Görzig & Ólafsson, 2011) on internet use across 25 European countries reveals that there have been substantial changes between 2005 and 2013. In 2005, 70 per cent of 6–17-year-olds in the European Union used the internet and by 2010, this figure had risen to 93 per cent. The most striking rise has been amongst younger children: By 2008, 60 per cent of 6–10-year-olds were online and in 2010, one third of 9–10-year-olds who used the internet went online daily. There has also been a substantial change between 2005 and 2012 concerning the location of use. In 2005, use of the internet at school was as common as home use. By 2010, 87 per cent of 6–17-year-olds were much more likely to use the internet at home (Livingstone & Haddon, 2009) and by 2012, many children were also using mobile devices to access the internet (Livingstone, 2011).

Most research exploring children's online behaviour has focused on North America and Europe, but there is some research from developing countries which also suggests increased internet usage amongst children. In Asia, internet access has also grown exponentially. Usage in Bangladesh, for example, grew by 143 per cent between 2000 and 2005; there are now over half a million people with internet access in the region (UN ITU, 2014). A recent survey of schoolchildren undertaken in Nepal suggests that 81 per cent of 14–18-year-olds (of a sample of 1430) were accessing the internet on a weekly basis, 51 per cent of the sample had home access and many children were using internet cafes (CWIN Nepal, 2011). In Bahrain, internet use grew from 40,000 (5.7% of the population) in 2000 to 402,900 (55.3%) in 2009 and continues to grow (UN ITU, 2014). In Russia, recent research from the Foundation for Internet Development (2009) on children and teenagers' online attitudes and perceptions shows that the internet is the primary information source ahead of television, books and printed mass media for both 14–15-year-olds and 16–17-year-olds. Approximately 65 per cent of 16–17-year-olds said that their parents allowed them free use of the internet and did so without imposing any time limit.

With regard to *how* young people connect online, there has been growth in the use of alternative devices. Mobile phone use is widespread amongst children and young people and an increasing number access the internet using a mobile phone or alternative mobile device. Young people make extensive use of the internet using interactive services such as games, social networking sites and instant messages, increasingly found as mobile phone applications (or 'apps'). The most significant difference between internet usage amongst children in industrialized and developing countries appears to be the mode of access, with children in developing nations increasingly gaining access using mobile phones. It has been estimated that there are approximately 376 million subscribers to cell phone technology in the African continent, where this form of technology is more affordable and more easily accessed than personal computers.[1]

Alongside the method of connection, gender appears to be a key issue in terms of internet access and usage, with different patterns emerging. A recent UK survey of schoolchildren examined the difference in use of technology between girls and boys. It revealed that girls were more likely than boys were to use mobile phones and digital cameras, with boys more likely than girls were to play computer and console games (Eynon, 2009). However, recent research suggests that in some developing nations, girls are less likely to have frequent access to the internet than boys are (Gasser, Maclay & Palfrey, 2010). A large survey of 10,000 girls in ten Indian cities found that only 4 per cent of 'girls on the street' had even heard of the internet and awareness about the internet varied enormously by city (Plan India, 2010, p40).[2] Access to the internet ranged from 13–18 per cent of the total sample, with wide variation by city. For example, in Kolkata (where poverty is high), only 5 per cent of girls had access compared to 36 per cent in Pune. Only 10 per cent of girls using the internet knew how to report online abuse, with a complete lack of awareness amongst the sample about potential online risks noted. The report concludes that girls who are socially disadvantaged are more often denied access to new technology. In contrast, research conducted in Bahrain suggested no significant gender differences in terms of online communication: boys were just as likely as girls were to use the internet to communicate with friends (61% and 62%, respectively). However, girls were less likely than boys were to play online games (36% of girls compared to 50% of boys) (Davidson & Martellozzo, 2011).

Although children's use of the internet is globally widespread, cultural differences help define what is considered acceptable practice. Whilst little research has been conducted in the Middle East, two studies note that interaction on social networking sites between unrelated female and male adolescents is considered unacceptable in some communities (Davidson & Martellozzo, 2012; Hijazi-Omari & Ribak, 2008). This has resulted particularly in the harsh punishment of girls by their parents,

as has the removal of the hijab or veil in social networking site profile pictures (Davidson & Martellozzo, 2012). It is clear that the focus
on internet behaviour in the West has led to a somewhat narrow view,
which fails to take into account geographical and cultural differences in
the context of usage.

Offenders online

Internet-perpetrated crimes are fairly recent phenomena, and include
a number of different behaviours, with offenders who use the internet to sexually abuse children also falling into overlapping categories.
Specifically, these include offenders who groom children for the purpose
of sexual abuse and offenders who produce and/or download indecent illegal images of children from the internet and distribute them
(Quayle & Taylor, 2002, 2003; Davidson, 2007; Davidson & Martellozzo,
2008). We have very limited knowledge regarding the nature of the
link between online abuse and contact offending, despite a few studies conducted that explore online offender behaviour (Beech, Elliot,
Birgden & Findlater, 2008; Elliott & Beech, 2009; Seto, 2009). This lack
of knowledge understandably underpins the insecurity and anxiety of
those within the criminal justice system tasked with making decisions
about the nature of these offences and the risk they pose to vulnerable
groups within our society (Davidson, 2007).

Child grooming refers to actions deliberately undertaken with the aim
of befriending and establishing an emotional connection to a child in
order to lower the child's inhibitions in preparation for sexual activity with the child. A recent report from the Centre for Missing and
Exploited Children described 2660 incidents of adults using the internet
to befriend and establish an emotional connection with a child in order
to entice them into meeting. What is clear is that the sexual abuse of
young people online is an international problem – a crime without geographical boundaries. This refers to the widespread and international
nature of the crime, but also to the possibility of groomers meeting
their victims outside of their own country. The potential for children
or young people to have contact with sexual offenders increases the
more they use the internet to network with friends. There is, however, limited parallel information available about the behaviours of
internet sexual offenders to inform effective risk-management strategies for policymakers, law-enforcement agencies, parents and young
people. Existing offender research has focused almost exclusively on
*intra*personal aspects of offending, ignoring the *inter*personal, group
and situational factors that influence the perpetration of online sexual

offences against children and young people. Quayle and Taylor (2003) comment on the possible motivations of online child sex abusers. They argue that sexual offenders perceive the internet as a way of generating an immediate solution to their sexual fantasies. Factors which encourage offenders to go online include presumed anonymity, disinhibition and ready accessibility. It is also acknowledged that the unique structure of the internet may play a major role in facilitating online child abuse. Whilst the internet itself does not create online abuse, some theoretical approaches to sexual offending emphasize the importance of the context in which offending occurs and how it can be facilitated by the internet (Wortley & Smallbone, 2006). The internet has unique characteristics that can sustain child sexual abuse, including through indecent image collection and online grooming. Findings from the European Online Grooming Project (EOPG) described in this book (Webster, Davidson, Bifulco, Gottschalk, Caretti, Pham et al., 2012) support this contention, as described in later chapters.

Legislation and policy

The last two decades have seen an increasing awareness of the need to provide a global safety net to protect children and ensure their wellbeing; this goal has been instigated and expressed at international level by the United Nations. In 1989, the UN Commission on Human Rights appointed a special reporter to consider matters relating to the rights of children and to consider how universal standards could be translated into action at the national level. This led to the United Nations Convention on the Rights of the Child (UNCRC) in 1990; a groundbreaking international convention requiring signatories to take all appropriate measures to prevent harm to children. The UNCRC gives children a raft of cultural, socio-economic and political rights, underwritten by a covenant that ensures that the child's best interest is the primary consideration for policy. All countries have now ratified the UNCRC with the exception of the United States and Somalia. Since the instigation of the UNCRC, a number of international instruments have strengthened child rights further, including the International Labour Organization (ILO) Convention 182 concerning the Prohibition and Immediate Action for the Elimination of the Worst Forms of Child Labour (1998), the ILO Protocol to Prevent, Suppress and Punish Trafficking on Persons, especially Women and Children, supplementing the UN Convention against Transnational Organized Crime (2000) and the Protocol on the Sale of Children, Child Prostitution and Child Pornography (2000).

The UNCRC is clear regarding under 18 being the age of consent to sexual relations, but there is geographically wide variation. The age of consent is essentially the legal definition of *child,* so such wide variation is clearly problematic and continues to prove a barrier to any international consensus on child safeguarding laws. In the United Kingdom, leading human rights Queen's Counsel Baroness Kennedy has recently argued that the only solution to this problem is to introduce an internationally unified age of consent and to introduce international law courts to address global child abuse (War Child, 2013). This seems particularly pertinent in the context of global internet-mediated crimes against children and the need for effective cross-border policing.

The UNCRC also contains important general principles which should be taken into account throughout all relevant legislation and measures, including the principle that the child's best interests should be considered in actions which affect them. There is also an optional protocol to the CRC on the sale of children, child prostitution and child pornography; this is the only universal treaty specifically addressing this topic. The Committee on the Rights of the Child has been set up to monitor the implementation of the convention by different states, but it is unfortunate that the convention has no real legal jurisdiction and so cannot force individual nations to implement its recommendations.

Political initiatives at national and European levels

Studies that have explored the prevalence of 'sexual solicitation' or 'grooming' (i.e. an adult encouraging a child to talk about or do something sexual or to share personal sexual information; Ybarra, Espelage & Mitchell, 2007) in the general child population have produced a variety of results depending upon the research sample studied and the method employed. For example, one study surveying an adult online population reported that 7.1 per cent of the adult participants had communicated about a sexual topic with unknown adolescents and 0.5 per cent with children (Schulz, Bergen, Schuhmann, Hoyer, Santtila & Osterheider, 2014). In a recent survey, 9 per cent of adolescents in America aged 10 to 17 reported having experienced unwanted sexual solicitation (Jones, Mitchell & Finkelhor, 2012). In comparison, 15 per cent of 11–16-year-olds in Europe had received a sexual message online (Livingstone et al., 2011).

Although there is no certainty regarding the incidence of online 'grooming', the concept has legal status in many countries. The EU Directive on combating child sexual abuse and sexual exploitation (including online grooming) and child pornography, seeking to curb the exploitation of children on the internet, required implementation by member states by the end of November 2013.[3] Grooming legislation has been in place in some EU countries for a number of years – for example, in England and Wales (SoA, 2003: s15), Finland (RL, code, 1998:563) and Sweden (SFS, code, 2009:343). The concept of sexual grooming is well documented in the sexual offender literature (Finkelhor, 1984; Seto, 2013) and is now filtering into legislation policy, crime detection and prevention initiatives. The United Kingdom was the first member state to introduce the new offence category of 'grooming' in 2003. The Sexual Offences Act (2003) in England, Wales and Northern Ireland and the Protection of Children and Prevention of Sexual Offences Act (2005) in Scotland include the offence of 'meeting a child following certain preliminary contact' (Section 1). 'Preliminary contact' refers to occasions where a person arranges to meet a child who is under 16, having met with or communicated with them on at least two previous occasions (in person, on the internet or by using other technologies), with the intention of performing sexual activity on the child. The definition of UK 'grooming' legislation is provided by the Crown Prosecution Service (CPS) (England and Wales) as follows:

> The offence only applies to adults; there must be communication (a meeting or any other form of communication) on at least two previous occasions; it is not necessary for the communications to be of a sexual nature; the communication can take place anywhere in the world; the offender must either meet the child or travel to the pre-arranged meeting; the meeting or at least part of the journey must take place within the jurisdiction; the person must have an intention to commit any offence within or outside of the UK (which would be an offence in the jurisdiction) under Part 1 of the 2003 Act. This may be evident from the previous communications or other circumstances e.g. an offender travels in possession of ropes, condoms or lubricants etc; the child is under 16 and the adult does not reasonably believe that the child is over 16.
>
> (CPS, 2007)

Prior to the introduction of the EU Directive, the only other European countries to have adopted the grooming legislation were Norway (in 2007), Sweden (in 2009) and the Netherlands (in 2010). The relevant section in the General Civil Penal Code (*straffeloven*) concerned with sexual offenders in Norway is Section 195.

Any person who engages in sexual activity with a child who is under 14 years of age shall be liable to imprisonment for a term not exceeding 10 years. If the said activity was sexual intercourse the penalty shall be imprisonment for not less than 2 years. Section 196 refers to any person who engages in sexual activity with a child who is under 16 years of age shall be liable to imprisonment for a term not exceeding 5 years.

Section 201a is the new grooming section in Norwegian criminal law. This section was included in the General Civil Penal Code in April 2007:

with fines or imprisonment of not more than 1 year a liable, person is someone who has arranged to meet a child who is under 16 years of age, with the intention of committing an act as mentioned in sections 195, 196 or 200 second section and has arrived at the meeting place or a place where the meeting place can be observed.

In Norwegian law, the grooming section refers to 'the intention of committing an act'. However, the perpetrator must actually appear for a meeting with the victim; the intention to meet alone is not enough to evidence criminal behaviour.

The 'meeting place' is identified as the potential scene of the crime, the location where the offence is intended to take place and where the offender has arrived, or where the offender can observe the potential crime scene from where he is located. The crime description is neutral in terms of reference to technology. Here, the way in which the child and adult came into contact and agreed to meet is considered important. The key criterion is that there is an agreement to meet in person. There is no requirement that there is an explicit agreement to meet. It is sufficient that the offender has a reasonable expectation to meet the child at a specific location within a specific time frame. It is also irrelevant to identify who initiated the meeting.

The Swedish legislation on grooming targets adults that contact children for sexual purposes. However, a report by End Child Prostitution, Child Pornography and Trafficking of Children for Sexual Purposes (ECPAT) Sweden suggests that the legislation has not been acted upon effectively (ECPAT, 2012a). The legislation came into force on 1 July 2009 and has so far resulted in only one conviction. The report describes the current legislation as 'weak and ineffective'. In the Netherlands, three convictions had been made under the legislation (Article 248e

Dutch Criminal Code) by May 2011 (Kool, 2011), although substantially more convictions have been made in the United Kingdom.

In recent years, there has been a concerted attempt to enhance the protection of children through political initiatives at EU level. In 2003, the European Union adopted a Council Framework Decision on 'combating the sexual exploitation of children and child pornography', committing EU member states to bringing their national laws in line with the standards it contains, including criminalizing child pornography and other child sexual exploitation offences. In November 2011, the Council of the European Union introduced a directive aimed at introducing legislation to address the sexual exploitation of children. The legislation provides for the removal or blocking of websites containing child indecent images, introduces measures against online grooming and criminalizes child sex tourism. All member states had two years to ratify the provisions into national law. The minimum sentences stipulated in the new legislation are three years in prison for producers of child indecent images and one year for consumers; and forcing children into sexual acts will be punishable by a ten-year minimum custodial sentence.[4]

The difficulty remains that whilst states will be forced to adopt the legislation, the legal definition of child at national level remains determined by the legal age of consent, which, as noted earlier, still varies widely across Europe and is as low as 13 in some countries such as Spain. There is a need for international consensus regarding the age of consent if such attempts to standardize the law are to succeed. The experience of EU member states that have already introduced the grooming legislation suggests that it results in few criminal convictions (Davidson & Gottschalk, 2011b). This difficulty may be to do with a reluctance to enforce the law actively at national level. But it may also be due to the precautionary nature of this particular criminal law that often requires compelling evidence regarding the 'intention' to offend, which is sometimes difficult to obtain (Kool, 2011). However, if member states do not ratify the legislation, they will be fined by the European Commission. International policing agencies such as Interpol and Europol are currently drafting strategies to address the new directive (Davidson & Hamerton, 2014).

International collaboration: Protecting children online

It should be imperative to encourage appropriate and safe use of the internet by assisting children and young people to feel comfortable and supported in navigating the information highway. However, online child protection is an issue demanding a collaborative multi-agency approach that includes law enforcement, health and social services, educators, parents and the IT industry. At national level, governments should take a lead role in coordinating the collaborative effort. In the United Kingdom government policy is informed by the UK Council for Child Internet Safety (UKCCIS), an organization established following the Byron Review in 2007. UKCCIS has an executive board, comprising experts from the government, industry, practice, academia, non-governmental organizations (NGOs) and charities. Sub-groups provide ongoing guidance on internet-safety education, industry regulation, engagement and research evidence. The Byron Review was also responsible for the introduction and roll out of internet-safety education in the UK schools' national curriculum.

Awareness raising has been a central focus of the European Commission's Safer Internet Action Plan and this is implemented across Europe through the INSAFE[5] network of national awareness-raising nodes. The Safer Internet Day is organized by INSAFE each year to promote safer use of online technology and mobile phones. The UK INSAFE network is represented by a consortium of the awareness nodes: the Child Exploitation and Online Protection Centre (CEOP), the Internet Watch Foundation (IWF) hotline and the helpline Childline. There are now awareness centres belonging to the INSAFE network in 27 European countries.[6] On a broader international scale, such centres can also be found in Argentina, Australia, Russia and the United States. Another international initiative is the International Association of Internet Hotlines (INHOPE), also founded under the European Commission's Safer Internet Action Plan in 1999. The principal goal of INHOPE is to represent and support a global network of internet hotlines in their attempts to respond to reports of illegal content. Their educational efforts with policymakers and stakeholders aim to provide a way towards better co-operation internationally.

In addition, the G8[7] countries have agreed a strategy to protect children from sexual abuse on the internet. Key aims include the development of an international database of offenders and victims to aid victim identification; and offender monitoring and the targeting of those profiting from the sale of indecent images of children. Work has also been conducted with internet service providers (ISPs) and organizations such as the Association for Payment Clearing Services in the United Kingdom and other credit card companies in different countries to attempt to trace individuals using credit cards to access illegal sites containing indecent images of children. An attempt has also been made to put mechanisms into place to prevent online payment for illegal sites hosted outside the United Kingdom.

There is still much work to be done in educating ISPs. Research by the IWF (2005) suggests that 72 per cent (of a sample of 1000 senior IT professionals) were unaware of the implications of amendments to the Sexual Offences Act 2003 for their industry and only 56 per cent had even heard of the IWF. ISPs have, however, taken some action to address child safety online: British Telecom's Operation Clean Sweep resulted in the closure of all of its chat rooms, following concerns over sex offenders' use of the service to target children. Other providers such as MSN and Yahoo[8] have also taken some action to protect children in chat rooms. A Scottish company (Net ID) has launched the world's first virtual ID card, which aims to protect children and young people online. The card aims to remove the anonymity of the internet, thus preventing paedophiles posing as children in chat rooms to gain their trust (Lunchtime Scotland Today, 2 August 2006).

In addition, many police forces in both the European Union and the United States are working to trace internet sex offenders and their victims. In the United Kingdom, national and local High Technology Crime Units currently investigate the grooming of children on the internet and indecent online images of children. Successful prosecutions have been brought under the Acts in Scotland, England and Wales, both for 'grooming' online and for the possession of indecent internet images following Operation Ore. This operation was launched following information provided to the UK police by the Federal Bureau of Investigation in the United States, regarding peer-to-peer technology being used to share indecent images of children. The National Crime Squad (which targets serious and violent crime) has made 2200 convictions since 2002 under Operation Ore.

Organizations such as the Virtual Global Taskforce (VGT) and the IWF are making some headway in attempting to protect children online. The VGT is an organization that comprises several international law-enforcement agencies from Australia, Canada, the United States, the United Kingdom and Interpol. Through the provision of advice and support to children, the VGT aims to protect children online and has set up a bogus website to attract online groomers. The IWF is one of the main government watchdogs in this area. Although based in the United Kingdom the IWF is a part of the EU's Safer Internet Plus Programme, and is part of the International Association of Internet Hotlines

(INHOPE) network. As Robbins and Darlington (2003) have pointed out, this programme has four main aims:

- to fight illegal internet content;
- to tackle harmful internet content;
- to promote a safer internet environment; and
- to raise awareness about internet dangers.

The first three of these objectives have until now largely been the province of institutions and organizations. However, the fourth has immediate implications for the everyday use of the internet by the members of the public and, most significantly, by children. This in turn has led to initiatives to teach online safety to children and young people.

International law enforcement in the internet sexual abuse area has developed considerably in recent years, but barriers to effectiveness include the preponderance of a small number of well-resourced policing units in industrialized countries leading the way and continuing considerable differences in domestic law. Effective international law enforcement is essential in combating internet child abuse given the global nature of the offending behaviour and good international links should be established at local level. As discussed earlier, the development of international law courts would also help to standardize practice at national level (Kennedy, 2013) but this would not address the problem unless a common legal definition of child can be agreed across jurisdictions.

That said, Interpol has a network of 187 countries and facilitates the sharing of information between police forces, and provides the principal focus for much international law-enforcement activity against child abuse online. However, the effectiveness of Interpol activity in different countries is limited by the extent to which treaty agreements and conventions have been ratified in national law. Interpol activity extends to many different geographical regions. Some regions have sub-directorates. For example, the aim of the African Sub-Directorate is 'to support regional and national crime-fighting activities in Africa by providing quality operational and administrative services on a daily basis through a regionally-based geopolitical structure'.[9] Interpol formally entered into a co-operation agreement with the UN in October 1996. This agreement outlines several areas in which the two organizations might cooperate, including responding to the needs of the international community in fighting crime; assisting states in their efforts to combat organized crime; co-operating in the implementation of the mandates of international judicial bodies; carrying out joint investigations and other police-related matters in the context of peace-keeping; and establishing joint databases related to penal law.[10]

The International Child Sexual Exploitation image database (ICSE DB) is managed by Interpol and is a powerful intelligence and investigative tool which allows specialized investigators to share data internationally with police forces. Available through Interpol's secure global police communications system (I-247), the ICSE DB uses sophisticated image-comparison software to make connections between victims and locations. Backed by the G8 and funded by the European Commission, the ICSE DB was launched in March 2009 as the successor to the Interpol Child Abuse Image Database (ICAID), which had been in use since 2001.

There have been some significant global activities. In 1996, the First World Congress against the Commercial Sexual Exploitation of Children (CSEC) was held, leading to a global declaration and timetable for action that was adopted by 122 countries. The Second World Congress was held in 2001, resulting in the Yokohama Global Commitment, which commits states to national action following the First Congress. This commitment required states to address harms caused by new technologies. The Third World Congress led to the development of the Rio Pact, which specifically referred to the prevention of online indecent child images and grooming.[11] The VGT now has member agencies in the United States, Canada, Australia and Italy. The VGT claim that law-enforcement agencies, including members of the VGT, have made 'substantial headway' in facilitating cross-jurisdictional investigations and information sharing.[12]

Finally, Microsoft, Facebook and the National Center for Missing and Exploited Children (NCMEC) have developed a PhotoDNA program to combat indecent images of children. NCMEC's program, using image-matching technology created by Microsoft Research in collaboration with Dartmouth College in the United Kingdom, will provide online service providers with an effective tool to take proactive action to stop the distribution of known images of child sexual abuse online. The PhotoDNA is now provided free of charge to appropriate organizations.[13]

The role of industry in online safety

Partners from industry play a key role in many aspects of online safety for children and young people as the providers of internet access through devices that enable us to get online. Examples of collaboration between the IT industry and law enforcement have already been described. The United Nations International Telecommunications Union (UN ITU) has produced the Guidelines for Industry on Child Online Protection,[14] which address four key components of the industry:

- ICT industry as a whole;
- Broadcasters;
- Internet Service Providers;
- Mobile operators.

The guidelines contain some key areas for consideration, which are a helpful starting point for countries embarking on the creation of an online safety strategy. However, the guidelines are very descriptive and may not be applicable in countries where a comprehensive child-protection legislative framework does not exist. In promoting safety, a balance is needed between effective law enforcement, educational awareness and technical solutions which allow users to make informed choices. This is set against the context of a comprehensive legislative framework. A positive relationship with industry is crucial in establishing the most effective online safety provision and there are examples where such partnerships have produced positive outcomes. Collaboration between industry and the European Commission has led to the development of the Safer Social Networking Principles and the Groupe Speciale Mobile Association (GSMA) has produced a framework for safer mobile use for young people to which all members have subscribed. More information on both initiatives is given further below. Additionally, it is encouraging to see that Facebook has recently introduced anti-grooming software in collaboration with law enforcement, although its impact has yet to be independently evaluated.

Perhaps one of the most significant actions taken by the IT industry in this arena is in the fight against online child sexual abuse images. The Mobile Alliance against Child Sexual Abuse Content is an alliance founded by an international group of mobile phone operators within the GSMA with the key aim of obstructing the use of the mobile environment by individuals or organizations wishing to consume or profit from child sexual abuse content.

Key measures include:

- Implementation of technical mechanisms to prevent access to web sites identified by an appropriate agency as hosting child sexual abuse content.

- Implementation of notice and takedown processes to enable the removal of any child sexual abuse content posted on their own services.
- Supporting and promoting hotlines or other mechanisms for customers to report child sexual abuse content discovered on the internet or mobile content services.

The Alliance is keen to encourage all mobile operators worldwide to participate, regardless of their current access to technology.[15]

The Safer Social Networking Principles for the European Union

A further positive development has been the Safer Social Networking Principles[16] developed by social networking providers in consultation with the European Commission in 2009. There are seven important principles, but the document allows each individual service provider to determine exactly where and how to apply the specific recommendations, rather than regulating for this. The principles are as follows:

1. Raise awareness of safety education messages and acceptable use policies to users, parents, teachers and carers in a prominent, clear and age-appropriate manner.
2. Work towards ensuring that services are age-appropriate for the intended audience.
3. Empower users through tools and technology.
4. Provide easy-to-use mechanisms to report conduct or content that violates the terms of service.
5. Respond to notifications of illegal content or conduct.
6. Enable and encourage users to employ a safe approach to personal information and privacy.
7. Assess the means for reviewing illegal or prohibited content/conduct.

The impact of this initiative needs to be evaluated to determine how far these recommendations have been pursued.

European framework for safer mobile use by younger teenagers and children

This framework was developed by the mobile phone industry in Europe (GSMA) with the support and endorsement of the European Commission. It is a series of recommendations which aim to ensure that younger teenagers and children are able to access content safely on their mobile devices. The recommendations relate to the classification of commercial content. Here, mobile operators' own and third-party commercial content should be classified in line with existing national standards of decency and appropriateness, to identify content unsuitable for viewing by younger teenagers and children.

A key area for industry is that of 'moderation and takedown'. All services which host online content need to take responsibility for the removal of material which is deemed illegal or inappropriate. Countries should develop guidance and accepted protocols for the moderation of content. At a minimum, service providers must have their own acceptable policies which make clear to users online what can and cannot be done on their sites. Due to the volume of user-generated content online, given the serious challenge to moderate all material, many providers rely on users of their sites to report or flag inappropriate material. This presents problems in terms of locally accepted definitions of 'inappropriate' in an environment which is in fact not 'local'. Online safety advocates are campaigning for more transparency from service providers with regards to takedown times and response times to the reporting of inappropriate content. Many users have found that after reporting content, they are unclear as to whether action is being taken. However, good-practice guidance for moderation does exist and is being used successfully with the full support and co-operation of industry. There are in fact a number of approaches to moderation that industry can adopt – the UKCCIS document 'Good practice guidance on the moderation of interactive services for children' provides a useful summary of some of the possible approaches.[17]

It is common practice now for sites hosting user-generated content to provide mechanisms for the general user to flag content needing to be assessed by a moderator. The more mainstream sites also provide extensive guidance for users on how to report problems and get help or advice. However, this content has been criticized as being too complex to understand, too difficult to find and not user-friendly. Service providers of user-generated content are now working to establish improved controls and support for their users. For example, Facebook released a new suite of tools to protect users from bullying earlier in 2011, which was intended to 'foster a stronger sense of community in the social network' and 'create a culture of respect among Facebook users'. Similarly, YouTube allows users to block content which has been flagged as inappropriate for younger people. Whilst the technology is often available to enable parents to have more control over the content available to their children, they do not always make use of the opportunities available. This requires greater awareness raising and maybe more technological up-skilling more generally.

Empowering users with the ability to report inappropriate or offensive content is very important in addressing online abuse. There are several steps which need to be in place in order for online users to be able to successfully report content which they feel is inappropriate:

1. ISPs need to clearly define what is meant by inappropriate behaviour or content on their site and this information must be easily accessible to all users. For educational and awareness-raising purposes, individuals who are not members of a specific service should also be able to access this information.
2. Internet users should be able to easily report inappropriate behaviour from another user.
3. The procedures for reporting should be age-appropriate, simple and easily accessible.
4. Individuals submitting reports should be kept informed about the progress of their referral or complaint.

The Safer Social Networking Principles for the European Union give clear guidance on the reporting of inappropriate content and contain detailed information of what users should expect. The 'teachtoday' website provides guidance on reporting inappropriate content on the major sites. Aimed at teachers and professionals working with young people, it is a useful reference point for anyone needing support in the removal of such content.

Alongside these principles, the 'red police button' was introduced in Norway in September 2008. The red button is located on web pages for children, where grooming may occur. The red button can be pressed by children and others who experience abuse behaviour on that website. When the button is pressed, an automatic message is sent to the Norwegian national criminal police (*Kripos*) (Døvik, 2008). Three alternative options emerge on the screen: sexual exploitation of children (*Seksuell utnytting av barn*), human trafficking (*Menneskehandel*) and racial expressions on the internet (*Rasistiske ytringer på Internett*). Microsoft in Norway has taken the lead in installing this system, which is to be found on all online sites used by children. Norway therefore has a number of initiatives at policy and practice level for intervening in internet safety for children and young people, which ideally need to be followed by other European countries and further afield.

Is industry doing enough? The challenge of self-regulation

Two recent cases in the United Kingdom involving the abduction, sexual abuse and murder of children, where the offenders were found to have indecent child image collections on their computers, provoked a political debate. This concerned the role of search engines in providing access to such illegal content.[18] In response to political pressure, Google has increased its funding of the IWF to improve its regulatory work. However, whilst it is undeniable that industry has a responsibility for child safeguarding, it is doubtful that the majority of offenders seeking images would use such a search engine; it is much more probable that they would be linked to offender networks and that they would know how to access images at an informal level. These cases have nevertheless highlighted the need for industry to become fully engaged with the online safety debate and to be proactive on child protection. As a consequence of political pressure, Google has agreed to block searches for child abuse images.

As the gatekeepers to online content, a great deal is expected of industry and there are many who suggest that more could be done to protect users, particularly from harmful and inappropriate content. There are ongoing discussions involving industry representatives and government officials to establish more effective self-regulatory systems and countries should seek to further engage with colleagues from industry in this debate. Most mobile devices and games consoles provide some form of parental control or means of restricting access to inappropriate content. There is, however, an argument that providers of mobile devices should provide more restricted models for younger users which would prevent them accessing inappropriate online content.

Conclusion

There are great benefits of the internet for research, education, leisure and social communication, now used on a scale never before experienced. Children continue to be avid users of digital media. Recent research with children suggests that digital media has become so much an integral part of their daily lives that they do not recognize the distinction between being 'online' and 'offline', with the environment becoming increasingly converged (Davidson, Lorenz & Martellozzo, 2011; Davidson & Martellozzo, 2012). The incidence of technology-mediated crime also continues to increase alongside the potential for children to be targeted and victimized. Research exploring online abuse is still in its infancy, and relatively little is known about both perpetrators and child victims, and the circumstances in which they engage. However, the findings from the research described in this book will shed light upon offender grooming and victim selection. Findings have already informed the development of grooming legislation in Belgium and sentencing policy on sexual offences in the United Kingdom.

However, challenges remain. First, whilst the development of child online wellbeing and safety policy and practice, underpinned by a strong research evidence base, is advancing well in Europe and the United States, the exponential rise in the use of mobile technology by young people in the developing world and some of the cultural challenges that this represents have been largely ignored. Given the global nature of the internet, wealthier countries have a responsibility to ensure that children are afforded the same level of protection regardless of their geographical location. Second, the development of collaborative and effective international legal frameworks that have a shared definition of *child* and that recognize all forms of abusive behaviour, whether perpetrated online or in the real world, remains a fundamental and essential first step in addressing cross-border child abuse.

Notes

1. Available at: http://www.independent.co.uk/life-style/south-africas-facebook-captivates-young-cell-phone-users-2113547.html.
2. It is estimated that India has approximately 11 million 'street children': children with no fixed abode, living and working on the streets (Plan India, 2010, p41).
3. Available at: http://www.consilium.europa.eu/uedocs/cms_data/docs/pressdata/en/jha/126068.pdf.
4. Available at: http://www.consilium.europa.eu/uedocs/cms_data/docs/pressdata/en/jha/126068.pdf.
5. Available at: http://www.saferinternet.org/
6. Details of these awareness nodes can be found at: http://www.saferinternet.org/web/guest/centre-european-map.
7. Canada, France, Germany, Italy, Japan, Russia, the United Kingdom and the United States.
8. Yahoo were forced into action in 2005 by a New York State Attorney General's Office investigation, which found that users were creating chat rooms explicitly for the purpose of grooming children for abuse. Yahoo then agreed to put into place procedures to ensure that the creation of such chat rooms would not continue.
9. Available at: http://www.interpol.int/Public/Region/Africa/Default.asp.
10. Available at: http://www.interpol.int/Public/ICPO/IntLiaison/UN.asp.
11. Available at: http://www.ecpat.net/EI/pdf/Jaap_Doek_Presentation_WCIIIFU.pdf.

12. Available at: http://www.ecpat.net/EI/pdf/Jaap_Doek_Presentation_WCIIIFU. pdf.
13. Available at: http://www.microsoft.com/presspass/features/2009/dec09/12-15photodna.mspx.
14. Available at: http://www.itu.int/osg/csd/cybersecurity/gca/cop/guidelines/industry/industry.pdf.
15. Available at: http://www.gsmworld.com/our-work/public-policy/mobile_alliance.htm.
16. Available at: http://ec.europa.eu/information_society/activities/social_networking/docs/sn_principles.pdf.
17. Available at: http://media.education.gov.uk/assets/files/pdf/i/industry%20guidance%20%20%20moderation.pdf.
18. Available at: http://www.huffingtonpost.co.uk/2013/05/31/april-jones-murder-raises-debate-about-child-porn_n_3364173.html.

2
The Theoretical Context of Online Child Sexual Abuse

Julia Davidson and Stephen Webster

Introduction

In Chapter 1, the policy and legislative context influencing the management of online sexual abuse has been discussed. This chapter examines research evidence about the influence of the internet on online sexual abuse together with some of the key theoretical approaches that have been used to explain sexual offending behaviour both offline and online. To provide important context to the theoretical discussion, we begin by describing some of the methodological challenges inherent in conducting research into online abuse.

Researching online offending: Methodological challenges

Research exploring online child sexual abuse has focused on two groups or types of sexual offenders. First, those who use the internet and mobile phones to target and 'groom' children (Quayle, Allegro, Hutton, Sheath & Loof, 2012; Webster, Davidson, Bifulco, Gottschalk, Caretti, Pham et al., 2012; Whittle, Hamilton-Giachritsis, Beech & Collings, 2013); and second, those who produce and/or download indecent illegal images of children from the internet and collect and distribute them (Quayle & Taylor, 2002; O'Brien & Webster, 2007). There has also been some focus on a potential link between image collection and contact sexual abuse (Bourke & Hernandez, 2008; Long, Alison & McManus, 2013). The key issue is that these two groups are not mutually exclusive, which makes meaningful segmentation within research designs challenging.

As noted in Chapter 1, the global surge in online communication is relatively recent. Thus, the evidence base about the risk factors and psychological functioning of online sexual offenders is still developing.

It remains difficult to estimate the incidence of internet-related child sexual abuse reliably. But with increased use of the internet amongst the general population, it seems likely that offenders will increasingly use digital media as part of their modus operandi (Bourke, Ward & Rose, 2012). This is supported by the work of Middleton and colleagues, who note that in the United Kingdom between 1999 and 2005, there was almost a 500 per cent increase in convictions for internet-related sexual offences and by 2005, online sexual offences accounted for almost one third of all sexual offence convictions (Middleton, Elliott, Mandeville-Norden & Beech, 2006).

Research about child sexual abuse has traditionally relied on convicted male offender self-reports (O'Brien & Webster, 2007; Webster et al., 2012; Seto, 2013) or on the accounts of police officers (Finkelhor, 2012). Whilst the former is usually considered more informative, it poses certain constraints over issues of confidentiality and immunity from prosecution, which may compromise accurate findings (Kaplan, 1985). Whilst better information collection is likely to result from offenders, assurances of confidentiality can also constitute an ethical dilemma concerning respecting participants' privacy versus concealing information regarding possible sexual offences committed against children. Most ethical boards would probably require some mandated reporting of revelations of abuse in such cases, which could hamper the ability to collect such data. Other variables are also important in determining the extent to which offenders are forthcoming in interview and treatment settings; Marshall (2005), for example, suggests that interviewing style makes a difference, with participants more willing to discuss their offending and offending history when working with a person showing empathy. It does however seem clear that accounts of offending behaviour obtained directly from offenders are more informative than those of professionals alone are.

Estimating the prevalence of online grooming is methodologically problematic, as prison samples represent only those offenders caught and convicted. To extend the range, there is a parallel body of research that has relied on victim self-reports of online grooming. For example, Finkelhor and colleagues have conducted two surveys (YISS-1, 2000 and YISS-2, 2006) in North America, which used telephone interviews with national samples of young people aged 10 to 17 (Finkelhor, Kimberly & Wolak, 2000; Wolak, Mitchell & Finkelhor, 2009b). The work is critical of much of the research which characterizes online abusers as predatory paedophiles taking advantage of young people. Finkelhor and colleagues suggest rather that in the majority of cases, victims are aware that they are conversing online with adults and freely engage (Wolak, Finkelhor, Mitchell & Ybarra, 2010).

The position of Finkelhor and colleagues seems to be challenging the consensus in the literature that we summarize in subsequent chapters. From a methodological perspective, their findings could also reflect underestimates of online abuse due to reluctance on the part of some young victims to discuss abusive experience in a research-interview setting. In particular, where the abuse is unreported to services and where the interview has been conducted on the telephone potentially in the presence of a parent or other family member. Indeed, recent research conducted by Quayle, Jonsson and Lööf (2012) suggests that some young victims of online grooming actively conceal the relationship prior to discovery but usually come to realize only later that the relationship was abusive. Despite these methodological challenges, there is a need to attempt to understand the prevalence of online offending so that law-enforcement, victims' services and offender management resources can be appropriately estimated and deployed. First, we need to consider issues around sexual abuse in general, not only that which occurs online.

The prevalence of child sexual abuse

The prevalence of childhood abuse (not only that online) is notoriously difficult to assess given its largely secret nature.[1] However, figures are available for those cases presented to social services for child protection plans in the United Kingdom. This shows that in 2013, there were 2030 cases, which is virtually the same as the 2000 coming to services in 2009 (DoE, 2013). These figures are substantially lower than for rates of physical abuse, neglect or emotional abuse. In order to establish a representative rate retrospectively, a large survey was conducted on behalf of the National Society for the Prevention of Cruelty to Children in the United Kingdom (NSPCC: Radford, Corral, Bradley, Fisher, Bassett, Howat et al., 2011). The research included interviews with over 6000 young adults, adolescents and parents of younger children. Participants were asked whether anyone had 'tried to make them do anything sexual whilst they were 18 years old or younger'. Parents of children aged less than 11 years responded on their child's behalf. Older teenagers and young adults were also asked if they had done sexual things with an adult when they were still under 16 years or with an adult in a position of trust whilst they were still under 18 years. The study used a definition of sexual abuse that included any unwanted sexual activity, as well as criminal sexual activity with an adult, where physical contact took place. It excluded non-contact sexual abuse (such as indecent exposure or saying sexual things) as well as 'consensual' sexual activity between adolescents. The findings showed one in 20 children/young people (4.8%) experienced contact sexual abuse. For those abused, over 90 per cent were abused by someone they knew; 34 per cent who experienced contact sexual abuse by an adult did not disclose this to anyone, with as many as 82 per cent who experienced contact sexual abuse from a peer not disclosing the incident. Highlighting abuse in the media can have an impact of victims coming forward to report abuse, sometimes involving historical abuse. For example, in the United Kingdom, reporting rates for sexual abuse increased by 77 per cent in London during 2013, attributed to the *Yewtree effect* (Spindler, 2013) and the unprecedented impact of high-profile arrests for retrospective child sexual abuse perpetrated during the 1970s following the Savile enquiry.[2] This illustrates some of the factors that can have a bearing on prevalence estimates based on reporting to services often masking the true extent of child sexual abuse.

It is equally difficult to estimate the extent of online child abuse. In the United Kingdom, the Child Exploitation and Online Protection Centre (CEOP) receives approximately 1000 reports of online child victimization each year but states that the number is 'unquantifiable' (CEOP, 2013). CEOP also estimates that at least 50,000 known individuals in the United Kingdom downloaded or produced child indecent images during 2012 (CEOP, 2013). There are however some estimates of children or young people receiving sexual messages on the internet. The EU Kids Online reports described earlier (Livingstone, Haddon, Gorzig & Olafsson, 2011) show that 15 per cent of 11–16-year-olds and 22 per cent of 15–16-year-olds say they have seen or received sexual messages in the prior year. Meeting in person a 'stranger' met online was also fairly common, at 28 per cent in the United Kingdom. This is discussed further in Chapter 7.

The role of the internet in facilitating child abuse

As described earlier, existing offender research has focused almost exclusively on *intra*personal aspects of offending, ignoring the *inter*personal, group and situational factors that influence the perpetration of online sexual offences against children and young people. The European Online Grooming Project (EOGP) study reported in this book goes some way to address this gap by exploring offender behaviour in the context of the online environment. Also, Quayle and Taylor (2003) comment on the possible motivations of online child sex abusers. As outlined in Chapter 1, they argue that sexual offenders perceive the internet as a means of generating an immediate solution to their fantasies through the presumed anonymity, disinhibition and ready access to children online. It is also acknowledged, however, that the unique structure of the internet may play a major role in facilitating online child abuse, as outlined in Chapter 1, however the context in which the offending occurs is also of significance (Wortley & Smallbone, 2006). The internet has unique characteristics that can both sustain and direct child sexual abuse.

The number of indecent images of children on the internet is difficult to estimate, but during 2011, the US National Centre for Missing and Exploited Children (NCMEC) received 161,000 reports of indecent images and reported a growth of 86 per cent in reports from 2009 to 2010. NCMEC's analysis of these reports concludes that the growth in such images has risen exponentially, with increasingly violent images depicting sexual abuse perpetrated against even very young children and infants (cited in Report of the Supreme Court of the United States, 2011). This figure represents a fraction of those images reported and, in reality, it is recognized that millions of indecent child images are currently in circulation online (Carr & Hilton, 2010).

Early groundbreaking research in this area conducted by Quayle and Taylor (2002, 2003) explored the behaviour of offenders collecting and distributing indecent child images and suggested that the material found in offender collections ranged from pictures of clothed children, through nakedness and explicit erotic posing, to pictures depicting the sexual assault of the child photographed. This constitutes what Taylor and colleagues have referred to as a continuum of increased deliberate sexual victimization (Taylor, Holland & Quayle, 2001). This ranges from everyday and perhaps accidental pictures involving either no overt erotic content or minimal content (such as showing a child's underwear) to pictures showing actual rape and penetration of a child, or other gross acts of obscenity at the other extreme.

Therefore, attention is focused not on just illegality as a significant quality of the pictures, but on the preferred type of pictures selected by the collector, and the value and meaning pictures have to collectors:

> The images then are seen as not only reflecting the ways in which children are victimized but also how such victimization is mediated by the use to which the images are put.
>
> (Quayle, 2009, p10)

However, it is not necessary for the picture to depict an actual assault on a child for it to be used in an abusive or exploitative way (Quayle, Lööf & Palmer, 2008), as offenders may collect images for their own use and/or may swap images with other offenders. Carr's (2004) study, in which he analysed the images used by offenders, indicated that the vast majority selected material portraying Caucasian and Asian children. In addition, Baartz's (2008) Australian data described mostly white females aged between 8 and 12 years as being portrayed in the images. In the United Kingdom, a CEOP analysis of child indecent images collected between 2010 and 2012 found a 70 per cent increase in female victims under 10, and that 91 per cent of victims were white and they found a substantial increase in more serious images circulated (CEOP, 2013).

The extent to which online groomers are likely to have an indecent image collection and/or to perpetrate contact abuse is an important issue, with research evidence inconclusive at present. Seto and colleagues found that an online grooming sample were more likely than contact offenders to have viewed child indecent images, and were more likely to report haebephilic (i.e. post-pubertal victim) sexual interests (Seto, Wood, Babchishin & Flynn, 2012). (See Chapter 5 for a discussion of paedophilic and haebephilic definitions.) A recent study by Long and colleagues (2013) found that half (60 of 120) of adult males convicted for indecent child-image-related offences had a previous contact child sexual offence conviction. The EOGP research findings on indecent image collections in relation to online grooming behaviour are discussed in more detail in Chapter 4.

The psychological and social impact of online sexual abuse on victims has only recently been explored and is still little understood. This includes the psychologically abusive aspects of humiliation, emotional blackmail, exploitation, abuse of trust and terrorizing, which can accompany grooming, and public distribution of abuse images, creating feelings of shame and guilt (Palmer & Stacey, 2004). Further research is needed to establish the effects of technologically aided sexual abuse in order to inform interventions for victims and appropriate sentencing for offenders. For this, a more detailed exploration of psychologically abusive techniques in the grooming and abuse process need elucidating, alongside the psychological damage this has on victims. This is discussed more fully in Chapter 7.

As Quayle and colleagues argue, whilst sexual offences against children are clearly not created by the internet, it does appear that technology affords opportunities to sexually offend (Quayle, Allegro, Hutton,

Sheath & Loof, 2012). Davidson and Gottschalk (2011) describe a number of internet characteristics that may have relevance. These include 'disconnected personal communication, mediating technology, universality, network externalities, distribution channel, time moderator, low-cost standard, electronic double, electronic double manipulation, information asymmetry, infinite virtual capacity, independence in time and space, cyberspace, and dynamic social network'.

There are a number of different ways of communicating online, research has however focused on the role of social networking sites (SNSs). Research conducted by Mitchell and colleagues has explored the various ways in which SNSs are used to facilitate the sexual exploitation of young people (Mitchell, Finkelhor, Jones & Wolak, 2010). A nationally representative survey of over 2500 local, state and federal law-enforcement agencies in the United States was conducted. The results suggest that SNSs played a role in an estimated 2322 cases of internet sex crimes against young people. Specifically, SNSs were used to initiate sexual relationships, to provide a means of communication between victim and offender, to access information about the victim, to disseminate information or pictures about the victim and to get in touch with the victim's friends. The reported 1696 SNS-related sexual grooming arrests involved police acting in an undercover capacity. The majority of such cases were initiated in chat rooms (82%). The authors suggested that SNSs could be useful in aiding law enforcement to detect online grooming (Mitchell et al., 2010). However, it is likely that SNSs simply provide another platform for offenders to perpetrate abuse. It will be interesting to see if the recent move away from SNSs by young people (Ofcom, 2013) will impact upon offenders' choice of ICT platform in the future.

As discussed, there has been limited research exploring the motivations and behaviours of offenders who use the internet to perpetrate child abuse. There are even fewer studies based upon direct offender interviews. Both the EOGP study reported in this book and the Risk-taking Online Behaviour: Empowerment through Research and Training (ROBERT) parallel project funded by the European Commission served to address this gap in knowledge through offender and victim interviews, respectively. See Chapter 7 for more details on the ROBERT project victim findings. The ROBERT project also included a small qualitative study focusing upon offender experience. The research aimed to develop 'a tentative exploratory model of the ways that offenders selected children online and the methods used to engage them sexually both online and offline. We were also interested in exploring the attributions that they made about their behaviour' (Quayle et al., 2012, p13).

The research identified two theoretical categories of online abuse: 'creating a private space' in which to offend and 'targeting minors' (Quayle et al., 2012, p13). Creating a private space referred to what offenders described as the need to create a physical and literal space separate from other aspects of their lives. The spaces often afforded the opportunity to network and interact with other offenders. The findings also suggest that offenders showed selectivity in terms of the platforms targeted, preferring those providing easy access to young people. The research shows that offenders preferred SNSs, chat rooms and instant messenger, with evidence of migration to mobile phones once contact was made (Quayle et al., 2012). This finding is supported by research conducted by Wolak and colleagues (2010). Quayle and colleagues go on to argue that the use of a web camera (webcam) altered the nature of the interaction with the young person, as this offered the opportunity for visual contact.

The ROBERT project research explored reasons identified for needing the space and found that sexual offenders referred to personal and adult relationship difficulties as contributory factors. Quayle and colleagues rightly refer to the literature on blame attribution here (e.g. Gudjonssen, 1984; Finkelhor, 1984), with early research conducted with child sexual abusers before internet use having produced similar findings (Davidson, 2006; Seto, 2013). Another interesting finding from the ROBERT study is that offenders described relationships with young people as less threatening than those with adults. These findings relate to the concept of 'emotional congruence with children', well evidenced in studies with sexual offenders before the internet became a mainstream mode of communication (Finkelhor, 1984; Davidson, 2006; Mann, Webster, Wakeling & Marshall, 2007; Seto, 2013). Finally, the ROBERT research described a process of targeting, involving selection of victims on the basis of their SNS profile and physical appearance (derived from a profile and avatar). The characteristics and markers of similar offending behaviour found in the EOGP study are described fully in chapters 4 and 5.

Theories of child sexual abuse

Although limited, the research literature published to date suggests there is enough 'crossover' between online and offline sexual offending to warrant the application of theories of offline sexual abuse to an online sexual offending context. Numerous explanations have been offered regarding why adults sexually assault children. These tend to be: physiological focusing on brain abnormalities (Langevin, 1990); psychological, for example, pointing to the importance of early childhood experience (Kline, 1987) as well as looking at cognitive, affective and behavioural models; sociological, stressing the central role of structural factors such as power relations (Kelly, 1988); and theories combining sociological and psychological thought (Finkelhor, 1984). These will be described in turn.

Physiological and biological theories

The literature pointing to physiological explanations of sexual offending in males has concentrated on offences involving adult victims and offences against children. Langevin (1990) claimed to show a link between temporal-lobe impairment in the brain and deviant sexual behaviour in male sexual offenders. However, given the small number of cases involved in his experiment, and the correlational nature of his work, it is not known if the relationship between sexually deviant behaviour and brain impairment is a causal one. More recent research in this area found frontal-temporal anomalies amongst paedophiles, but not in rapists of adult victims (Joyal, Black & Dassylva, 2007). Cantor and colleagues have also looked at the brain-matter volumes of the temporal and parietal lobes amongst paedophiles, and report significantly less white-matter volumes in the temporal and parietal lobes in paedophiles (Cantor, Kabani, Christensen, Zipursky, Barbaree, Dickey et al., 2008).

Studies focusing on testosterone levels in male sexual offenders assume that unusually high levels of the hormone prompt sexual abuse (Lanyon, 1991; Rada, Laws & Kellner, 1976). Berlin and Hopkins (1981) reported higher testosterone levels in a large number of child sexual abusers, whilst Rada and colleagues reported that abusers' testosterone levels were similar to non-abusers (Rada, Laws & Kellner, 1976). The evidence in this area appears contradictory and inconclusive. Hucker and Bain (1990), in their review of the literature in this area, conclude that the majority of such studies should be treated with caution as the broad generalizations made are in fact based on very small clinical samples and findings are often incomplete or inconclusive.

However, this is an important area of work, as research informs the debate regarding the efficacy of chemical castration of sexual offenders. This involves using hormonal drugs to reduce sexual violence. The first reported attempt of hormonal manipulation to reduce pathological sexual behaviour occurred as early as 1944, when diethylstilbestrol was prescribed to lower testosterone levels. Similarly, medroxyproges-terone acetate and cyproterone acetate have been used throughout the United States, Canada and in some European countries to dimin-ish sexual fantasies and sexual impulses in sexual offenders. A more recent development in the treatment of paraphilias used luteinizing hor-mone releasing (LHRH) agonists such as leuprolide acetate and goserelin. In 1996, California became the first state in the United States to autho-rize the use of either chemical or surgical castration for certain sexual offenders being released from prison into the community. This legisla-tion was extremely controversial at the time in terms of human rights concerns. However, other states have subsequently passed laws that provide some form of castration for offenders applying for parole or probation.

Testosterone is the major hormone associated with libido and sexual function, and several studies have reported that violent sexual offenders have higher levels of androgens than do non-violent comparison groups and that androgen levels correlate positively with both prior violence and the severity of sexual aggression (Rada, Laws & Kellner, 1976; Brooks & Reddon, 1996). However, some have questioned the effectiveness of hormone-replacement treatment in preventing reoffending (Kingston, Seto, Ahmed, Fodoroff, Firestone & Bradford, 2012).

Surgical castration reportedly produces definitive results, even in repeat paedophilic offenders, by reducing recidivism rates to between 2 per cent and 5 per cent compared with expected rates of 50 per cent. For example, Sturup (1968, 1971) reported a 1 per cent reconviction rate for 900 sexual offenders followed up for 30 years after surgical castration, with similarly low reconviction rates reported by Heim and Hursch (1979) and Ortmann (1980). Chemical castration using LHRH agonists reduces circulating testosterone to very low levels and also results in very low levels of recidivism despite the strong psycholog-ical factors that contribute to sexual offending. Chemical castration has some advantages over surgical castration. First, although chemical castration is potentially lifelong for some offenders, it might allow sex-ual offenders undertaking psychotherapy interventions to have normal sexual activity. Second, some sexual offenders may voluntarily receive chemical castration. Third, chemical castration may be a more real-istic restriction than electronic ankle bracelets or surgical castration. Fourth, unlike surgical castration, the effects of anti-libido medication are reversible after discontinuation. Finally, the general public may feel relieved knowing that sexual offenders are undergoing chemical castration.

However, Grubin and Beech (2010) warn that this approach runs the risk of causing doctors to focus on public safety rather than on the best interests of the offender/patient. They do however argue that if clinical treatments are shown to be effective, then they should be offered to sexual offenders for informed acceptance. This could be problematic however, especially if not engaging with clinical treatment may result in a longer prison sentence (Rice & Harris, 2003).

Psychological theories

Psychology has arguably made the most significant contribution to the study of child sexual abuse and its impacts on the individual. Relevant psychological theory ranges from psychodynamic theories beginning with the Freudian psychoanalytic school to more recent cognitive behavioural theories. These are described in turn below.

Psychodynamic theories

Psychoanalytic theory originates in the work of Sigmund Freud and has had an impact upon both the treatment and theoretical explanation of child sexual abuse. It was Freud's belief that all personality disorders, such as sexual deviance, arose from unresolved sexual problems in childhood. Unsatisfactory resolution of the 'Oedipus complex' in males (the 'Electra complex' in females) was seen as one of the primary causes of sexual deviation in Freud's later work. The Oedipus complex refers to the belief that male children desire sexual relations with their mother, wish their father dead and fear castration from their father by way of retribution. The child comes to resolve this dilemma through identification with the father and a happy relationship is resumed (Freud, 1952). Adult sexual problems are suggested to arise following the unsuccessful resolution of this complex in childhood.

Post-Freudians such as Weldon (1988) have blamed the unsuccessful resolution of the Oedipus complex on poor parenting on the part of the mother, whilst others such as Kline (1987) point to the inadequate development of the superego, implying that childhood desires are taken into adult life and inappropriately directed towards children (Lanyon, 1991).

The complexity of this theory makes it difficult to investigate empirically; however, the basis of the claims has been challenged. First, Freudian theory has been criticized on methodological grounds, as it was based on the therapeutic work conducted by Freud with a small number of middle-class Viennese women who may not be representative. Second, post-Freudians such as Kline (1987) have failed to explain the existence of female child sexual abusers focusing exclusively on males. Third, whilst women as mothers are implicated in ultimately giving rise to abuse via the poor parenting of male children (Weldon, 1988), no consideration is given to the fact that victims tend to be female (Salter, 1988).

The influence of Freudian thought is widespread in present-day psychology. Groth (1979) (in Lanyon, 1991), for example, developed classifications for child sexual abusers and rapists, which have informed approaches to treatment. It is suggested that abusers are motivated by unresolved life issues occurring in childhood; abusers are characterized as either fixated or regressed. The fixated abuser has a consistent primary sexual interest in children and is unable to maintain long-term relationships with adults. The regressed abuser has formed relationships with adults but will regress into relationships with children under certain circumstances, such as when rejected by an adult. Later psychoanalytic approaches have focused upon the family. Mrazek and Kemp (1981) claim that the absence of a good marital bond and previous incestuous behaviour on the part of male family members make for a dysfunctional family, in which incest is likely to occur. Whilst De Young (1982) suggests that incest arises when discontented males who are too inhibited to seek sexual gratification outside the family abuse their daughters.

De Young views incest as symptomatic of the dysfunction. It could, however, be argued that the presence of a child-abusing male in any family unit would cause that family to be dysfunctional whereby the dysfunction is probably symptomatic of the incest (Kelly, 1988). Treatment approaches do not now tend to locate the origins of abuse within the family, as more has been discovered about the way in which abusers target and manipulate children (Elliot, Browne & Kilcoyne, 1995). As Barker and Morgan (1993) state: 'it becomes increasingly logical to see dysfunction in incestuous families as an effect of the offender's manipulation of that family, rather than the cause of the incest' (p9).

More recent psychodynamic theories have developed consistent theoretical models to understand sexual deviance. The most important are listed below:

The object-relations model: based on Kernberg's (1984) early work with severe personality disorders, this approach argued that extreme sexual deviance found in many sexual offenders is based on a narcissistic personality organized at a psychotic or borderline personality disorder level, where the domination of the victim is the desired objective of a triumphant and omnipotent self (e.g. De Masi, 2007).

The trauma-dissociation model: based on original work by Sandor Ferenczi in the 1930s. He was a psychoanalyst who argued against Freud in stating that sexual abuse reported by patients was based on real experience. Ferenczi argued that the sexual abuse from a parent occurs from a severe distortion in the parent's interpretation of the child's desire to be cared for and loved. The caregiver's misinterpretation of the child's attachment requests for tender interaction may lead, amongst those adults who are psychologically disturbed, to wrongly detecting a sexual 'language' in the affective communications coming from the child, as if they were a request for sexual interaction (Gutiérrez Peláez, 2009). This leaves the child feeling culpable and blameworthy, because of the introjection of the unconscious guilt of the perpetrator, through the psychic processes of the identification with the aggressor, which in turn may lead to the 'cycle of abuse' (e.g. De Zulueta, 2009).

The mentalization-based model: based on recent influential work of authors such as Fonagy and Target (1999) in the United Kingdom, this approach postulates that child sexual abusers lack mentalizing abilities; that is, the ability to make sense, implicitly and explicitly, of one's own behaviour and that of another, in terms of subjective states and mental processes. Child sexual abusers, having poor mentalizing ability, may lack empathy and behave in response to a specific mental state (e.g. excitement) rather than reflecting on the consequences of their behaviour. See Chapter 5 for psychodynamic approaches to the categorization of disorder and treatment of sexual offending in relation to online grooming.

A final element to emerge from psychodynamic theory is that of attachment theory, formulated by John Bowlby. This similarly uses a lifespan developmental approach but with a focus on interpersonal style and the distortions that can arise in relating based on early life experience with carers (Bowlby, 1988). This approach has had a major impact on parenting and the intergenerational transmission of risk (Cassidy & Shaver, 2008), it now also covers forensic psychological issues in relation to problem solving in addressing violent offending (Fonagy, 1999). There is to date only relatively minor application of this theoretical approach to sexual offending (e.g. Ward, Hudson, Marshall & Siegert, 1995; Ward,

Hudson & Marshall, 2006), but it has not been applied to the victim's behaviour online. This will be discussed further in Chapter 7.

Cognitive behavioural theory

Behavioural learning theories within psychology originate in the early work of Pavlov in the late nineteenth century and Skinner in the 1920s (cited in Sparks, 1982), who studied learned responses to external stimuli amongst animals. The implications for child sexual abuse is that learning theorists attribute offender behaviour to the misdirected learning of behaviour. In keeping with Pavlov's original study of the manner in which dogs could be conditioned to respond to external stimuli, learning theorists argue that the sexual abuse of children occurs when abusers associate childlike characteristics with sexual arousal. Abusers may become aroused by a small childlike body, for example (Marshall, Laws & Barbaree, 1990); the impact of the stimulus is such that the characteristics become the prompt for sexual arousal.

Other learning theorists such as Wolf (1984) argue that a childhood history of sexual, emotional or physical abuse can lead to the development of sexual deviancy. It is suggested that through such experience, children learn inappropriate behaviour; the abusive experiences serve to act as 'potentiators' for the child to learn inappropriate behaviour. Wolf states that the more potentiators there are, the greater the risk that the child will become a sex offender. The presence of potentiators coupled with other stimuli such as alcohol, drugs or pornography is proposed to lead to deviant sexual fantasy, which provides the backdrop to future offending. According to Wolf, events leading to feelings of powerlessness and worthlessness reinforce deviant sexual fantasies which are often masturbatory. This acts as a rehearsal for future offending.

Cognitive theory concerned with the development of a person's thought processes (or cognitions) is now an important approach in psychology. It looks at how thought processes influence how we understand and interact with the world. These mental processes include memory, perception, thinking and language (Simon & Kaplan, 1989). The main assumption of the cognitive approach is that information received from our senses is processed by the brain and that this processing directs how we behave or at least justifies how we behave the way that we do (Ellis & Young, 1997). Cognitive psychology has been influenced by developments in computer science and analogies are often made between how a computer works and how we process information. Based on this computer analogy, cognitive psychology is interested in how the brain inputs, stores and outputs information (Kuhn, 1970; Simon, 1980).

However, we are much more sophisticated than computer systems and an important criticism directed at the cognitive approach is that it often ignores the way in which other factors, such as past experiences and culture, influence how we process information (Baron-Cohen, Jollife, Mortimore & Robertson, 1997). Cognitive theories have been particularly useful in understanding psychological disorder (e.g. the work by Aaron Beck in identifying the negative thinking in depression). As with psychoanalytic theory, this also fits in a developmental framework linking distortions in thinking to adverse childhood experience. From this has emerged cognitive behaviour therapy (CBT), now one of the most popular and well-evidenced treatments for common psychological disorders. It is a psychotherapeutic approach that addresses dysfunctional emotions, maladaptive behaviours and cognitive processes and contents through a number of goal-orientated, explicit systematic procedures (Marshall, Anderson & Fernandez, 1999). This technique acknowledges that there may be behaviours that cannot be controlled through rational thought. CBT is 'problem focused' (undertaken for specific problems) and 'action orientated' (the therapist tries to assist the client in selecting specific strategies to help address those problems).

These approaches have been used to understand and treat sexual offenders. For example, Finkelhor's approach to defining grooming has had a significant influence on the current use of CBT approaches in this arena. Finkelhor's (1984) model describes four preconditions that act as a precursor to the abuse. These are the thinking stage; overcoming internal inhibitions or 'giving permission'; external inhibitions or 'creating the opportunity'; and overcoming the victim's resistance. Many later formulations have been based upon this approach, although subsequent writers afford grooming a more central position in sexual offending (Craven, Brown & Gilchrist, 2006; Hall & Hirschman, 1992; Sullivan, 2009; Ward & Siegert, 2002), with Sullivan (2009), for example, having developed this work referring to a spiral of abuse.

The design of effective interventions for online groomers requires an understanding of how online groomers behave, their barriers and enablers to change, and what influences their behaviours in general. To that end, three additional approaches are outlined as a useful framework by which to understand online grooming which combine both cognitive behavioural and psychodynamic elements.

Self-regulation and disinhibition

The first of these is Ward and Hudson's (1998) *self-regulation model of the sexual offence process*. The central premise of Ward and Hudson's theory is that different self-regulation styles, involving the internal and external processes that allow an individual to engage in goal-related behaviour, underpin the sexual offence process. Two styles of goals are discussed: approach and avoidance. Approach goals concern the successful attainment of a state or situation and involve approach-focused behaviours. For example, an individual tailoring their online profile page in order to attract the interest of a particular young person. In contrast, avoidance goals involve the reduction of a particular state whereby attention is focused on negative information signalling failure rather than success. An example here may be an online groomer who masturbates to their collection of indecent images of children in order to suppress the desire to contact a young person online. Intrinsically linked to approach and avoidant goals are three self-regulation styles. The first, *under-regulation*, refers to individuals who may behave in a passive or disinhibited manner. *Mis-regulation* describes the misplaced effort to avoid offending due to a lack of knowledge about the impact of the response selected, as in the example above. Finally, individuals who consciously think out a sequence of behaviours in order to commit an offence do not show emotional under-regulation or mis-regulation as a feature of their offending and thus form a third group. For these individuals, their emotional state is likely to be positive and they do not see their behaviour as particularly problematic.

In addition to setting the sexual offence process in the context of self-regulation theory, Ward and Hudson's seminal paper also suggests that comprehensive models of the sexual offence process should encompass three further features: the integration of cognitive, affective and behavioural factors that underpin the sexual offence; a demonstration of the dynamic nature of the sexual offence that accounts for the various phases or milestones of the offence process; and, identification and the description of the psychological mechanisms that drive and inhibit the relapse process.

Alongside theories specific to sexual offending is Suler's (2004) model of the *online disinhibition effect,* Suler's work contains three dimensions that describe the influence of online space on behaviour that may help develop understanding of online groomers' behaviour. The first dimension, *dissociative anonymity,* refers to the internet providing people with the opportunity to separate their actions from their real-world identity, making them feel less vulnerable about opening up. Suler argues that individuals believe that whatever they say or do online cannot be directly linked to the rest of their lives. Consequently, individuals do not have to own their behaviour by acknowledging it within the full context of who they really are.

Invisibility refers to the online individual not being physically seen, with many people unaware that the individual is there at all. Suler argues that invisibility gives people the courage to go to places and do things that they otherwise would not. Although there is clear overlap with anonymity, Suler suggests that with the user physically invisible, the disinhibition effect is amplified. That is, unlike in face-to-face interaction, invisible individuals do not have to worry about looking or sounding foolish and do not have to attend to other accepted conversational norms indicating displeasure or disinterest such as a frown or shake of the head.

Dissociative imagination refers to the belief that the online persona along with online others live in a make-believe dimension, separate and apart from the demands and responsibilities of the real world. Here, individuals dissociate online fiction from offline fact, whereby online life consists of games, rules and norms that do not apply in actual living. As such, Suler states that once the computer is turned off and daily life returned to, individuals believe they can leave that online game behaviour and their game identity behind.

Researchers and clinicians who have worked with online groomers note that some sexual offenders may be susceptible to the social influence of other groomers and like-minded individuals in cyberspace (Harkins & Dixon, 2010; Seto, 2013). That is, this online 'community' appears to shape the thinking patterns and beliefs of online groomers, eventually influencing the degree and rate of their behavioural disinhibition online. Therefore, it may be that it is not just the de-individuating characteristics of the internet (dissociative anonymity, invisibility and dissociative imagination) that have an influence on the groomer, but also the actual 'community' of sexual offenders. Here, the online groomer's social identification with and 'immersion' in the community of like-minded individuals in cyberspace may further influence behaviour through a process of de-individuation. The theory of de-individuation (Zimbardo, 1969) proposes that factors such as anonymity, loss of individual responsibility, arousal and sensory overload contribute to a state of de-individuation and behavioural disinhibition where established norms of conduct may be violated.

Conclusion

This chapter has outlined the theoretical context of child sexual abuse and considered recent research literature focusing upon online abuse. Research is inconclusive regarding whether internet use actually encourages sexual offending or whether technology has simply made it easier for perpetrators to target larger numbers of victims, network and collect indecent child images. Some combination of the two seems likely. The internet effectively provides a supportive context for the perpetration of abuse and for networking with other offenders. The psychodynamic approach (which emphasizes themes such as power and narcissism, affective states and defensive processes) has been outlined alongside the cognitive behavioural approach, which emphasizes distorted thinking and goal-orientated behaviour. Problems in self-regulation and disinhibition take into account elements of both. But in addition to both these psychological approaches, the socio-environmental context needs to be considered in relation to victim access opportunities and to circumstances and behaviour that make victims pliable and unlikely to disclose. These combined approaches can provide valuable insight into offender online behaviour: concepts like individuals offence-supportive beliefs (denial, attribution errors and so on) remain central, but should be viewed in the wider context of the interplay between the offender, technology and victim. The unique impact of the internet cannot be ignored. For example, in identifying whether the disinhibiting effect of the internet interacts with offenders' tendency to attribute blame. Also, in identifying the relationship between increased anonymity and offender denial in the grooming process. More research is needed to explore some of these central issues and they are discussed further in subsequent chapters.

Notes

1. Available at: http://www.nspcc.org.uk/Inform/research/helpline/helpline-highlight-sexual-abuse-pdf_wdf93060.pdf.
2. Jimmy Savile was a children's entertainer working for the BBC during the 1970s. It has recently transpired that Savile used his celebrity status to perpetrate a series of child sexual abuse attacks over several decades.

3
The European Online Grooming Project Study Design

Stephen Webster

Introduction

Until relatively recently, there has been a dearth of high-quality studies that have examined internet sexual offending. In 2008, the need for a robust evidence base to develop policy became more acute. To that end, Action 3.1 of the then European Commission Safer Internet Plus Programme invited proposals for projects that enhanced the knowledge of the online sexual abuse of young people, with a particular focus on online grooming. From this call for proposals, the European Online Grooming Project (EOGP) was developed. The EOGP (Webster, Davidson, Bifulco, Gottschalk, Caretti, Pham et al., 2012) is a cross-discipline research consortium of experts from the United Kingdom, Belgium, Italy and Norway. The project was funded by the European Commission for 30 months between 2009 and 2012, and at the time of the study, the work represented the most comprehensive examination of online grooming commissioned.

Given that the EOGP is the foundation of this book, this chapter provides an overview of the study design, methods and analytic approaches taken in the programme of research. The chapter plan is to begin by offering a definition of online grooming in the context of limited consensus in the literature, then by examining evidence on the prevalence of online grooming. The chapter will then provide a description of each of the qualitative research phases and samples used. The concluding section supports the use of the qualitative approach within an online offending evidence base dominated by quantitative research that can vary considerably in terms of quality.

Defining online grooming

Within the literature about online harm, there is no clear consensus regarding a definition of grooming. As Schulz, Bergen, Schuhmann, Hoyer, Santtila and Osterheider (2014) state, the terms 'sexual solicitation' and 'online grooming' have been used interchangeably. Sexual solicitation is defined as, 'encouraging someone to talk about sex, to do something sexual, or to share personal sexual information even when that person does not want to' (Ybarra, Espelage & Mitchell, 2007, p32). In contrast online grooming has been defined as a process of socialization that, independently of virtual or real context, serves to establish trust and aims at soliciting a minor for sexual purposes (Whittle, Hamilton-Giachritsis, Beech & Collings, 2013a). These diverse definitions present challenges for interpreting research results and for those wanting to replicate earlier studies.

The EOGP research team defined online grooming as, 'the process by which a person befriends a young person[1] online in order to facilitate online sexual contact and/or a physical meeting with the goal of committing sexual abuse'. However, this original definition did assume that the online groomers' behaviours involved 'socialization' of their victims, which was yet to be tested by the evidence provided. Whilst the study was of online grooming, the extent of the 'solicitation' or 'luring' involved was a matter for empirical investigation.

Prevalence of online grooming

Despite the lack of consensus about grooming definitions, within the literature there are three main sources of data used to estimate the rate of online grooming. First, there are studies of police reports or official records that have recorded a sexual offence that involved an online component (Mitchell, Jones, Finkelhor & Wolak, 2011). Here Mitchell and colleagues analysed 2006 arrest data from the National Juvenile Online Victimization Study, a nationally representative longitudinal study of more than 2500 local, county, state and federal law-enforcement agencies across the United States. Findings show that an estimated 569 arrests for internet-facilitated commercial sexual exploitation of children occurred in the United States in 2006. Of those 569 arrests, 36 per cent of cases involved those who used the internet to purchase or sell access to identified children for sexual purposes. Within this group are men who have contacted children to make and distribute indecent images of children, as well as those who made contact online with the intention of grooming a child for offline sexual abuse. Turning to data from the United Kingdom, the Child Exploitation and Online Protection Centre (CEOP) described 1536 reports of suspected online grooming (66% of the total CEOP caseload) received from the UK public between April 2009 and March 2010 (CEOP, 2010).

Alongside surveys of law-enforcement officials and the analysis of official records, there have been a number of studies in North America and Europe that have attempted to assess the prevalence of online grooming and solicitation by asking young people about their online experiences. As described in earlier chapters, using North American data, Mitchell, Finkelhor and Wolak (2007) found that 5 per cent of young people report that they had been sexually solicited and/or groomed by an adult over a one-year period. Interestingly, Mitchell and colleagues also report that the incidence of online sexual solicitations decreased over subsequent waves of the survey. Ybarra, Espelage and Mitchell (2007) report a further longitudinal survey of young people aged 10–15 over a three-year period. Here, 15 per cent of 1500 young people reported experiencing a sexual solicitation at the baseline survey encounter. A final North American study reported data from a convenience sample of approximately 2000 high school students and found rates as high as 65 per cent of girls and 53 per cent of boys reporting having been asked to meet a stranger offline who they had originally met online (Dowdell, Burgess & Flores, 2011). Thus, the prevalence of online grooming found is highly variable.

In Europe, the seminal research into young people's online experiences is the EU Kids Online Survey (Livingstone, Haddon, Gorzig & Olafsson, 2011). Funded by the European Commission, this survey covers a random stratified sample of 25,142 children and young people aged 9–16, drawn from 25 countries. Relevant here is a module of questions about perceived risks and harms, in particular the prevalence of new online friendships that result in offline meetings. Livingstone and colleagues report that 30 per cent of their sample made contact online with someone that they did not previously know offline, and 9 per cent had a face-to-face meeting with someone they had first met online. Of the 9 per cent that went to a meeting, only 1 per cent reported being 'bothered' by what happened at the offline meeting. Looking at the experiences of this 1 per cent in further detail, 22 per cent reported meeting an older teenager (defined in this survey as somebody up to 20 years old) and 8 per cent met an adult (aged 20 years or over). Finally, with regard to the content of those offline meetings, 11 per cent of the young people with a meeting reported the other person 'doing something sexual to me'.

The final (emerging) method of estimating the prevalence of online grooming/solicitation is to survey adults about their online sexual behaviour. Schulz and colleagues conducted an online survey amongst 1151 adult internet users from three countries who communicated online with strangers (Schulz, Bergen, Schuhman, Hoer, Santtila & Osterheider, 2014). Here, one in ten participants (n = 125) reported communicating about non-sexual topics with unfamiliar young people (aged 14–17) and 2 per cent (n = 24) communicated with unfamiliar children (aged 13 years or younger). Furthermore, 83 (7%) people reported that they had communicated in a sexual way with adolescents and six participants (0.5%) with children. A quarter of the participants with adolescent online contacts went on to meet an online contact offline and a third received sexual pictures from an adolescent online contact.

This indicates some obvious policy concerns about the behaviour of adults and young people online. However, the inconsistency of prevalence data about online grooming also indicates some inherent methodological challenges associated with research in this area. First, within different surveys, online harm/solicitation/grooming is defined in different ways. Second, there is no legislative consensus across nations about the age of sexual consent (although a person under 18 is defined as a child under the United Nations Convention on the Rights of the Child [UNCRC]) or on how online harm is to be defined. Within these diverse methodological and cultural contexts, comparing the prevalence of online grooming across studies is very challenging.

A further challenge with these survey methods is the potential for under-reporting online sexual offences. That is, some young people may be becoming desensitized to unwanted online sexual approaches to the extent that these approaches are seen as a 'hassle of life online'.

The final challenge with estimating the prevalence of online grooming relates to the nature of the internet itself. Suler's (2004) theory of online disinhibition whereby people can behave in ways online that they would not be able to offline has already been outlined. Online, people can easily create aliases and fail to disclose their true identity. In addition, Suler described how the internet could support people's fantasies, some of which may never be acted out offline. If the work of Schwartz and colleagues described earlier is set in the context of online disinhibition, it is impossible to be certain about the veracity of peoples' online identities (be that a single identity or multiple online identities (Schulz et al., 2014). The same challenge applies to the surveys of young people online, described above, in terms of the characteristics of people who had made unwanted sexual approaches. That is, there is no way of verifying the age and gender of the perpetrator.

EOGP research design

When the EOGP was commissioned, there was very limited evidence about online grooming. In an attempt to start to fill that evidence gap, the EOGP was tasked by the European Commission with meeting the following overarching objectives:

- Describe the behaviour of both offenders who groom and young people who are 'groomed' and explore differences (e.g. in demographics, behaviour or profiles) within each group and how these differences may have a bearing on offence outcome.
- Describe how information communication technology (ICT) is used to facilitate the process of online grooming.
- Further the current low knowledge base about the way in which young people are selected and prepared by online groomers for abuse online.
- Make a significant contribution to the development of educational awareness and preventative initiatives aimed at parents and young people.
- Contribute to the development of online sex offender risk-assessment and management knowledge.

To meet this challenging set of objectives, the research programme involved three distinct but related phases: a scoping study, interviews with online groomers and dissemination of awareness messages to key stakeholders.

A qualitative approach

The aim of qualitative research is to explore the experience of a selected group in order to gain a depth of understanding on a case-by-case basis. It does not select a sample that statistically represents the broader population of interest (in this case, men convicted of online grooming or stakeholders working in the online offending area). Nor can it undertake statistical analyses to indicate causal factors or generalize findings to a wider population statistically. It can, however, represent the population of interest symbolically and the final section of this chapter sets out generalizibility criteria appropriate to qualitative research. The main motives for choosing a qualitative approach were first the relatively small number of online groomers available in the criminal justice system, particularly in Europe, due to the very recent nature of the legislation, which precluded a large quantitative survey. Second, because the qualitative approach is the preferred method of exploring motivations and behaviour in some depth to develop a descriptive model of different types of groomers triangulating data from a number of sources.

Since a qualitative approach was used in the EOGP, it is important to understand how the findings should be interpreted. Lewis, Ritchie, Ormston and Morrell (2013) state that:

> Qualitative research cannot be generalized on a statistical basis – it is not the prevalence of particular views or experiences, nor the extent of their location within particular parts of the sample, about which wider inference can be drawn. Nor, of course, is this an objective of qualitative research. Rather, the value of qualitative research is in revealing the breadth and nature of the phenomena under study. It is this 'map' of the range of views, experiences, outcomes etc., and of the factors and circumstances that shape and influence them, that can be generalized to the parent population. (pp350–351)

To that end, qualitative samples are purposively selected to represent the range and diversity of the online grooming or professional stakeholder population symbolically. In accordance with these qualitative standards of good practice, the EOGP deliberately picked participants according to their particular demographic or offence-specific characteristics in order to include the full range and diversity of experience and views, rather than to establish prevalence. This strategy underpinned the extent to which findings from this research could be generalized and this is discussed in further detail in the final section of this chapter. Therefore, whilst the demographic and other characteristics of the online groomers are described, we cannot take the further step of saying therefore that all online groomers will have these characteristics. Instead, we can focus on the diversity and range of different types of individuals included to look at some individual differences in offenders' modus operandi.

The scoping phase

The aim of the scoping phase was to explore the background and context of internet abuse in each research-partner country so that the study could be set in the legislative and offender treatment context at that time. Alongside mapping the policy context, this phase also set out to ensure that phase two of the research, described below, was of the highest possible quality and represented good value for money. As such, the scoping phase aimed to ensure that questions asked of online groomers were based on the current most comprehensive information available about these individuals. The scoping phase drew on a combination of three distinct data-collection approaches, described below.

Scoping methods

Literature review

The key library sources for the literature review were the British Library and the British Library of Political and Economic Science at the London School of Economics (LSE) (Davidson, Grove-Hills, Bifulco, Webster, Gottschalk, Caretti et al., 2010). In particular, the joint JISC and ESRC-funded International Bibliography of the Social Sciences (IBSS). Specific government, academic and agency sites were used such as EU Kids Online at the LSE, the (then) Department for Children, Schools and Families (now the Department for Education), the CEOP and the Internet Watch Foundation. In addition, the European Commission website was searched to supplement the contributions sent from the consortium partners from each country. Alongside the sourcing of published materials, there was also use of unpublished articles from, for example, the G8 Carolina Symposium on 'Examining the relationship between online and offline offences and preventing the sexual exploitation of children'.

Review of police case files

Five case files were drawn from the United Kingdom Metropolitan Police High Technological Crime Unit and the Paedophile Unit. Four of the final report authors (SW, JD, AB, JGH) read the case files and recorded the key points on a Performa. Each case was then discussed by the research team, with the conversation digitally recorded. Case-file data was analysed using the Framework method, discussed in detail later in this chapter. In Table 3.1, the demographic and offence-specific characteristics of the case-file sample are described.

Interviews with strategic stakeholders

Stakeholder interviews were undertaken to ensure that a range of key professionals with expertise on the behaviour of online groomers were included to inform the wider analysis and the development of a model of online grooming. A brief review of these findings is presented in Chapter 4. In-depth interviews were conducted with 19 strategic

Table 3.1 EOGP case-file sample characteristics

	Case reference				
	1	2	3	4	5
Age	45	36	37	56	48
Ethnicity	White-British	White-British	White-British	White-British	White-British
Occupation	Professional	Professional	Skilled manual	Professional	Skilled manual
Marital status	Married	Married	Married	Partner	Married
Access to children	Yes	Yes	Yes	Yes	Yes
No. of own children	1	2	1	1	1
Exposure self on line	No	Yes – photos & webcam	No	Yes – photos	Yes – webcam
Images sent to YP	3 adult movies	None	None	Yes	Yes
No. of indecent images seized	510	259	Not specified	35	2
Class of indecent images	1 to 5	1 to 5	2 to 4	1 to 4	1 to 3
Travel to meeting with YP	No	Yes	Yes, arrested nearby	Yes	No, stated no intention

Source: Webster, Davidson, Bifulco, Gottschalk, Caretti, Pham et al. (2010, p30).

Table 3.2   EOGP stakeholder sample information

Country	Stakeholder number	Role
United Kingdom	1	Sexual offender treatment specialist
	2	Internet safety expert
	3	Police – overt investigator
	4	Police – covert investigator
	5	Young people treatment specialist
Norway	1	Young people treatment specialist
	2	Police – overt investigator
	3	Sexual offender treatment specialist
	4	Sexual offender treatment specialist
Italy	1	Police – national prevention co-ordinator
	2	Police – overt investigator
	3	Public prosecutor
	4	Information technology expert
	5	Police – overt investigator
Belgium	1	Police – human trafficking prevention
	2	Police – overt investigator
	3	Police – overt investigator
	4	Police – overt investigator
	5	Police – overt IT investigator

Source: Webster et al. (2012, p31).

stakeholders from the United Kingdom, Italy, Norway and Belgium. The characteristics of the stakeholder sample are presented in Table 3.2. The interviews were digitally recorded and carried out using a topic guide. The topic guide covered the key themes likely to be relevant in the interviews and helped to ensure a systematic approach across different encounters and countries.

Interviews with online groomers

UK sampling and recruitment: the sample of online groomers was provisionally selected from sexual offender assessment data collected by the National Offender Management Service (NOMS). Ethical approval was also granted by NOMS. Demographic and offence-specific data were interrogated to draw a purposive sample of online groomers. Recruitment was conducted in two phases. Phase one involved treatment providers seeking individual offender's consent for contact details to be passed to the research team. Phase two involved the research team contacting individuals who consented to releasing their details about participating in the study.

A total of 33 interviews were undertaken during 2010 with convicted male online groomers across Europe. In England and Wales, 26 interviews with online groomers were conducted in prisons. Each offender interview lasted approximately 1.5 hours and was digitally recorded for verbatim transcription. In the three partner countries/sites, five interviews were conducted in Norway and two in Belgium. These transcripts were sent to the United Kingdom for analysis. In Italy, researchers found it challenging to identify and recruit online groomers for the research largely due to the absence of grooming legislation at that time in Italy. To ensure there was still research coverage from Italy, two transcripts of Italian online offenders' chatlog interactions with children, captured by police in the course of convictions, were utilized in the analysis. These were used to cross-validate the offender interviews conducted and to highlight the offenders' likely psychological characteristics, strategies and defensive patterns (see Chapter 5). The demographic and offence-specific characteristics of the online groomer offenders are presented in Table 3.3 below.[2]

Focus groups with young people

Focus-group discussions were conducted across three of the four partner countries (the United Kingdom, Belgium and Italy) with normative groups of young people in the community. Schools opted in to the research and all the young people were provided with detailed information to make an informed decision about whether to take part. Signed consent was sought from each young person before each group started.

The purposive sample frame involved young people at secondary school with an age range of between 11 and 16 years. The research ensured that the achieved sample comprised of two age groups of 11–13 years and 14–16 years; a mix of boys and girls with two of the groups being single sex (girls only); and where possible, socio-economic diversity to identify any differences in awareness, behaviours and attitudes.

Twelve focus groups were delivered with 6–12 young people in each group. The strategy for including young people from a range of socio-economic backgrounds could not be consistently achieved across the different partner countries. In the United Kingdom, socio-economic representation can generally be achieved by selection of schools in a particular 'catchment area' but it is not necessarily a transferable method for other European countries. As such, in Belgium and Italy,

Table 3.3   EOGP online groomers' sample characteristics

Characteristic		N
Age	18–24	4
	25–34	7
	35–44	11
	45–54	7
	55 and above	4
IQ score	Less than average (90 or below)	5
	Average (91–109)	7
	Above average (110+)	15
	Don't know	6
RM2000 score	Low risk (0–1)	6
	Medium risk (2)	10
	High risk (3+)	10
Offence	Online grooming no meeting	2
	Online grooming meeting	8
	Images and online grooming – no meeting	5
	Images and online grooming – meeting	18
Offender access to children	Yes	17
	No	16
Sex offender treatment received this sentence	None	2
	Core programme	26
	Core plus other (Booster, Extended, HSF)	5
Sex offender treatment received (prior to sentence)	None	25
	Core programme	1
	Core plus other (Booster, Extended, HSF)	1
	Thames Valley SOTP	1
Pre-convictions	None	16
	Non-sexual	6
	Sexual – children offline	6
	Sexual – children online	5
	Sexual – children online and offline	0
	Sexual – adult offline	0
Victim age (of grooming)	5–9	1
	10–12	5
	13–15	27
Victim gender (of grooming)	Male	5
	Female	28
	Both	0

Source: Webster et al. (2012, pp32–33).

Table 3.4 EOGP focus groups' sample profile

Age	Gender		Total
	Male	Female	
11–13 yrs	17	22	39
14–16 yrs	29	30	59
Total	46	52	98

Source: Webster et al. (2012, p34).

the groups would be mixed. For example, in Belgium, the groups were young people in 'vocational' or 'general' education. Young people in vocational education tended to be from lower socio-economic group-ings and pupils had selected special subject streams such as hairdressing, horticulture and drawing. Confirmation of the different socio-economic backgrounds was provided throughout the discussions where references were constantly made to their circumstances, particularly the occupa-tion of parents or a similar indicator. The final sample composition is presented in Table 3.4.

A topic guide was used to shape discussion and covered four main areas: general nature of internet use; safety awareness, awareness and perception of groomers; their own online experiences; and attitudes to safety awareness training. The questions were mostly open with guidelines for suggested interviewer prompts where relevant.

Stakeholder dissemination events

Seven dissemination events were held with teachers, parents and pro-fessionals in Belgium, Italy, Norway and the United Kingdom to discuss key findings from the project. The groups included three with parents, three with teachers and one with forensic psychologists. All participants were provided with information before each event and gave consent to take part. The format included a presentation of key findings from the project, a period of discussion and then a standardized evaluation form to ascertain the usefulness of the messages. The EOGP sample is summarized in Figure 3.1 below.

EOGP qualitative analysis

The case-file and interview data was analysed using Framework (Ritchie & Lewis, 2003; Spencer, Ritchie, O'Conner, Morrell & Ormston, 2013), a systematic approach to qualitative data management. This involved a number of stages. First, the key topics and issues which

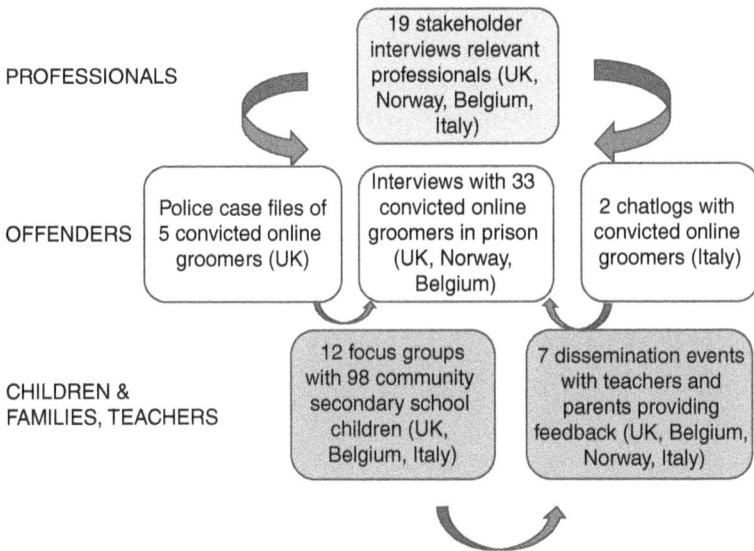

Figure 3.1 Overview of the EOGP sample

emerged from the research objectives and the data were identified through familiarization with the transcripts. An initial analytical framework was then drawn up and a series of thematic charts or matrices were set up, each relating to a different thematic issue. The columns in each matrix represented the key sub-themes or topics and the rows represented the individual interview participants. Data from each interview transcript was summarized into the appropriate cell and was grounded in participants' own accounts. The final stage of analysis involved working through the charted interview data in detail, drawing out the range of experiences and views, identifying similarities and differences, developing and testing hypotheses, and interrogating the data to seek to explain emergent patterns and findings. The findings from the study are described in the next chapter. However, before doing so the last section of this chapter sets out the criteria through which qualitative research can be generalized and the limitations of such analysis.

Appraising qualitative research

As outlined in the introductory chapters, research undertaken to understand the attitudes of behaviours of sexual offenders has tended to be dominated by the use of quantitative methods, in particular psychometric tests (Webster & Marshall, 2004). A recurrent theme advocating the use of quantitative methods revolves around the quantitative markers of quality control including objectivity, representativeness, reliability and validity. When compared against quantitative research standards, qualitative research can be perceived as less trustworthy, as it cannot demonstrate rigour according to those accepted quantitative criteria (Webster & Marshall, 2004).

However, Lewis and colleagues (2013) argue that comparing qualitative research against quantitative measures of rigour is inappropriate due to the epistemological and ontological differences between quantitative and qualitative research:

> given the different epistemological basis of qualitative research from the natural sciences and quantitative social science these concepts arguably have very limited value in determining the quality or credibility of qualitative research data and investigation. Certainly, statistical tests or measures of reliability and validity are wholly inappropriate for qualitative investigation and would cause considerable confusion if applied. (p354)

The view of Lewis et al. (2013) is very compelling. If qualitative research such as the EOGP is to be judged against quantitative standards then of course it could be seen as lacking in scientific rigour. The EOGP did not draw on a random probability sample of online groomers across Europe, and the research team have not enumerated and statistically tested the views of the sample against other sub-samples of online sexual offenders.

However, the key issue to note is that the EOGP did not set out to conduct a *quantitative* study. Lewis and colleagues (2013) propose that the extent to which a *qualitative* study is generalizable can be appraised against the following linked criteria:

- *Representational* – whether what is found in a research sample can be generalized to, or held to be equally true of, the parent population from which the sample is drawn.
- *Inferential* – whether the findings from a particular study can be generalized, or inferred, to other settings or contexts beyond the sampled one.
- *Theoretical* – whether theoretical propositions, principles or statements can be drawn from the findings of a study for wider application. (p349)

It is clear that when set against this generalizability framework, the EOGP fulfils the requirements of a high-quality study. As will be described in Chapter 4, a key finding of the EOGP is that online groomers can be classified into certain mutually exclusive behavioural groups. Whilst the research does not attempt to draw any conclusions about the relative prevalence of these groups or the views within each, the study makes a *representational generalization* that this categorization reflects the behaviour of online groomers that would be found in the parent population of convicted online groomers.

In Chapter 4, the features of online grooming that can involve up to six behavioural phases are described. These phases are under-pinned by various 'maintenance' and 'risk-management' factors. The extent and sequence within which these phases, maintenance and risk-management strategies are relevant to each individual, depends on which of the three behavioural types each online groomer fitted. Although further research (including quantitative research) is needed to confirm the robustness of these findings, these categories may have wider relevance for offender community management, risk-assessment and treatment programmes; for example, a fuller understanding of the characteristics associated with the different types has implications for offender treatment programmes. The findings will provide an *inferential generalization* that the different online groomer types and their pathways to offending are also likely to be found amongst other men convicted for online grooming offences, many of whom may be taking part in offending behaviour treatment programmes.

Finally, the EOGP study explored the key factors associated with dif-ferent patterns of online grooming. In doing so, the research highlighted the role of online disinhibition (Suler, 2004), cognitive dissonance (Festinger, 1962) and the offender's goals (Ward & Hudson, 1998) in maintaining online grooming behaviour. These theories are used to support the derived categorizations and also to challenge offender treat-ment programmes to consider the key role that online context plays in understanding and intervening in online groomers' sexual offending. In this way, the research can be used to make theoretical generalizations to inform higher order offender theory about how people can change sexual offending behaviours that of course carry serious risks to society.

In making this statement of generalizibility, the EOGP will call for fur-ther testing, replication and challenges regarding the findings. But with the hope that future research with online groomers and sexual offend-ers per se will be of high methodological quality, whether qualitative or quantitative.

Notes

1. For the purpose of this research, young people were defined as those aged 16 years or younger.
2. Data for the RM2000 score and access to treatment interventions was not available for the Norwegian sample, thus these frequencies do not total 33.

4
Understanding Online Grooming: Findings from the EOGP Study

Stephen Webster, Julia Davidson and Petter Gottschalk

Introduction

The majority of published literature to date about online sexual offending against children and young people has focused on the proliferation of indecent images of children online and on the people who access these indecent images (O'Brien & Webster, 2007; Elliott & Beech, 2009; Elliott, Beech, Mandeville-Norton & Hayes, 2009; Seto & Eke, 2005; Seto, Canter & Blanchard, 2006; Seto, 2013). However, online sexual offending is a term that can be applied to a diverse range of different attitudes and behaviours. In keeping with earlier chapters, a definition of online sexual offending encompasses not only the viewing, production and/or distribution of indecent images of children, but also the 'online grooming' of children and young people. Here, online grooming involves an interaction and in some cases socialization between an offender and a child/young person aged 16 years or younger, during which an offender prepares him/her for sexual abuse (Sexual Offences Act 2003 – Article 15). Within this definition, sexual abuse can occur online, offline or in both contexts.

This chapter begins by reviewing research literature about the characteristics of online groomers. The chapter then provides analysis of the interviews in the European Online Grooming Project (EOGP) followed by a review of features of the internet, technology and offending behaviour that can serve to 'maintain' or 'reinforce' online grooming of children and young people. Here, the chapter examines the use of web cameras (webcams), indecent images of children and online communication between people with a sexual interest in children and young people. The chapter concludes by discussing typologies of online groomers and the implications for further research.

Characteristics of online groomers

Existing research indicates that offline sexual offenders are not a homogenous group (Marshall, Anderson & Fernandez, 1999), but whether the same applies to online groomers requires further investigation. One particularly important question relates to how online groomers compare to men who use indecent images of children but who do not solicit young people online. Alexy, Burgess and Baker (2005) compared traders of indecent images with men convicted of online solicitation of children and a group convicted of both indecent image and solicitation offences. They report little difference between the groups, with the exception that the solicitation offenders were less likely to be classified as professionals when compared to the offenders who collected indecent images.

In a review of 22 online grooming offender case files, Young (2005) reported that none had any previous convictions or any known previous sexual contact with children or young people. The majority of the group were white-collar professionals with minimal indecent image collections, contradicting the earlier findings. In a further descriptive study of 31 online grooming cases, Malesky (2007) found that 71 per cent had previous convictions for sexual offences and 97 per cent engaged in explicit sexual chat online. Finally, 29 per cent lied about their age and had changed their identity to that of a young person online.

Seto and colleagues (2012) reviewed 146 cases from a North American sexual offender screening and notification database and compared three groups: online groomers/solicitors, indecent image of children offenders and offline contact sexual offenders. They found that contact sexual offenders had lower academic attainment than online groomers had and were more often living with a child than the indecent image or solicitation offender groups were. The online groomers were also more likely than contact sexual offenders were to have viewed indecent images of children, to report haebephilic sexual interests (i.e. in post-pubertal young people) and to have problems maintaining a stable adult relationship.

In the EOGP sample of 33 men convicted of online grooming in the United Kingdom, Belgium and Norway, demographic and offence-specific characteristics reported are similar to those described above. The men ranged in age from 18 to over 55, half the sample had a Full Scale Intelligence Quotient of 110 or more and had regular access to children offline. Only a few had previous convictions for sexual offences against children before their current convictions for online grooming.

There is a growing body of literature on the likely targets for online groomers and Chapter 7 looks in detail at the behaviour of young people online. Research has found that girls are at greater risk of being targeted than boys (Mitchell, Finkelhor & Wolak, 2007; Whittle, Hamilton-Giachritsis, Beech & Collings, 2013a; Wolak, Finkelhor, Mitchell & Ybarra, 2010). The EOGP data revealed a similar pattern with most (but not all) the online groomers interviewed having mainly described targeting girls. This data should not however detract from a law-enforcement and research focus on male victims of online sexual abuse. Given online abuse is heavily under-reported, this may under-estimate the experience of male victims of online sexual abuse (O'Leary & Barber, 2008).

Evidence points towards adolescence as a key risk period for victimization through online grooming (Baumgartner, Valkenburg & Peter, 2010; Quayle, Jonsson & Loof, 2012; Whittle et al., 2013a, Wolak et al., 2008). This was consistent with the EOGP data with the 33 online groomers interviewed mainly approaching young people aged 13–15. A contributory factor may be the amount of time adolescents spend online compared to younger children (although there is evidence to suggest that younger children are increasingly online and using mobile technology) (Ofcom, 2013) and the greater range of online media available to them. Livingstone and colleagues (2011) report that 38 per cent of children aged between 9 and 12 have a social networking profile compared to 77 per cent of those aged 13–16. More recent research funded by the National Society for the Prevention of Cruelty to Children (NSPCC) suggests that as many as 84 per cent of 11–16-year-olds use a social networking site regularly and more than a quarter of these young people (28%) have had an experience which had upset or bothered them in the last year (NSPCC, 2014).

Although there is quite extensive literature on the behaviour and sites of interest to young people online (Livingstone et al., 2011; Ofcom, 2013), there is very little reported about the information communication and technology (ICT) competence of online groomers and the locations they target to make approaches to children and young people. The EOGP study found the extent of formal education or training in ICT *was not* a barrier to achieving a sophisticated understanding of personal computing and the internet – learning that could then be utilized during contact with young people. Groomers interviewed without a formal training in ICT talked about learning in two ways – in the workplace and at home by observing the behaviour of their partners or children online. However, instruction from family was not always overtly requested by the groomers. For some offenders, observing their children's online behaviour 'over their shoulder' was described as helpful in terms of knowing the language and symbols/emoticons used by young people when social networking. This knowledge could then be transferred to develop 'credible' conversations with young people online. The map of the sites and chat rooms accessed by EOGP participants encompassed five broad areas and are shown in Table 4.1.

It is worth noting that in the fluid online environment, preferred sites are likely to change fairly regularly. However, this map highlights two issues that are important in understanding online grooming. First, offenders cross over from adult to young people's online domains to abuse. Second, some sites are accessed to support or legitimize the grooming process using indecent images, chat or abuse-specific essays/narratives/fantasies.

Models of online grooming

In this section, three existing models of online grooming are reviewed, compared and contrasted: O'Connell's (2003) seminal model of the grooming process and the Williams, Elliott and Beech (2013) model of grooming themes and sub-themes. These are compared with the features of online grooming and solicitation described in the EOGP study.

O'Connell (2003) presents a linear process model of online grooming that is comprised of a number of distinct phases. She gathered her data over a five-year period by posing online, usually as a young girl aged 8, 10 or 12. The conversations she had with adults took place in chat venues/forums intended for children or teenagers. The fictitious profile she created was of a child that had recently moved, who had not made friends at her new school and whose parents did not get along and argued frequently. Consequently, O'Connell presented as a vulnerable young girl with characteristics that can be specifically 'targeted' by some online groomers.

From her study findings, O'Connell (2003) argues that online grooming has a number of distinct stages that typically occur in sequence. First, there is the 'friendship-forming stage'. Here, the offender attempts to get to know the child at first contact, with the time spent varying from one offender to another. Second is a 'relationship-forming stage', an extension of the 'friendship-forming stage', whereby the offender may talk about topics such as life at school and home. Here, the offenders are 'presenting an illusion of being the child's best friend' by encouraging trust and subsequent disclosure of personal information. The 'risk-assessment stage' involves questions by the offender aimed at appraising the risk of

Table 4.1 Map of sites disclosed by the EOGP sample

Genre	Intended target group of site		
	Adults and young people	Adults	Young people
Social networking	Facebook Multiply JayDoCity		Bebo Coolbox (Belgium) Faceparty High 5
Instant messaging	Mobistar (Belgium) Proximus (Belgium) Skyblog MSN Chatavenue Flikster MySpace Yahoo Messenger Netlog		
Online dating/ romance		Adultfinder Ladslads BoysZone BoyBliss Datingdirect Love at Lycos Hot or Not	MyLoL
Indecent image exchange	Limewire Kazaa Flickr eMule WinMax		

Sexual abuse sites		Men who Like
		    Young Boys
		Boylovers
		Cherry-
		    Popping
		Daddies
		Young Petals
		Nifty
		ImagesRU	

Source: Webster et al. (2012, p40).

being caught, for example, asking about the location of the computer in the home (child's bedroom versus public place in view of parents/care giver/older siblings). Next is the 'exclusivity stage' where the offender presents the 'relationship' as a friendship built on trust, the sharing of secrets and personal issues. O'Connell talks about the concept of 'mutuality' at this point whereby the offender will present the 'friendship' as 'a mutual respect club that must remain secret from other people'. She argues that this behaviour lays the foundations for stage five (the 'sexual stage') where intimate and sexual issues are then raised.

During the sexual stage, O'Connell (2003) defines three potential pathways that the offender will take. First, there is 'gentle boundary pressing' whereby the offender will ask questions such as 'have you ever been kissed or touched'. These questions will seem quite innocuous given the build-up of conversations and the trust that has formed in the preceding stages. The second pathway is 'reducing inhibitions' where the child is sent pornography and/or indecent images of the child are requested by the offender. The third pathway involves 'fantasy re-enactment' with fantasy requested through 'mutuality', as if in some form of online relationship, or by using coercion or aggression where the child is threatened if non-compliant with the offender's demands.

O'Connell's (2003) study was the first detailed descriptive account of online grooming. The research also presented a framework and a number of hypotheses to be tested, challenged and expanded by future studies. Ten years after the study was published however, questions arose about the model's validity and its generalizability to a broader population of online groomers. The idea that online grooming is a linear process, with a relatively heterogeneous group of offenders all passing through the same sequence of behaviours has been questioned as unlikely to represent the full range and diversity of online offenders' modus operandi. A second limitation of this work (and some other subsequent studies) is that the data is not 'naturally occurring' with O'Connell posing as a child online to collect data. This casts doubt on whether the online behaviour was a reliable mirror of a child's online presentation. It also fails to cover the grooming stages and behaviours applicable to young boys online. Finally, the risk-assessment description, although appropriate at the time of publication, has been dated by more recent developments in online technology. This is a problem with all online offending studies, requiring a continual updating of research information.

A more recent conceptualization is the Williams, Elliott and Beech (2013) map of sexual grooming themes used by internet sexual offenders. In developing their work, they analysed data from the Perverted Justice Website, a not-for-profit foundation based in the United States whose adult volunteers enter child-orientated online chat rooms to present themselves as children. If the adult 'decoy' suspects the other adult is in the chat room to initiate sexual activity with a child, the decoy will engage the adult to gather enough information to pass on to the relevant law-enforcement agency.

The authors conducted a qualitative thematic analysis of eight of these online transcripts. All the adults were told that they were conversing with a female between 12 and 14 years of age. From this analysis, three higher order themes are presented: rapport building, sexual content and assessment. Williams and colleagues (2013), however, suggest that not all offenders move through these themes in a linear sequence. Instead, the men in their sample spent a greater or lesser amount of time on the behaviours, some of which seemed to be cyclical within the same grooming encounter.

'Rapport building' sets out the process of the offender seeking to create a friendship or relationship with a child. Three sub-themes in this category are identified. First is 'coordination' where the offender 'synchronises their identity and behaviour with that of the child'. For example, describing offender age as much younger to reduce any actual or perceived gap between them and the child. The next sub-theme within rapport building is 'mutuality', where offenders will look to discover the interests and attitudes of the young person and then mirror or support those views to build rapport and a bond between them. At this stage, advice and guidance can also be offered to the child as a form of online mentoring/guardianship, characterized by friendliness, empathy and warmth. The final theme in rapport building is 'positivity'. Here, the offender looks to portray themselves as somebody with positive characteristics, whether playful or advice giving, to create the illusion that they do not have any harmful intentions and can be trusted by the young person.

The second higher order online grooming theme in this model is 'sexual content'. As with the description of rapport, Williams and colleagues (2013) suggest two broad sub-themes: introduction and maintenance/escalation. When sexual content is first 'introduced', four offender strategies are proposed: discussing sex is 'a game'; that the offender is providing 'advice' and so supporting the presentation of an online mentor; that the discussion is in fact a 'mutual fantasy' thereby subtly placing some responsibility for the interaction on the young person; and 'force' whereby the offender will explicitly set out their demands. With regard to the maintenance/escalation stage, it is suggested that the offender uses repetitive requests for sexual interactions with the young person over a short period of time as well as some more forceful or threatening approaches.

The third and final higher order theme is 'assessment'. Sub-categories within this theme cover the assessment of the child and the environment. With regard to 'child assessment', the offender is constantly appraising the extent of 'trust' the young person has in them and the degree to which they are 'vulnerable' to the sexual approaches. In contrast, 'assessment of the environment' involves probing for information that involves appraising the degree to which there is an opportunity to sexually offend, and understanding and overcoming any obstacles to their offending behaviour. For example, the geographical location of the child; the extent to which the child is supervised by their parents; the location of the computer in the home and so on (Williams et al., 2013).

One of the strengths of the Williams et al. model is that it presents a conceptualization of grooming behaviours not following a linear process. It is clear from the broader literature that young people do not present as a homogeneous group online (Baumgartner et al., 2010; Mitchell et al., 2007; Whittle, Hamilton-Giachritsis, Beech & Collings, 2013b). They have diverse backgrounds, needs and behaviours, so it seems likely that some online groomers will tailor or adapt their approaches to meet 'the needs' of the particular young person.

Alongside the strengths set out above, there are some challenges to the Williams et al. (2013) model. The findings cannot be generalized to a broader population of online groomers. First, Williams et al. (2013) said that the themes presented were displayed by all eight participants, albeit with different degrees of intensity. For example, friendliness, empathy and warmth were described as core characteristics of rapport building. It is debateable whether this conceptualization is showing the full range and diversity of online grooming behaviour. Specifically, warmth and empathy may not be displayed in all online offenders modus operandi.

The second challenge is that the profile of the 'decoy' online was that of a young female. It is therefore debatable whether the findings apply to online groomers that are targeting young boys. The third observation is related to the method of qualitative analysis presented. That is, statements such as 'four of the eight people said theme X' are presented to support the thematic conceptualization. There are a number of problems with this approach, and enumeration of qualitative analysis is difficult to support due to the small sample size and the non-random way in which qualitative samples are developed (Lewis, Ritchie, Ormston &

Morrell, 2013). In addition , the model presents a reductionist approach to a method of analysis that is designed to map the range and diversity of behaviours (Ritchie & Lewis, 2003; Lewis et al., 2013).

The EOGP model of online groomers

As noted in Chapter 3, the first phase of the EOGP research programme was to gather the views of professionals working with sexual offenders convicted of online offences and those working with survivors of online sexual offences. Alongside the analysis of convicted online groomer case-file material, the scoping phase interviews facilitated the development of a hypothetical model of online grooming that the research team could then test and refine during and after the interviews with convicted online groomers.

The case-file review and interviews with stakeholders led to the development of a hypothetical nine-stage model of online grooming. The phases identified were offender vulnerability factors; grooming style; preparation and scanning; identity assumed 1; initial contact; identity assumed 2; desensitization; offence maintenance and intensity; and outcomes (Webster et al., 2010).

A key advantage of this phase is that it allowed the research team to incorporate research design requests from stakeholders into the main-stage interviews with online groomers described in the remainder of this chapter. For example, to identify whether there are any further grooming types aside from the 'planned' and 'opportunistic' styles that some stakeholders were familiar with in 2010 and to understand the role of online websites and networks in maintaining online sexual offending behaviour:

> I would also like to understand the experiences of other colleagues as well. To obtain more details on the profile of this sort of abuser to help us work well.
>
> (Belgium, SH4, Police)

> I want to understand how online grooming activity is connected to other kinds of risk activities and offensive activities and what are the underlying dynamics in the grooming process as such.
>
> (Norway, SH4, Treatment provider)

> You want to understand as a treatment provider what made him want to do it, what enabled him to do it, what triggered it, what maintained it, all that kind of thing. At the moment a lot of the

research isn't very helpful as internet offenders are often split into two groups and compared without people thinking 'how valuable is this and what does it explain?'

(UK, SH1, Treatment provider)

Using the stakeholder-developed model of online grooming as a baseline platform for testing, analysis of the online groomer interviews led to a model of grooming shown in Figure 4.1. The EOGP findings

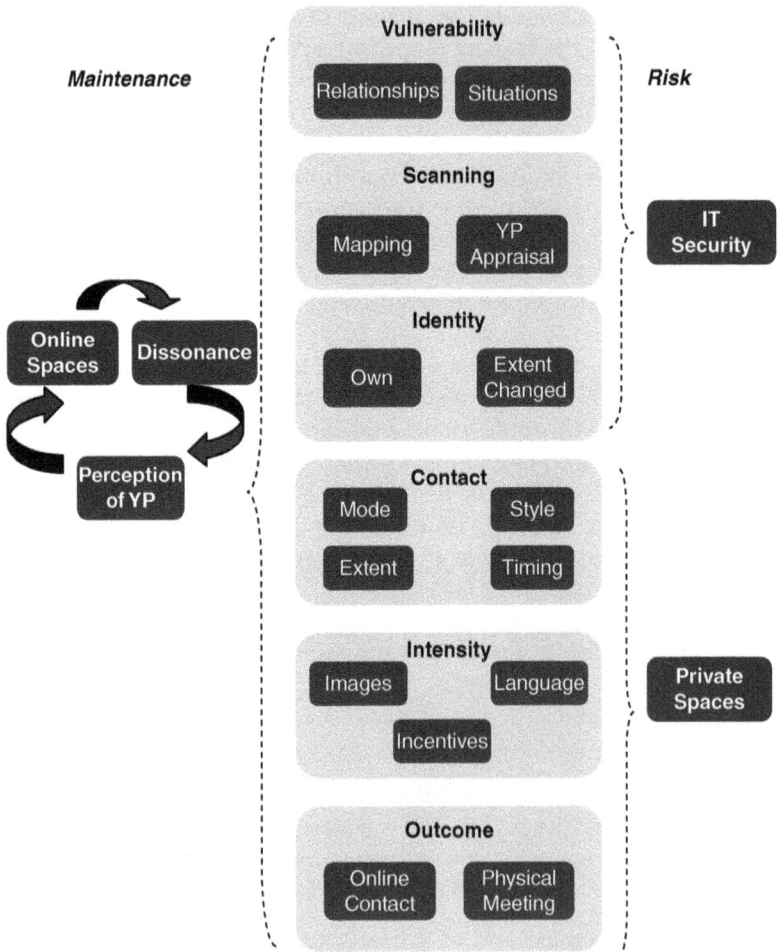

Figure 4.1 The features of online grooming described by the EOGP sample
Source: Webster et al. (2012, p42).

describe movement through the different features of online grooming as neither unitary nor linear. Instead, the model developed indicated a cyclical process, involving a pattern of adoption, maintenance, relapse and re-adoption over time. For this reason, the features described in Figure 4.1 are not numbered so as not to indicate a linear process. Additionally, it was found that according to groomer accounts, the actual process of online grooming could take minutes, hours, days or months. Online groomers appeared to remain at different behavioural points for various lengths of time according to a dynamic inter-relationship between their goals and needs and the style or reactions of the young person.

The salient aspects of each online grooming feature are then summarized in subsequent paragraphs.

Vulnerability

The men interviewed described event(s) that made them vulnerable and low and so triggered their underlying goal or desire to contact and groom a young person. Situational factors included life events such as redundancy or the loss of the home:

> ... losing my job, I suppose it knocked me for six when I couldn't find a job quickly after that. It knocked my confidence and I thought 'am I any good in this field, can I get another job' and a lot of self-doubt crept in.
>
> (UK offender)

Alongside the situational factors, the second set of vulnerability events tended to involve the breakdown of interpersonal relationships, such as a partner or spouse leaving the offender, or an argument with a friend or acquaintance. Irrespective of the type of relationship challenge, this vulnerability factor was underpinned by feelings of low self-worth. Low self-esteem is a common feature amongst offline sexual offenders (Webster, Mann, Thornton & Wakeling, 2007) and can be a significant risk factor in the offending process.

> I'd lost all self-respect, I wasn't functioning as a person, more ... mechanically.
>
> (UK offender)

This finding is also supported by some earlier research based upon in-depth interviews with convicted child abusers (pre-internet) which explored the circumstances in which abuse occurs (Davidson, 2006).

Scanning

Some of the men said they did not immediately begin to groom the first young person encountered online. Instead, some offenders scanned the online environment to make an 'informed' decision about who to approach for sexual contact. Scanning included *being in online spaces* where young people meet to identify the nature of different conversations and what friends were saying about other young people in the forum. Scanning also involved *appraising the characteristics* of particular young people online. Three types of appraisal emerged: virtual-sexual meant interpreting the screen name or forum tag:

> I'd always aim for someone with a sexy name because obviously, they'd be into sex. Usually BigTits or whatever; it wouldn't be a normal name or anything. It was some sexy name.
>
> (UK offender)

> You then have normal exchanges with people in chat-rooms until an opportunity comes along. 'Hmm, that girl has a pretty racy alias.'
>
> (Belgium offender)

Idealistic/romantic scanning denoted looking for young people who would be good in a 'relationship':

> The young person looked fun, fun to be around and with.
>
> (UK offender)

Finally, physical characteristics described the use of images of the young person to identify whether they were physically developed enough to warrant potential online contact. In contrast to those scanning, there were men who did not hide an immediate and explicit desire for sexual contact with young people:

> The girls I was interested in, they had to look mature enough.
>
> (UK offender)

> Ideally I looked for people age 14/15 as more physically developed and I saw younger people as too young.
>
> (UK offender)

Identity

Online identities were described as being shaped to present the men in the most positive way possible to young people. There were men that described making 'minor' changes to their identity such as changing their name, age, marital status or using a younger (perhaps more attractive) photograph of themselves.

> I said I had an athletic body rather than skinny, but otherwise my profile was true.
>
> (UK offender)

> The only thing on my profile that was not true was that was I said I was more social than I actually was.
>
> (UK offender)

Some men made these minor changes to their identity based on unsuccessful previous attempts at contact:

> At first I was honest about my age but sometimes I got negative reactions and was called a 'peado'... so I then used a younger age as girls were then more likely to respond to me.
>
> (UK offender)

There were also people that made major changes to their identity. Here, changes went beyond amending age or name and could involve pretending to be a young girl or woman. Some offenders also talked about using multiple concurrent identities online and switching between them to maximize the opportunity of contact:

> You can put any picture up and say it's you, you can invent all sorts of stories. I got a kick out of it. The manipulation is part of the game. Why? You're certainly not going to come out and say 'I'm 30 years old and I would like to get to know you'.
>
> (Belgium offender)

> I sometimes created a new identity and would speak to the victim as real and fake me. That way I could transfer information about me through two channels. I would typically pretend to be a younger girl as girls tend to talk more openly and honestly to other girls.
>
> (Norway offender)

Finally, there were online groomers that did not change their identity either before or during their online encounters with young people. Alongside listing legitimate details, some men were also explicit about their sexual interest in young people. That some of these men went on to develop contact with young people raises important questions about the vulnerability of some young people online. This is discussed in detail in Chapter 7.

> I said I was 28 and I did this job, got my own place, got a car ... I wanted to be honest with her, because I wanted her to make, to make the decision about whether to talk to me or not.
>
> (UK offender)

Contact

Having contact with young people online was described as being made and sustained in four ways. First, there was the *mode* of contact which included forums and chat rooms that were used for text communication that continued until the encounter with the young person ended or escalated into a physical meeting. Alongside text chat, some offenders also described using webcams[1] as a key part of their offending behaviour. Webcams reinforced, strengthened and maintained grooming by bringing some offenders' fantasies to life:

> I was at home and had the opportunity to get on the internet quickly, and she happened to be on there. And so, you know, it sexually aroused me. So I said 'do you want to see my webcam' and she said she did. She didn't have a webcam, she just watched me. I just typed about what I'd like to do to her, and masturbated on the webcam.
>
> (UK offender)

Phones were also used to contact young people, and were described as being a more immediate and intimate method of contact.

> I got her phone number and started phoning her, and then sort of, the conversation did turn sexual on the telephone. No images, just well, phone sex I suppose you'd call it.
>
> (UK offender)

> It's easier to talk on the phone, when I was talking on the phone it was like I was right next to them, like I was face-to-face with them.
>
> (UK offender)

Finally, online game platforms were used by some men that were attempting to groom young boys. Grooming using game platforms helped to reinforce the fantasy aspect of offending behaviour and gave the men credibility in the eyes of the young men being approached:

I spent a lot of time playing [name of online war game] with boys. I
was good, it was a 'shoot em up'.

(UK offender)

The second aspect of contact was the *extent* of interactions described
with young people online. As expected in such a diverse group of
offenders, the number of contacts varied considerably. For example, the
number of young people online across time zones meant that some men
had sexual conversations with dozens of young people concurrently.
In contrast, some online groomers were very particular about whom
they spoke to. For those groomers speaking to a number of young people, keeping on track with multiple conversations was a challenging task
particularly when some used multiple identities. To manage this, some
described strategies such as logging conversation histories on MS Excel
spreadsheets, or using other coding schemes to monitor conversation
'progress':

It was difficult because I was talking to so many young boys online,
I mean I must have had over 200 on MSN at any one time. It was
difficult remembering what we talked about so I started to put a tick
by his name or a star by his name.

I: And what did the tick and star mean?

A tick would be a non-sexual chat and a star was a sexual chat.

(UK offender interview segment)

The third aspect of contact described was that of *style*. Here, a 'typical'
grooming approach was not always used. For example, the identity of
some men online was denoted by a picture of their flaccid penis, or
their avatar or a profile name would be an explicit descriptor such as
PussyLicker69 – limited conversation and an instant sexual request/act
characterized approaches that used this 'style':

I'd just go online and say straight out 'what's your name, what's your
bra size'. And they would reply back with a size and I'd say 'that's
nice and big'.

(UK offender)

For those men who did not make instant sexual requests, a deliberate
process of gentle socialization was described. Here, the approach was
tailored to meet the needs of the offender and/or the perceived needs

of the young person and encompassed 'complimentary approaches', for example, using language to explicitly flatter the young person:

> She had a very low self esteem of herself because she was slightly overweight. She'd always say 'oh I'm really fat, I'm ugly' and I would say 'no you're not you're good looking', I was very supportive.
>
> (UK offender)

'Mentor' meant presenting themselves as somebody who could discuss and solve the young person's problems:

> I fitted the criteria for a couple of boys, they wanted a father figure and they saw me as a sort of father figure, as it were. It was the way they said things, calling me 'daddy' and stuff like that.
>
> (UK offender)

Finally, 'experience congruence' was about approaching young people that shared similar interests or life experiences. In addition, some men said they adopted a style of text to present themselves favourably. This included using being up to date with music favoured by young people and using *text-type* (*'Hi gorgeous hope to cu l8r'*) and *emoticons*.[2]

> I'd get on their side and talk about music. So I was well up-to-date with all the teen, the chart stuff. So I knew all the names and what have you and groups and songs, and that was always a good progression. It's on their wavelength; that's it, they're interested, and it's finding, basically finding out their interests.
>
> (UK offender)

The fourth aspect of contact involved *timing*. Participants said they spent seconds, minutes, days, months and in some cases even years talking to young people. For those offending quickly, the internet has speeded up the process of child sexual abuse. That is, the anonymous, disinhibiting properties of the internet allowed the offenders to behave in a sexually explicit way, at a speed that would be almost impossible to replicate face-to-face with a stranger offline.

Intensity

Contact with young people was described as being intensified using three desensitization techniques. *Visual desensitization* involved sending young people adult pornography and/or indecent images of children.

Where online groomers talked about a gradual process of offence intensity and escalation, images were used to instigate sexual discussion. Use of images also intensified the abuse process for the offender. For example, it was not uncommon for some offenders to describe masturbating to ejaculation whilst discussing images with young people:

> I sent them pictures of, of some of the bits that I had or videos or images. I'd send them through and we would comment on the, on the person in the image. About sort of whether they were attractive or not ... and maybe talk about what I wanted to do with, what I want to do with the girl and sometimes we had conversations about, even with the young girls about what I want her to do with the young girl as well or want her to do with me and what the three of us could do together, those sorts of conversations.
>
> (UK offender)

Running concurrently to visual desensitization, some men created further process momentum by using *language* to encourage and reassure the young person. Here, a 'sexual test' was given to young people that could involve an explicit or subtle sexual discussion. The choice of approach was influenced by how the young person was presenting online. For example, a young person's provocative screen name could be used to introduce sexual topics. Where there was nothing to indicate a sexualized young person, sex was more subtly introduced. In addition, 'competitions' to masturbate to ejaculation or telling sexual jokes helped promote sex as entertainment:

> After a while I would ask her to go on web-cam 'with a short skirt on, like'.
>
> (UK offender)

> You test her by saying stuff like: 'Are you slutty, are you horny?' If she's receptive, then we can take it a step further. If not, you move on to something else.
>
> (Belgium offender)

The third aspect of intensity was the *'incentives'* described by men in our sample. These were either gifts or threats. Gifts included topping up mobile phones, providing new phone handsets, sending webcams to young people and offers of money. Providing gifts to young people as part of the sexual offence process is also a common tactic used by men who sexually offend offline (Marshall et al., 1999). In contrast, the type of threat selected depended on whether the groomer wanted the young person to begin sexual contact or continue behaving sexually. Where the young person had not yet acted sexually, there was an example of one offender hacking into the computers of young people to encourage them to act out sexually. If the young person had been behaving sexually online, some offenders also talked about making explicit threats to encourage the young person to continue. For example, threatening to make public indecent images of the young person:

> ... you have a direct link between their computer and yours, so once that's established you can go into the, the DOS prompt and you can find their IP address, which is very easy to do. Once you've got their IP address, if they have no protection or little protection on their computer it's very easy to just use a simple programme to hack straight into their computer. If they do have some protection you can send a virus ... that allows me to get into their computer through those open ports. When they were open, I could access their files, I could control their computer as though I were sat in front of it ... so if, if I spoke to the girls and they wouldn't do what I wanted to do, I would hack in via those means and then say, you know, look, I can do this, I can do that: do what I want or I'll, you know, mess up your computer, delete files, whatever.
>
> (UK offender)

Outcomes

For some online groomers, being able to continue to collect images and engage with young people in a sexual way was the desired outcome – a meeting or any longer term contact for these offenders was not the goal driving their offending behaviour:

> As long as they looked more mature, that was all I was kind of interested in really. At the time, because it wasn't anything long-term, it wasn't a case of I'd even want to speak to them the next day. It was just for that moment, so there was no real specific target in there.
>
> (UK offender)

However, there were also accounts of a physical meeting between the young person and offender as the final outcome. Meetings were held in hotels, car parks, parks, bus stops and in the offender's or young person's bedroom. Meetings could take place on single or multiple occasions with the same young person. The profile of men who tended to want to meet young people physically is described later in this chapter.

Risk management

Throughout the different features of online grooming, the management of risk was described in three ways. First, ICT was adapted by some men to manage the risk of detection. These steps included using *multiple hardware*, for example, purchasing a laptop or smartphone for the sole purpose of offending that was then hidden to avoid probation monitoring:

> I got myself a laptop for the purpose of going back on chat. I got a (prevention order) saying not to go in chat rooms. So I went back online undercover on this laptop that was hidden under my bed if, if I ever got raided. I was using a different internet connection than the main computer when I first started to contact my victim... Obviously for cover up, again.
>
> (UK offender)

Multiple ISP addresses and multiple proxy servers[3] were also used to hide the actual location of the offender:

> ...when I got further into like technological knowledge I started setting up virtual personal networks and proxy servers, so that the internet believed that I was from a different country... because there are certain websites out there which are illegal in this country but aren't illegal in other countries.
>
> (UK offender)

File labelling and storage management encompassed changing file extensions of indecent images; filing indecent images in a hidden hard drive, directory or folder; and using external devices to store indecent material:

> I used to zip them up in a zip file, then change the name of the zip file so that someone couldn't just stumble across it and open it up.
>
> (UK offender)

Second was *conversation management*. Here, a chat in any open space was described as risky, so some online groomers asked for the *private email address, postal address* or *mobile telephone number* of the young person.

A sexual chat would always have taken place in one of the private places...never in the open because anybody could see it. I suppose there was an element of hiding protection of being caught in that.

(UK offender)

The *language* used in some encounters was also tailored to minimize the risk of detection and so encourage the young person not to disclose the abuse:

All I used to say is, 'this is our secret, don't tell anyone'.

(UK offender)

Finally, some online groomers picked young people and meeting *locations* far away from their own homes so they were less likely to be recognized in a new environment. This behaviour was particularly pronounced amongst the groomers from Belgium and Norway.

Proximity is important as well. For example, I'm from xxxx, I'm not going to meet with someone from xxxx because I'll risk getting caught. So I'm going to choose girls who live further away, where no one knows me, if I want to meet them.

(Belgium offender)

However, not all online groomers adopted risk-management behaviours. For some individuals, their view was that they were not doing anything wrong and so there was no need to hide their actions. This is explored later in the chapter where three types of online groomer are described.

There are a number of similarities in the EOGP model and in that of O'Connell (2003) and Williams et al. (2013). All describe the tailoring of online identities by some men with a sexual interest in children, as well as the concepts of mutuality, offence intensity and escalation. It is important that these frameworks be further tested, particularly given the speed at which online technology is changing. It is possible that grooming behaviours will be adapted as the mobile internet continues to develop and that these models need to evolve over time.

Factors maintaining online grooming

Adults with a sexual interest in young people are aware that the general public finds such behaviour abhorrent. Offenders themselves may also be disgusted or unsettled with their sexual attraction towards young people but feel that they do not have the strategies or power to resist such urges (Mann, Webster, Blagden, Lee & Williams, 2012). Given the clear personal and social risks associated with online grooming, understanding how some offenders actively tried to deal with these threats has important implications for offender management and internet safety policy.

In this next section, three factors that are proposed to have a bearing on the maintenance of online grooming are discussed: the role of online networks, online technology and indecent images of children. Additional analyses of EOGP data will be used to illustrate the discussion points.

Online networks

There are a number of online organizations that unite people with a sexual interest in children and these can be examined in terms of their size and structure. Examples of groups with a large membership and structure include the North American Man-Boy Love Association (NAMBLA), the British Paedophile Information Exchange (PIE) (Harkins & Dixon, 2010) and Girlchat and Boychat (Holt, Blevins & Burkert, 2010; O'Halloran & Quayle, 2010). These groups tend to advocate a lowering of the age of consent alongside the demythologizing of adult sexual behaviour with children (De Young, 1988). More recently, these networks have also been found to facilitate the online sexual abuse of children and young people. An example of this is the 'Orchid Club' that was operating in North America (Beech, Elliott, Birgden & Findlater, 2008).

A number of scholars have analysed the cognitive distortions prevalent within online paedophile group discussions (see Durkin & Bryant, 1999; Malesky & Ennis, 2004; De Young, 1988). However, these studies tend to describe cognitions and behaviours, rather than explain what people actually get from membership and the bearing the membership can have on the maintenance of online grooming and contact sexual abuse. One of the few studies that has described and explained the role of cognitions within networks is the EOGP. Here, some of the offenders talked about accessing child abuse sites such as Men who Like Young Boys, Boy-lovers, Boy Bliss, Cherry-Popping Daddies and Young Petals. In addition, some men described these groups as 'educational', as evidenced by a quote from one offender in the study:

It's the fact that I could talk to other boy-lovers, as it were, and see how they would do things. I would post things on there and they would post messages back. They would give me advice, as to what the next step was.

(UK offender)

The function of organized online networks may also meet other needs in men with a sexual interest in children. In particular, there is some data from the EOGP that suggests forums help people come to terms with their interest, in effect managing any cognitive dissonance (Festinger, Riecken & Schachter, 1956). In particular, making people feel 'normal':

For me it goes back to about being, wanting to be accepted, feeling people wanted to talk to me and everything.

(UK offender)

It cannot be inferred that such acceptance causes people to escalate their offending interests and subsequent behaviour. However, this data suggests that a 'need for continued support' does have some bearing on offending. For example, one offender described how despite knowing that his behaviour was unacceptable, he began to provide an online group with sexual fantasy material about a young relative to maintain their contact:

I suppose looking back now I had a fear that if I, if I stopped giving him stuff that he wanted to hear he would have stopped being my friend and I would lose that contact.

(UK offender)

Evidence from the EOGP research indicates that online networks are not always clearly labelled, structured and organized. Offenders included men who had communicated online with one or two other people about a sexual interest in young people. However, the key difference here is that the interaction was characterized by deceit. In effect, some online groomers who were perhaps more sophisticated seemed to be grooming other men with a sexual interest in children in order to meet their 'offending needs'. The extract below is from a case where the participant sent indecent images of a young relative to another sexual offender he met in a chat room. The sexual offender was posing in the chat room as a woman with children who could invite people to 'parties' where sexual offences against 'her' children would take place. Similar to the case described in the preceding section, the need to belong and to act out

the sexual interest seemed to influence an escalation in this participant's
own offending behaviour:

I: Where did you first meet this other person [name] online?
O: I can't remember exactly. It was over a long period of time, it was
small things, small conversations, I was curious, I was interested,
and I also was seeking her attention.
I: Did you have any idea that [name] wasn't actually [name]?
O: No. I genuinely thought it was a woman. At one point, the first
time I took the pictures [of his young relative] and then she disap-
peared, I did think, God, it was the police, you know, or some sort
of sting operation reeling me in.
I: What sort of things did you talk about?
O: We talked about her daughters, for instance, and she might start
talking about how, you know, someone came round from another
family and they'd swap children, and what they did in terms of the
sexual acts they would perform on people, on each other...that
type of conversation.
I: What did you think about that?
O: To begin with I was horrified, but I was intrigued and I wanted to
keep her attention, because I enjoyed her attention. So eventually it
became normalised. It was just completely normal.

(UK offender)

There remains a dearth of research on the bearing of online networks on
the prevalence of online and offline sexual abuse. The EOGP has provided some initial data that indicates this is a concern. However, larger
scale testing of these findings is required to inform law enforcement,
policy and offender intervention practice.

Technology: Webcams

In September 2013, the Child Exploitation and Online Protection
Centre (CEOP) in the United Kingdom described the use of webcams
in the online grooming and sexual abuse of children as a key emerging online threat. The CEOP (September, 2013) stated that in the past
two years they had been involved in 12 operations where blackmail-
ing children into performing sexual acts had been a clear motive of the
offender. In that same period, it has also discovered – using information
from police forces in the United Kingdom and abroad – that 424 children have been a victim of online sexual blackmail, with 184 from the
United Kingdom.

Despite the use of webcams being high on the policy and public agenda, there is very limited research on this issue, particularly the offence-specific and psychological needs that this type of offending seems to meet. An exception is the EOGP, whereby a key finding of the study was that not all of these offenders wanted to physically meet a child offline – having a young person perform a sexual act on a webcam was a 'desired outcome' for some men in itself. Webcams were also used as a tactic to escalate the sexual nature of the encounter with the young person (see Figure 4.1 above). Here, some offenders were able to control the computers of some young people remotely as a way of compelling them to act out sexually on a webcam:

> I found the IP address and I got in very easily. I said look what I can do to your screen and I kind of switched it off then she blocked me on [chat room name] and then I turned their screen blank. I said turn it back on now or I will start deleting files. They said 'don't delete anything this isn't my computer' and I said 'well, if you do what I'm asking you to do, then I won't' so they went along with it ... they then sent me topless photos and indecent images.
>
> (UK offender)

Alongside explicit offence escalation, webcams can also be used to meet an individual's paraphilic behavioural needs, such as exhibitionism and voyeurism (Seto, 2013). The EOGP provides some support for Seto's contention. Exhibitionism was demonstrated by some men exposing themselves to unsuspecting young people using a webcam, as well as adult men and women on particular websites.

Voyeurism was evidenced by one participant that subscribed to hidden camera websites. These sites encourage the surreptitious photography of girls under desks, in showers and so on, with the images taken then posted online:

> There were websites where they were advertised as sort of hidden camera websites. You pay a bit of extra money and you see an office webcam under a desk or one in the shower block and things like this.
>
> (UK offender)

Indecent images

The proliferation of indecent images and videos of children online is a significant public health concern. Prichard, Watters and Spiranovic

(2011) found that 'child pornography' search terms were in the top 300 terms listed on isoHunt – a peer-to-peer network engine. The advent of freely available file-sharing software, peer-to-peer networking and the significant number of images available makes effective law enforcement challenging (Seto, 2013). As noted earlier in this chapter, the past ten years has seen a significant amount of work on the demographic, offence-specific and psychiatric characteristics of indecent image users (Elliot & Beech, 2009; Elliott et al., 2009; Krueger, Kaplan & First, 2009; Babchishin, Hanson & Hermann, 2011). Other studies have concentrated on comparing the characteristics of indecent image users to offline child molesters and online groomers (Alexy, Burgess & Baker, 2005; Young, 2005; Malesky, 2007; Seto et al., 2012).

Although this stream of comparative analyses is a valuable contribution to the literature, it could be argued that they describe indecent image use more than they actually explain the role of images in maintaining or escalating the sexual abuse of children. A recent exception to this is the work of Long, Alison and McManus (2013), who examined a sample of 120 adult males convicted of offences involving indecent images of children. Of the 120 offenders, a sub-sample of 60 offenders – 30 offenders that used images and had a contact sexual offence and 30 offenders that had 'only' used indecent images – were examined in terms of the quantity and type of indecent image used and their offending behaviour. Long et al. (2013) report that the two offender groups could be discriminated between by previous convictions, access to children, and the number, proportion and type of indecent image viewed. From this analysis, Long and colleagues (2013) conclude that there may be an association between the type of indecent image collected, victim selection and offending behaviour.

Data from the EOGP suggests some support for the hypothesis of an association between indecent image use and the sexual abuse of children either online or offline. Here, this type of escalation took two forms. First were men that described moving from adult pornography to indecent images to online chat and then the grooming of children.

> I found myself looking at younger and younger pornography pages. I mean, some of them, one of them was a website called U18, you know, and the models were, like, 18 years old, but they looked younger. You know, I was finding myself sexually turned on more by those.

> (UK offender)

The second type of escalation involved a process of saturation whereby harder and more violent indecent images of children were sourced over time:

> Well I started off looking at images of like teenagers from Eastern European countries where it's not so illegal to look at images of that age. Then I also started using file share software to download images off other people. It escalated because when I first started it was just the odd pornographic image I was looking at, and by the time I was arrested my computer could be on 24 hours a day downloading off file share software... I think I was looking for higher level images, to get the same satisfaction. You'd start off at level one, two images, and then it progressed to images of three and four and the odd level five image, just to be able to get the same kick that I was getting at the beginning.
>
> (UK offender)

In some cases, men were very clear that looking at indecent images normalized the offending behaviour to the extent that it encouraged them to talk to young people and adults about fantasies and sexual abuse online:

> When I first got the images there was a sexual excitement to them... it was very much about what's out there, what can I see... a whole new sphere of things that I hadn't ever seen before. Later on [it was about using images] with conversations and actually creating fantasy conversations with some of the images that I was trying to interweave the two together. Later on, the images were secondary and it was about having conversations with people and then being able to say 'I've got some images here', send them to them, then having a chat with them about sexual fantasies involving young children.
>
> (UK offender)

Taking all the evidence to date, it cannot be said with any certainty that looking at indecent images of children *causes* contact sexual abuse. However, from the work of Long et al. (2013) and the EOGP findings reported here, there is an indication of an association that requires urgent research attention. This of course would have benefits for law-enforcement case prioritization and intervention efforts with online groomers.

Types of online groomers

Earlier sections of this chapter have described research that has high-lighted the diversity of online sexual offenders, particularly those convicted of indecent image offences. It is plausible to suggest that online groomers are equally heterogeneous but there is little pub-lished work examining this. One study of relevance is by Briggs, Simon and Simonsen (2011), who examined a sample of online groomers and distinguished between fantasy-driven and contact-driven offend-ers. Fantasy-driven offenders were characterized by online activities that could be classed as 'cybersex' with young people. For example, sexually explicit chat, masturbation in front of a webcam and so on. In con-trast, the contact-driven offenders are described as having briefer online activities that were all geared towards meeting with a child offline.

The EOGP findings provide some support for the Briggs et al. (2011) concept of the fantasy-driven offender. For example, some men described being able to 'see through' some online child abuse narratives. That is, the behaviours and acts were perceived as simply not 'credible':

> There were a couple [on a child abuse forum] that were saying that they had their son who they were doing stuff with, but I was think-ing, 'well if that's the case, why are you telling everyone?' So, I didn't know whether to believe it or not.
>
> (UK offender)

> I have told people [details] but it never was like big fantasies. Some people used to ask 'what's the youngest you've done' or some-thing...some of the conversations were just proper dirty. One per-son was talking about kidnapping someone or stuff...but [when challenged] he said he was joking.
>
> (UK offender)

Seto (2013) suggests that whilst the Briggs et al. (2011) typology is appealing, the reliability of the typology will, to some extent, be depen-dent on the sample of solicitation offenders. To support this view, if you consider the networking, webcam and image use of the men described in the section above, they could be the cybersex or fantasy behaviours defined by Briggs et al. (2011). However, a number of the men inter-viewed in the EOGP went on to meet a child offline and commit a sexual offence. It would therefore not be possible to classify the men in the EOGP sample within the two types suggested by Briggs and colleagues (2011).

To account for this heterogeneity, the EOGP sample was classified according to their behaviour across the following nine dimensions:

- whether the offender had any previous convictions for sexual offending;
- if they used their own or another identity;
- the nature and extent of indecent image use;
- if they contacted other offenders online;
- the type of offence-supportive beliefs described;
- the speed of contact made with young people;
- how contact was made and sustained;
- the outcome of the offence (online offending and/or offline meeting).

From this qualitative analysis, three types of online groomer were proposed. These are described in the section below with composite case-study material to illustrate the dimensions within each behavioural type.

Men in the *intimacy-seeking* group did not have any previous convictions for sexual offending. They had offence-supportive beliefs that involved seeing contact with the young person as a 'consenting relationship'. As such, they did not change their identity in any way, as they had a desire to be liked for who they were, and they did not get involved in other online behaviours that indicated to them, and others, that they were sexually offending. Consequently, men within this group did not have any indecent images of children and they did not have any contact with any other sexual offenders online. This group also seemed to spend a significant amount of time online talking to the young person before they met the victim. All men in this group met with the victim to develop or further the 'intimate relationship'.

Composite case study: Intimacy-seeking online groomer

Tom was a 42-year-old single parent bringing the children up after his partner had left him. Tom had a steady job but had recently been made redundant. At the time of the offence, he was concentrating on looking after his children. He said that he sometimes felt lonely being at home all day. He had never been in trouble with the police before. As he was at home all day, Tom talked about having lots of time to go online and do things like looking for houses, looking for jobs and downloading films for him and his children. One day when surfing the internet, Tom talked about feeling particularly low, so he wanted to meet somebody. He then went on MSN as he had heard that was a good meeting place. Tom used his own name and details on his profile page. At first, Tom talked about playing other online games with other adults and some young people, with no suggestions of any sexual conversations.

Tom's internet use steadily increased and he found himself spending more and more time online playing games with adults and teenagers. On one occasion, he said 'hi' to a 15-year-old girl and they began talking about all sorts of things, but nothing sexual at first. Over a period of weeks, Tom and the girl decided to exchange phone numbers and conversations moved from MSN to phone chat. Tom said that the girl was chasing him as much as he was she and that she would sometimes call him up for a chat. Eventually, they both decided to meet, and did so on several occasions over a few months. During the meetings, they would spend the day together and then go to a hotel where the sexual offence took place. Looking back, Tom said that sex was never the main aim of his relationship with the girl – he was looking for company and friendship. He said that whilst the grooming was taking place he knew what he was doing was wrong but that he could not stop as he was like a 'love-struck' teenager. Tom reacted angrily when asked whether he had seen or used indecent images of children, saying he was 'disgusted by such behaviour'.

Source: Webster et al. (2012), p81.

From the description and case-study material, Table 4.2 shows the features of online grooming, maintenance and risk management that are pertinent to understanding the 'intimacy-seeking' groomer. Shaded dimensions refer to the factor not emerging from the data as prevalent for that particular grooming style.

The *adaptable online groomer* tended to have previous convictions for sexual offending against children. They had offence-supportive beliefs that involved their own needs and they viewed the victim as mature and capable. Unlike the intimacy-seeking offenders, they did not seem to have discussed the encounter in terms of a relationship. Some men in this group had collections of indecent images of children but they

Table 4.2   Features of online grooming pertinent to the 'intimacy-seeking' groomer

	Dimension	Attitudes and behaviour
Grooming features	Vulnerability	Emotional loneliness, emotional congruence with young people.
	Scanning	
	Identity	Own, wants to be accepted for who he is, it's a 'consenting open relationship'.
	Contact	Prolonged and frequent, sexual conversations not introduced early, slow build-up, as if getting to know a friend.
	Desensitization & Intensity	
	Outcomes	Physical meeting to develop the relationship further. Meetings can take place on numerous occasions.
Maintenance	Online Environment	Feels more confident online; helps increase low sense of self-efficacy.
	Dissonance	No indecent images or chat with other offenders. Offence-supportive beliefs involve feelings of a 'consenting relationship' and feeling 'love struck'. Idealized romantic fantasy.
	Perceptions of Young People	Consenting to a relationship and also wanting affection.
Risk Management	IT Security	
	Private Spaces	Regular telephone contact, but not described in risk terms, more in terms of increased intimacy or 'the obvious thing to do in a relationship'.

Source: Webster et al. (2012, pp81–82).

were not significant collections in terms of size. They also tended not to have significant contact with other sexual offenders online. *The key characteristic of men in this group is that they were adept at adapting their identity and grooming style according to how the young person presented online and reacted to their initial contact.* Similarly, the speed at which contact developed could be fast and/or slow according to the how the victim responded to contact. Risk management was a feature of this type of groomer's offending, with hidden folders for images, and sometimes extra computers or phones that could be used exclusively for online grooming.

Composite case study: Adaptable online groomer

Derek was a 49-year-old man living alone. He had previous convictions for contacting young people online and so was under regular probation supervision. Since his last offence, Derek talked about trying to stop his online offending and managed to stay offline for a couple of months. However, he said the urge to go back online and talk to young people overcame him so he found himself back in chat rooms. Derek said that he was aware of the risk he was taking, so he brought a new laptop that he would use only for his online chats. The other computer was 'clean and safe' to be monitored by the Probation Service.

Derek said that he felt quite adept at talking to young people sexually from his previous experiences. He said that when he first went online, his profile was of his own age and details. However, he said that lots of young people would laugh at him in forums and tell him to 'piss off'. Consequently, Derek adjusted his identity to that of a 19-year-old man and used a picture of a handsome young man as his avatar. Derek talked about spending lots of time in chat rooms, and over time, he came to know who to approach for a sexual chat. That is, if the young girl had a sexual screen name or talked sexually to her friends, she was obviously 'sexually mature'. Derek would make contact with several girls at the same time, and within a matter of minutes, turn the conversation to sex by asking them about their physical characteristics or what they liked to do sexually. In tandem with these chats, Derek would request images from the girls and would also go on his webcam to show the girls images of him masturbating. Derek said that sometimes he would go on to meet the girls where the sexual offence would take place. Derek would sometimes bring gifts or things the girls said they were interested in to the meetings. On other occasions, the sexual conversation would stay online and never develop into a meeting. Derek said that he had spoken to other offenders online but not regularly. Usually, these conversations were brief and involved indecent image requests or exchanges.

Source: Webster et al. (2012, p82).

Table 4.3 Features of online grooming pertinent to the 'adaptable' groomer

	Dimension	Attitudes and behaviour
Grooming features	Vulnerability	Acute sexual interest in young people, lack of ability to manage or cope with the sexual interest.
	Scanning	Sexual screen names of young people, sexual chat, sexual avatar picture.
	Identity	Own, but can also tailor his 'legend' to fit the needs of the conversation at that particular time. Adaptable offenders also had the ability to have multiple identities running concurrently.
	Contact	Typically short, sexual conversations can happen in a matter of minutes. Contact with one particular person can be one off or regular, depending on how things are developing.
	Desensitization & Intensity	Asks a sexual question quite quickly, requests an image or webcam contact. Also tends to send pictures of himself. Men in this group could also use threats to intensify the relationship, typically involving blackmailing the young person into continuing contact.
	Outcomes	Physical meeting for sexual contact, or online image sharing only.
Maintenance	Online Environment	Talk about fantasy life online, sometimes not feeling real. Feelings of anonymity also.
	Dissonance	Some indecent images and some chat with other offenders. In some cases, chat can be intense and involve sharing fantasies about young people online. Offence-supportive beliefs involve feelings of a 'mature sexual young people' and feeling that 'young people can stop this' if they want to.
	Perceptions of Young People	Young people are inherently sexual, as evidenced by sexual screen names, photos and chat.
Risk management	IT Security	Evidence of multiple hardware, hiding images and multiple ISP addresses.
	Private Spaces	Some phone contact and private mail chat. Not really to increase intimacy, but due to awareness of the risk of talking sexually in an open space.

Source: Webster et al. (2012, pp83–84).

As with the first example, Table 4.3 illustrates the features of online grooming, maintenance and risk management that are pertinent to understanding the 'adaptable' groomer.

The *hyper-sexualized* group of men were characterized by extensive indecent image collections of children and significant online contact with other sexual offenders or offender groups. Some men in this group also had significant collections of extreme adult pornography. They adopted different identities altogether or had an identity picture that was not of their face, but of their genitals. Their contacts with young people were highly sexualized and escalated very quickly. Their offence-supportive beliefs involved 'dehumanizing' young people. They tended not to personalize contact and so did not seem to be using the phone or other personal media like the other groups of offenders. In this group, meetings were less prevalent than with the adaptable and intimacy-seeking groomers. Some of these men also had previous convictions for having indecent images of children.

Composite case study: Hyper-sexualized online groomer

Bob was a 29-year-old man living in a flat with this friend. He had previous convictions for having indecent images of young people. He talked about not being too social and spending a large amount of time online, surfing, chatting or looking at pornography. Bob said that he was fascinated by pornography and that often there was not really a dividing line between adult pornography and images of child abuse. When his computer was seized, a significant amount of extreme adult pornography was found (bestiality, for example) alongside hundreds of indecent images of children. Bob also talked about having some extreme fantasies about young people and would sometimes discuss these online with other men. Bob would talk about having some awareness of what he was thinking about being wrong, but his thoughts of young people in the images 'almost as not real' would override this.

Bob's online profile picture was of his flaccid penis; the name tag was not identifiable to him. When Bob engaged young people online, contact tended to be frequent, fast and very sexualized. He said that sometimes, within seconds, he would ask for an image or a graphic sexual chat. He sometimes would send the young people adult pornography at the same time. Bob did not seem to be perturbed by frequent rejection from young people online, as

(Continued)

he was not really looking for a relationship. The fact that he could quickly have a sexual chat with someone else also seemed to 'help' here. Bob was arrested having had a very fast sexual conversation with a young person, who turned out to be an undercover police officer. He was invited to a meeting and was arrested by police at the scene.

Source: Webster et al. (2012, p84).

Table 4.4 below shows the features of online grooming, maintenance and risk management that are pertinent to understanding the 'hyper-sexual' groomer. Shaded dimensions refer to the factor not emerging from the data as prevalent for that particular grooming style.

To date, this typology has not yet been further tested or replicated and this is a key next step for research if it is to have law-enforcement and intervention potential. In particular, a reconviction study looking at the reoffending rates of the three types and larger scale quantitative work would be helpful. In the next chapter, the typology is used as a basis for understanding forensic/clinical assessment with online groomers.

EOGP study strengths and limitations

The EOGP has some methodological limitations. First, the main thrust of data collection involved in-depth interviews and these can always be influenced by memory errors, bias and post hoc rationalizations by the offenders. There were no interviews with victims, so later categorizations are based on the offender accounts (see Chapter 7). Second, the qualitative purposive sample only reflected online groomers who had been convicted across four countries and jurisdictions. Third, the model developed was in no way intended to be a causal model, but is intended as an aid to understanding online grooming and as a basis for further investigation and testing.

However, the EOGP also stands apart from other work on grooming in a number of ways.

- Considerably more diverse behaviours have been mapped than in research that was only able to use chatlog data alone.

- Chatlog and detailed interview data has been triangulated for a very comprehensive picture of online grooming.
- It is the first study (to our knowledge) that has also looked in detail at the way in which young boys are targeted and groomed online. However, there remains a dearth of research in this area.
- The research has described the context of online groomers' attitudes and behaviour before they made contact with young people – this is key information for intervention programmes.

Table 4.4 Features of online grooming pertinent to the 'hyper-sexualized' groomer

	Dimension	Attitudes and behaviour
Grooming features	Vulnerability	Sexual obsession, possible saturation from collection of adult pornography.
	Scanning	
	Identity	Identity is not his own, or cryptic and not identifiable. Identity tag can also be explicit '*PussyLicker69*'. Only identifiable feature tended to be a picture of his penis as the avatar image.
	Contact	Very fast, literally seconds sometimes. Not really interested in developing relationships.
	Desensitization & Intensity	Fast, adult pornography or images of self sent.
	Outcomes	Tended to be characterized by image collection. However, some meetings evident but these men seemed particularly susceptible to undercover police operations.
Maintenance	Online Environment	Fantasy and anonymity online plays a big role. Extent of sexual material and chat online saturates and desensitizes.
	Dissonance	Significant collections of indecent images and extreme adult pornography. Offence-supportive beliefs tend to dehumanize young people.
	Perceptions of Young People	
Risk management	IT Security	Tends to be more limited than the adaptable type.
	Private Spaces	

Source: Webster et al. (2012, p85).

- The EOGP is the only study to date that has examined the influence of particular aspects of the online environment on groomers' attitudes and behaviours.

Conclusion

There is a clear policy and public health priority to ensure that young people are safe online. However, decisions about online safety initiatives, risk-management strategies and intervention programmes need to be based on solid empirical evidence. There is a strong body of work on users of indecent images, but there is a dearth of good evidence on the attitudes, behaviours and risk profiles of online groomers. There is also a need for more work looking at the role of networks in maintaining online grooming behaviours and on how online disinhibition (Suler, 2004) can be understood and managed to ensure the internet is a healthy place for all users.

Notes

1. A webcam is a video-capture device connected to a computer or computer network. Their most popular use is for video telephony, permitting a computer to act as a videophone or video-conferencing station. This can be used in messenger programs such as Windows Live Messenger, Skype, Yahoo messenger amongst others.
2. An emoticon is a textual expression representing the face of a writer's mood or facial expression. For example, :), :(and :D. They have now largely been replaced by pictures such as
3. A proxy server is a server that acts as an intermediary for requests from clients seeking resources from other servers. The main aim of proxy servers is to keep the machines behind it anonymous and help to bypass security/parental controls.

5
Psychopathology of Online Grooming

Vincenzo Caretti, Adriano Schimmenti and Antonia Bifulco

Introduction

In the previous chapter, findings from the European Online Grooming Project (EOGP) study focused on the experience of the groomers within a model which examined the likely motivations, processes of accessing children online and the social and technological environment that makes it possible. Thus the social environment within which online grooming takes place has been well documented.

However, another dimension to online grooming involves explaining the behaviour of groomers within a forensic psychological context. That is, to identify behaviours which might indicate underlying psychopathology. This would serve to further understand this type of sexual offending as well as assist in the provision of appropriate treatment programmes. This chapter will examine whether online groomers display particular disorders known to be common amongst sexual offenders and how these may fit into the model of online grooming developed by the EOGP. It offers a theoretical and diagnostic approach geared towards clinical practice, with speculation on how the information learned from the EOGP and the groomers' profiles may fit with aspects of disorders. This will be illustrated from data collected from chatlogs recorded by Italian police analysed as part of the EOGP.

Conceptualizing grooming

The study of sexual offenders shows the psychological conditions presented can be conceptualized in terms of clinical disorders or personality disorders. However, research indicates that it is difficult to cluster online groomers into a single diagnostic class as they are a heterogeneous group (Briggs, Simon & Simonsen, 2011; Webster, Davidson, Bifulco, Gottschalk, Caretti, Pham et al., 2012), as are other child sex offenders (Elliott, Beech, Mandeville-Norden & Hayes, 2009; McCarthy, 2010; Webb, Craissati & Keen, 2007).

The first challenge in understanding online grooming as a psychopathological process is with regard to its inclusion amongst the paraphilic disorders. Paraphilic disorders include individuals with atypical sexual interests as defined in the latest edition of the *Diagnostic and Statistical Manual* (DSM-5). These individuals' experience either personal distress about their interest (not merely distress resulting from society's disapproval); or sexual desire or behaviour that involves another person's psychological distress, injury or death; or a desire for sexual activity involving unwilling persons or persons unable to give legal consent. Paedophilic behaviour is defined as lasting over a period of at least six months, is recurrent and involves intense sexually arousing fantasies, sexual urges or behaviours involving sexual activity with a prepubescent child or children (aged 13 years or younger). The fantasies, sexual urges or behaviours cause clinically significant distress or impairment in social, occupational or other important areas of functioning. The paedophile is required to be at least 16 years old and at least five years older than the child or children involved (APA, 2013).

In their survey study with a stratified random sample of 2574 law-enforcement agencies, Wolak, Finkelhor and Mitchell (2004) noted that practically all (99%) of the groomers in their sample could not technically be defined as paedophiles, because their victims were older adolescents aged 13–17. There are other more appropriate terms to define sexual interest in postpubescent children, but they are less widely known, such as haebephilia or ephebophilia, which refer to a sexual interest in young people in the mid- to late-adolescent age range. There is some evidence that haebephilia and ephebophilia may be distinct from paedophilia, as individuals who report being preferentially attracted to adolescents show different sexual arousal patterns than do individuals who prefer prepubescent children (Miller, 2013; Seto, 2009b). In the EOGP, most victims were reported to be aged 13–17 and therefore the offenders would fall into the haebephilia or ephebophilia categories not formally covered in the DSM-5 categorization.

As Miller (2013) has argued, in the real world of clinical and forensic practice, the preferences of people who show sexual interest towards minors often fall along a spectrum. Here, some of these individuals are attracted only to children, whereas many others are attracted to the full younger age spectrum (from preschool children to high school

children). It is very unlikely that forensic or mental health practitioners would have doubts that a middle-aged male who starts grooming
an adolescent aged 14 for sexual purposes would fall into this type of
psychopathology. Such an individual would have difficulties with psychosexual development and the integration of social norms and values.
Thus, it is argued that the specific age of the victim should not be used
to restrict the inclusion of adults with such sexual interest in adolescents
being included into a category requiring investigation and treatment by
psychologists and related professionals.

Recent research suggests that neuropsychological abnormalities and
neurodevelopmental trauma may play a role in the development of
adults with a sexual interest in young people. For example, it is well
known that a deterioration in cognitive functioning together with a
reduction in sex drive may follow a brain injury (Zasler, 1994), and
a brain injury can produce an irritative lesion that can be associated
with abnormal sexuality, as with some cases of frontal and temporal
lobe lesions (Absher, Vogt, Clark, Flowers, Gorman & Keyes, 2000).
Therefore, some child molesters can suffer from a brain syndrome or
intellectual deficiency that makes them unable to control their impulses
or understand the wrongfulness of their actions (Miller, 1994, 2013).

Similarly, experiencing abuse and/or neglect as a child can at times
create a psychological template for abusive behaviours in later life.
In addition, childhood abuse and/or neglect may also be associated with
impairments in frontal and temporal brain regions related to affect regulation and behavioural control (Teicher, Ito, Glod, Andersen, Dumont &
Ackerman, 1997). Similarly, developmental problems may also be implicated in the early onset of behavioural disorders such as aggressive
unsocialized conduct disorder (ICD-10, WHO, 1992). This shows significant associations with violent behaviours in adulthood, including
sexual aggression (Soderstrom, Sjodin, Carlstedt & Forsman, 2004).
Moreover, substance abuse is also implicated; this may lower moral
inhibitions and the ability to control inappropriate social behaviour.
Amongst some individuals, the abuse of alcohol or drugs may reduce
moral constraints which contribute to sexual offending behaviours, and
this can apply to individuals who show sexual interest in children
(Langevin & Lang, 1990).

Finally, online groomers can differ not only in the age of their targets (children or teenagers) but also in their motivation to groom,
which in turn can be associated with their personality traits (Webster
et al., 2012). A well-known distinction has been made between online
groomers who use the internet and other technologies as a method

to connect with young people for the purpose of cybersex and mas-turbation (the so-called fantasy-driven offenders) and those who use internet social networks and chat rooms to locate and connect with young people with the intention of developing a sexual relationship with them (the contact-driven offenders) (Beech, Elliott, Birgden & Findlater, 2008; Briggs, Simon & Simonsen, 2011; Elliott & Beech, 2009; Krone, 2004). Both these categories are of relevance to the EOGP study reported here.

Whilst both these sub-types present child protection challenges, the latter contact-driven group is particularly important, and individuals in this group tend to have a criminal history characterized by a number of antisocial behaviours and are more dangerous in terms of risk for con-tact sexual offending against children. In fact, research on child sexual abusers suggests that children's risk for offline sexual abuse may increase when the groomer has a general propensity to antisocial behaviour. For example, a study by Seto and Eke (2005) on a sample of 201 adult male child pornography offenders showed that those individuals with prior criminal records were significantly more likely to offend again during the study follow-up period. In their study, those who had committed a prior or concurrent contact sexual offence were also the most likely to offend again, either generally or sexually.

An analysis conducted in the Butner Redux Study (Bourke & Hernandez, 2009) on 42 of 155 child pornography offenders looked at the age of onset for online and offline sexual crimes in the same offenders. Here, the majority of participants reported that they had in fact committed acts of contact sexual abuse *prior* to seeking child pornography on the internet. Another study from Briggs et al. (2011) examined the chat room transcripts of 51 inmates convicted of an internet-initiated sex offence. Briggs and colleagues found that a larger group (the fantasy-driven group) spent a significant amount of time in online chat rooms with a child (up to 180 days) as a primary social and sexual outlet. This group was motivated to engage an adolescent in online cybersex without an express intent to meet offline. Conversely, there was another smaller group of groomers (the contact-driven group) which was highly motivated to engage in offline sexual behaviour with an adolescent and was therefore more likely to envisage grooming as another method leading to the opportunity for contact (Elliott & Beech, 2009; Webster et al., 2012; Gallagher, Fraser, Christmann & Hodgson, 2006).

It is therefore possible that the groomers who show high levels of antisocial behaviour pose the highest risk for contact sexual abuse against children. Moreover, if the antisocial patterns are associated with severe psychopathic traits, the risk for children may increase further. Psychopathy is a well-known personality disorder in the forensic and clinical fields, characterized by a constellation of interpersonal, affective and behavioural characteristics. It involves features such as grandiosity, egocentricity, deceptiveness, shallow emotions, impulsivity, irresponsibility, lack of empathy, guilt or remorse, together with violations of social expectations and legal norms (Hare & Neumann, 2008). In fact, the clinical and empirical literature suggests that mental disorders per se have only a weak relationship with criminal behaviour unless associated with a psychopathic personality (Caretti, Ciulla & Schimmenti, 2012; Grann, Långström, Tengström & Kullgren, 1999; Hare, 1998; Miller, 2012).

The rest of this chapter will discuss the mental functioning and disordered personality traits likely to be associated with groomers' behaviours and how these personality traits may be associated with different subtypes of groomers. Two approaches to case formulation will be discussed to aid forensic practice across different European and US traditions of treatment and for the development of treatment/resocialization programs for online groomers. Approaches seeking to clarify diagnostic formulations for online groomers could help boost the research in this field and aid in formulating the development of specific prevention programmes for children, to avoid contact sexual abuse being perpetrated by online groomers. However, a note of caution is needed here: whilst theoretical models, typologies and manualized diagnostic procedures can aid professionals in understanding the psychological dimensions that underlie a crime, it is important to acknowledge that internet offenders, victims and the dynamics between the two are often unique and varied, as indicated by the EOGP findings and other recent research (Seto, 2013; Whittle, Hamilton-Giachritsis, Beech & Collings, 2013a & b).

Typologies of groomers

In recent years, a number of theoretical models about grooming behaviours and related typologies have been developed. Some of these represent stages of grooming, such as that by O'Connell (2003), who developed a typology of online exploitation of children which includes subsequential stages of grooming practices (friendship-forming stage, relationship-forming stage, risk-assessment stage, exclusivity stage and sexual stage). This was described in detail in Chapter 4. Other models are more focused on grooming practices. For example, the model developed by Craven, Brown and Gilchrist (2006) identifies three types of grooming: grooming the self; grooming of the surroundings and significant others; and grooming the young person. In particular, this model highlights the commonality between the processes used by groomers to prepare a child for the abuse and to prepare themselves for carrying out the abuse.

Other typological models are based on grooming motives. For example, Elliott and Beech (2009) have suggested typologies of individuals using the internet to access child pornography. These typological approaches broadly comprise of four groups: (1) periodically prurient offenders, consisting of those accessing impulsively or out of a general curiosity, who carry out this behaviour sporadically, potentially as part of a broader interest in pornography that may not be related to a specific sexual interest in children; (2) fantasy-only offenders, consisting of those who access/trade images to fuel a sexual interest in children and who have no known history of contact sexual offending; (3) direct victimization offenders, consisting of those who utilize online technologies as part of a larger pattern of contact and non-contact sexual offending, including child pornography and the grooming of children online in order to facilitate the later offline commission of contact sexual offences; and (4) commercial exploitation offenders, consisting of the criminally minded who produce or trade images to make money.

However, when typologies of groomers are presented within a psychopathological framework, the most important differences between them may be those related to their personality and mental functioning, for example, between the fantasy-driven and the contact-driven groomers. The EOGP has identified three types of online groomers across nine behavioural dimensions. These were described in Chapter 4 and include the intimacy-seeker, the adaptable and the hyper-sexualized groomer. These are discussed further below.

At the clinical level, the *intimacy-seeker* is likely to correspond to the fantasy-driven groomers described elsewhere. This category includes offenders who often face difficulties in real relationships and so may feel more accepted online (Whittle et al., 2013a). Here, they spend a significant amount of time talking to a particular young person online before meeting to develop or further the 'intimate relationship' (Briggs, Simon & Simonsen, 2011). The intimacy-seeker, as described in the EOGP findings, also has offence-supportive beliefs that involve seeing contact with the young person as a 'consenting relationship'. They therefore tend to fit in the 'fixated' or 'seductive' types of child sexual molesters (Holmes & Holmes, 1996). This indicates that their sexuality has been fixated at a primitive stage of psychosexual development and they find children sexually attractive and easier to relate to because these groomers are emotionally immature and may be socially inadequate. For them, the intimacy with the young person may be as important as the sexual acts committed later. So, they will court the young person with gifts and attention and are likely to rationalize about having a special relationship with the child based on mutual affection. Whilst they are not likely to physically harm the young person, they are dangerous because they manipulate and seduce children, distorting their affective development, often acting as an adult 'mentor' for their victims, in addition to the sexual abuse. From the EOGP analysis it was clear that the intimacy-seeking online groomer was also highly likely to meet the child ultimately.

The *adaptable groomers* manage their online identity and grooming style according to how the young person presents online and reacts to their initial contact. Therefore, they can be contact-driven offenders and, from a clinical perspective, are morally indiscriminate and may show more Machiavellian and psychopathic traits than the intimacy-seekers do. Some of them will have higher manipulative and deceptive traits than those that they use for luring the child. They will tend to have a low degree of empathy, accompanied by the belief that only their own needs matter, and that young people are sufficiently mature and capable of deciding to initiate sexual activities with them. In a US national survey, Wolak and colleagues (2004) found that the victims of online grooming (predominantly young teenagers) typically agreed to meet the groomer and to engage in sexual activity with the adult without force, coercion or abduction, knowing of the groomer's sexual interest. It seems likely that the groomers who sexually offended against the victims in their study belonged to this 'adaptable' type of groomer. This typology of groomers is understudied, but their mental functioning, behaviours and especially their ability to gain access to children may be even more concerning than those of the people in the hyper-sexualized group described below.

The *hyper-sexualized groomers* directly request children for sexual activities. Therefore they are likely to introduce sexual content to the online chat quickly, if not immediately, and their demands for sexual activity escalate rapidly. Effectively, they are not engaging in what is usually considered 'grooming' behaviour with this direct approach, even though they are luring their victims. Their offence-supportive beliefs involve a total disavowal of the psychological and developmental characteristics of children. Also, they tend not to personalize contact and they often dehumanize, grooming many children at the same time. In this category of online grooming, several types of child molesters are represented. This includes the sexually indiscriminate molester who has no particular preference for children but abuses them as part of a more generally omnivorous pattern of sexual behaviours, involving a wide variety of common and unusual sexual practices and partners (Holmes & Holmes, 1996). It may also include the sadistic paedophile whose erotic gratification is based on the fusion of sexual arousal and sadistic aggression (Miller, 2000, 2013).

However, whilst typologies can help differentiate offenders, they unfortunately cannot add much to the specific characteristics of a particular offender. This is crucial information for both forensic and clinical practice. Therefore, this chapter will introduce two possible ways of clinically assessing the online groomers' personality and their mental functioning, which relate to the risk of violence and the risk of recidivism amongst offenders (Grann et al., 1999; Rice, Harris & Cormier, 1992; Schimmenti, Craparo, Ciulla & Caretti, 2013). The first type of assessment is based on the DSM-5 model for personality disorders (APA, 2013). The second is based on the operationalization of personality disorders and mental functioning in the psychodynamic tradition, as described in the mental functioning axis of the *Psychodynamic Diagnostic Manual* (PDM; PDM Task Force, 2006).

Assessing the groomer's personality and mental functioning using the DSM-5

In the new edition of the *Diagnostic Statistical Manual* (DSM) used by clinical psychologists and psychiatrists internationally to diagnose disorder, the 'classical' categorical approach to personality disorders is provided (Section II), where the established criteria and thresholds for a given disorder are presented. A further alternative model to diagnosing personality disorders is outlined in DSM Section III. In this alternative model, personality disorders are conceived as characterized by impairments in personality *functioning* and pathological personality *traits* (APA, 2013, p761). This section includes six specific personality disorders (i.e. antisocial, avoidant, borderline, narcissistic, obsessive-compulsive and schizotypal), with each type defined by a specific pattern of impairments and traits. This approach also includes a diagnosis of Personality Disorder–Trait Specified (PD-TS) when a personality disorder is considered present, but the criteria for any specific personality disorder is not fully met. For this diagnosis, the clinician would note the severity of impairment in personality functioning and the problematic personality traits. Therefore, the PD-TS diagnosis allows for a more dimensional assessment of personality disorders. This can provide more clinically useful information on personality functioning and personality traits of individuals.

The elements on which personality functioning is appraised are related to both the self and interpersonal dimensions. The *self* dimension includes the facets of identity (experiencing oneself as unique, with clear boundaries between self and others; stability of self-appraisal and self-esteem; capacity for affect regulation) and self-direction (pursuit of coherent short-term and life goals; constructive and prosocial internal standard of behaviour; ability to self-reflect productively).

The *interpersonal* dimension includes the facets of empathy (ability to comprehend and appreciate the experiences and motivations of others; tolerance of different perspectives; understanding the effects of one's own behaviour on others) and intimacy (depth and duration of interpersonal connection; desire and capacity for closeness; capacity for mutuality as reflected in interpersonal behaviour).

The elements on which pathological personality traits are judged refer to five broad domains: negative affectivity, detachment, antagonism, disinhibition and psychoticism. These are widely derived from the well-validated five-factor model of personality (McCrae & Costa, 1987), and include 25 specific trait facets. Other criteria in this alternative model for diagnosing personality disorders involve the pervasivity and stability of the disordered personality functioning and personality traits, and alternative explanations for personality pathology (i.e. the differential diagnosis).

In this alternative model, many groomers fit in the proposed diagnostic criteria for antisocial personality disorders. The essential features of antisocial personality disorder are a failure to conform to ethical behaviour and an egocentric, callous lack of concern for others, together with deceitfulness, irresponsibility, manipulativeness and/or risk-taking in an individual at least 18 years of age. These features are accompanied by specific impairments in identity functioning and the presence of specific maladaptive traits in the personality domains of antagonism and disinhibition. Therefore, to diagnose antisocial personality disorder, there must be moderate or greater impairment in personality functioning and some specific pathological personality traits.

The impairments in *personality functioning* are manifested by several characteristics including those that are self-relationship based (identity, self-direction, empathy and intimacy) and those involving pathological personality traits. These are outlined in Table 5.1.

Table 5.1 Pathological personality traits in the DSM-5 and their association with an online groomer's personality

Emotional lability	Instability of emotional experiences and mood. The *intimacy-seeking* and the *hyper-sexualized* groomers may show high levels of affect dysregulation and low levels of affect tolerance triggering their behaviours.
Anxiousness	Feelings of nervousness, tenseness or even panic in reaction to diverse situations. High levels rarely apply to groomers' and psychopathic groomers may show very low levels.
Separation insecurity	Fears of being alone due to rejection by, and/or separation from significant others, based in a lack of confidence in oneself. May characterize some *intimacy-seeking* groomers, who see the relationship with the child as more reliable and safe than with adults.
Submissiveness	Adaptations of one's own behaviours to the perceived interests of others, even when not congruent with one's own interests. Only applies to some groomers who fake it to manipulate and exploit children.
Hostility	Frequent angry feelings and irritability together with nasty and/or vengeful behaviours. Applies to some *adaptable* groomers, who use bribery, force and threats.
Perseverance	Persistence in behaviour long after it has ceased to be effective, and continuance despite repeated failures or a clear reason for stopping. This trait shown by *intimacy-seekers* and *hyper-sexualized* groomers. It is related to an obsessive reiteration of maladaptive behaviours, important for understanding the 'type' of online groomer.
Withdrawal	Preference for being alone, avoidance and lack of initiation of social contact. On a continuum, the lowest levels of withdrawal can be observed in the psychopathic groomers, whereas the highest levels can be observed in the fantasy-driven fixated groomers.
Intimacy avoidance	Avoidance of close romantic relationships, attachment bonds and intimate sexual relationships. It is typical of people who are extremely dismissive in their attachment relationships. The lowest levels of intimacy avoidance observed in the *intimacy-seeking* groomers, and the highest levels characterize the psychopathic groomers in the *adaptable* and *hyper-sexualized* groups. It should be noted that the internet may facilitate the avoidance of real intimacy in favour of the development of manipulative relationships.
Anhedonia	Deficits in the capacity to feel pleasure and take interest in things. It is rarely observed as a trait amongst online groomers.

Depressivity	Feelings of being down or hopeless, pessimism about the future, pervasive shame and/or guilt, and feelings of inferior self-worth. Although some sexually fixated online groomers may show this trait, it is rarely observed. When prevalent, depressive feelings are usually counteracted through online grooming behaviours. If the depressive traits with shame and guilt are dominant, it can be positive for treatment purposes.
Restricted affectivity	Little reaction to emotionally arousing situations and constricted emotional affectivity and experiences. This trait is common amongst the adaptable and the *hyper-sexualized* groomers, and may sustain their lack of empathy towards the victims.
Suspiciousness	Expectations of, and sensitivity to signs of interpersonal harm, and feelings of being mistreated and used by others. It can characterize those online groomers who are particularly careful about managing the risks of their online behaviours and those who are more callous and opportunistic.
Manipulativeness	The use of subterfuge, including the use of seduction, charm, glibness and ingratiation to influence and control others. As online grooming involves manipulation, this is a key trait to help discriminate between the personality types of online groomers. The most manipulative online groomers are highly Machiavellian, their behaviour indicates limited attention to a child's perspective and associated expectations from society. Low levels amongst online groomers may be associated with relationally incompetent sexuality or with detached and opportunistic sexual behaviours. The internet may facilitate the expression of this trait.
Deceitfulness	Dishonesty together with misrepresentation of self. For example, when some online groomers present as younger than they actually are. High levels of deceitfulness observed in those online groomers who are particularly difficult to treat. Again, the online environment may facilitate the expression of this trait.
Grandiosity	Selfishness alongside feelings of entitlement and superiority. Together with other traits such as narcissism, this can sustain the online groomer's lack of empathy for the young person.
Attention-seeking	Behaviour designed to attract attention and facilitate admiration from the young person. This trait may be observed in those *hyper-sexualized* online groomers who use pictures of their genitals as their avatar representation online. In addition, some *intimacy-seeking* and *adaptable* men may use their knowledge to impress children and so take on a form of mentor role.

Table 5.1   (Continued)

Callousness	Lack of concern for the feelings of others alongside a lack of guilt or remorse about the negative effects of one's action on other people. This is a key trait that can help discrimate online groomers' personality styles. The most callous online groomers are relationally detached and psychopathic, with their lack of guilt or remorse a rationalization indicating limited empathy towards children and people per se. High levels of callousness may be observed in those online groomers that are particularly difficult to treat.
Irresponsibility	Disregard and lack of respect for obligations or commitments. This trait is usually associated with other antisocial traits related to a parasitic and impulsive lifestyle.
Impulsivity	Acting without plans or a consideration of outcomes, and a sense of urgency under emotional distress. High levels of impulsivity can be observed in *hyper-sexualized* online groomers and those people who struggle with affect regulation.
Distractibility	Difficulty focusing on tasks and maintaining goal-focused behaviours. *Hyper-sexualized* online groomers may show high levels of distractibility. In contrast, fantasy-driven online groomers in the *intimacy-seeking* group may be low in this trait.
Risk-taking	Engagement in dangerous activities without regard for the consequences, alongside proneness to boredom and impulsive acts to counter boredom. Some online groomers in the *hyper-sexualized* group are risk-takers as demonstrated by the way in which they are very clear about their needs and identity.
Rigid perfectionism	Insistence on everything being perfect without errors and faults, including own and others' performances. Low levels associated with other traits such as irresponsibility, impulsivity and risk-taking.
Unusual beliefs & experiences	The belief that one has unusual abilities, such as mind reading. When this trait is prominent and is not a strategy used to deceive and impress the child, it may be observed amongst online groomers who have developmental challenges, are immature and/or show other schizotypal or psychotic traits.
Eccentricity	Unusual behaviour, appearance or speech. The trait may be observed in online groomers who are socially inept, may have development challenges and/or may show other schizotypal or psychotic traits.
Cognitive and perceptual dysregulation	Unusual thought processes such as thought-control experiences, and/or depersonalization, derealization and other dissociative experiences. High levels of this trait suggest malingering in the frame of an antisocial personality with psychopathic traits. Otherwise it would be helpful to evaluate the presence of psychotic symptoms or dissociative disorders may be considered.

As Table 5.1 illustrates, online groomers tend to show several traits that are associated with antisocial personalities, but they may also present other traits that are critical for diagnostic and treatment purposes.

Assessing the groomer's personality and mental functioning using the PDM

Psychodynamic practice has a long tradition in the assessment of personality disorders and mental functioning and is utilized in many European countries and the United States (Bellak & Goldsmith, 1984; Cierpka, Grande, Rudolf, von der Tann, Stasch & the OPD Task Force, 2007; Clarkin, Levy, Lenzenweger & Kernberg, 2004; Kernberg, 1984; McWilliams, 2011; Shedler & Westen, 2004). The PDM (PDM Task Force, 2006) provides an alternative classification to the DSM-5 described earlier, and summarizes knowledge in an operationalized structure based on different axes that can be used for diagnostic purposes. For online groomers, important information can be derived from both its Personality Patterns and Disorder (P) Axis and the Profile of Mental Functioning (M) Axis.

In the PDM, evaluating the severity of personality disorders is conducted by assessing the following seven capacities:

(1) Identity: to view self and others in complex, stable, and accurate ways.
(2) Object Relations: to maintain intimate, stable, and satisfying relationships.
(3) Affect Tolerance: to experience in self and perceive in others the full range of age-expected affects.
(4) Affect Regulation: to regulate impulses and affects in ways that foster adaptation and satisfaction, with flexibility in using defenses or coping strategies.
(5) Superego Integration: to function according to a consistent and mature moral sensibility.
(6) Reality Testing: to appreciate, if not necessarily to conform to, conventional notions of what is realistic.
(7) Ego Resilience: to respond to stress resourcefully and to recover from painful events without undue difficulty. (PDM Task Force, 2006, p22)

Whilst online groomers may differ significantly in relation to these capacities, an accurate assessment of them individually may provide useful information for diagnosis and treatment. For example, the assessment of superego integration is critical for evaluating whether a groomer can benefit from psychological treatment or conversely will use the treatment offered as another way to learn strategies for manipulating and exploiting others. Another example is the assessment of object relations which may inform about the capacity of an intimacy-seeking groomer to form significant affective bonds away from children. Finally, the assessment of affect tolerance may provide information about whether online grooming behaviours are triggered by some specific emotional states. On a nosological level, the clinician should accurately assess if the groomer shows the characteristics associated with a psychopathic (antisocial), a narcissistic or a sadistic personality disorder. In fact, within a psychoanalytic framework, the online grooming behaviours are likely to be associated with these personality disorders.

The PDM has a definition of psychopathic (antisocial) personality disorder and does not differentiate between the two, as in the DSM-5. This is because in the psychodynamic tradition, antisocial behaviours may relate to many disorders but the specific constellation of psychopathic traits often includes antisocial or other immoral behaviours. The characteristic orientation of individuals who show a psychopathic personality disorder is towards expressing power for their own sake, being more preoccupied with self-definition (in terms of personal power and the ability to manipulate and exploit others) than with relationships.

The psychopathic personality disorder as described in the PDM is characterized by the following indicators:

(1) The contributing constitutional-maturational patterns involve aggression and a high threshold for emotional stimulation (which may reflect a disorder of early attachment).
(2) The central tension/preoccupation is about manipulating and being manipulated.
(3) The central affects are rage and envy.
(4) The characteristic pathogenic belief about the self is 'I can make anything happen'.
(5) The characteristic pathogenic belief about others is that everyone is selfish, manipulative and dishonourable.
(6) The central way of psychological defence involves reaching for omnipotent control.

The PDM also distinguishes between two sub-types of psychopathic personality disorder: the *passive/parasitic* sub-type, who is a more dependent, less aggressive, relatively non-violent manipulator, the 'con artist' type; and the *aggressive* sub-type, who is a more actively predatory and often violent offender. Both of these sub-types may relate to online groomers. For example, those pychopaths with parasitic tendencies may be observed amongst the adaptable groomers and those who are apparent intimacy-seekers, but are instead highly manipulative, contact-driven and thus adaptable groomers who use seduction and charm to gain access to the child. In addition, some of the hyper-sexualized groomers may show the psychological characteristics of aggressive psy-chopaths, and so may use threats, bribery or other aggressive behaviours to meet the child offline and to commit the sexual abuse. It is important to note that research to date tends to show that psychotherapy has little or even a detrimental effect on psychopathic individuals (Carney, 1977; Salekin, 2002).

The characteristic subjective experience of individuals suffering from *narcissistic* personality disorder is a sense of inner emptiness and mean-inglessness that requires recurrent infusions of external confirmation of their importance and value. Those with narcissistic personality disor-der therefore spend considerable energy evaluating their status relative to that of other people, and tend to define their self-esteem through a combination of idealizing and devaluing others. When they idealize someone, they feel more special or important by virtue of their asso-ciation with that individual. When they devalue someone, they feel superior. Narcissistic personality disorder involves preoccupation with inflated and deflated self-esteem; with central affects of shame, con-tempt and envy, with the characteristic pathogenic belief about the self of 'I need to be perfect to feel okay'. The pathogenic belief about others is that other people enjoy riches, beauty, power and fame. Therefore, the more one has of those things, the better one will feel. There are also two sub-types. First, the arrogant/entitled sub-type who behaves with an overt sense of entitlement, devalues most other people and perceives others as vain and manipulative or charismatic and commanding. Sec-ond is the depressed/depleted sub-type who behaves ingratiatingly, seeks people to idealize, is easily wounded and feels chronic envy of others seen as being in a superior position.

Narcissistic personality disorder, especially in its depressed/depleted sub-type, may be particularly associated with *intimacy-seeking* groomers who are seductive or socially inept offenders, and who may need the contact and appreciation of a child to increase their self-esteem. These individuals may use children to fulfil their need for being idealized and being seen as superior. However, this in turn could generate a further need to be confirmed and appreciated as a sexual partner. For these individuals, psychotherapy can be difficult, because the grooming behaviours are likely to respond to a psychological need for being seen as perfect that is embedded in the individual's personality. When the narcissistic traits are not accompanied by other psychopathic or sadistic traits, the prognosis may be more favourable.

Sadistic personality disorder is organized around the theme of domination, with overriding motivations involving control, subjugation and forcing pain and humiliation on others. Therefore, the hallmark of sadistic personality disorder is emotional detachment and the guiltless enthusiasm with which the individual pursues domination and control. This in turn has the effect of dehumanizing the victim. Sadistic personality disorder is characterized by the central preoccupation about suffering indignity and inflicting suffering. Accompanied by hatred, contempt and pleasure based on 'sadistic glee', the characteristic pathogenic belief about the self is 'I am entitled to hurt and humiliate others'. The pathogenic belief about others is that people exist as an object for sadististic domination. Psychological defence involves detachment, omnipotent control, reversal (turning of impotence into omnipotence) and acting out. The PDM also distinguishes the intermediate manifestation of sadomasochistic personality disorder, where there is an alternation of sadistic and masochistic attitudes and behaviours. These are much more emotionally alive and capable of attachment than those with psychopathic, narcissistic or sadistic personality disorders. Their relationships however are intense and explosive.

Online groomers who present with a sadistic personality disorder are perhaps the most dangerous. They are particularly expected to be found in the *hyper-sexualized* group, but could also be amongst the intimacy-seeking and the adaptable groups. They tend to use the child to fulfil a need for domination and humiliation. Children can be perfect targets for them because children are weaker, powerless and candid – particularly online. The naïve openness and subsequent vulnerability of some young people online is discussed further in Chapter 7. Children online can be relatively easily lured into the perpetrators' offending behaviour. To the best of our knowledge, to date there is no psychological treatment which has been demonstrated to be effective for this disorder.

A further important aspect that can be assessed using the PDM is an individual's mental functioning and its role in shaping personality (Schimmenti et al., 2013). This can be conducted using the Profile of Mental Functioning (the M Axis) – which examines in detail the features that contribute to an individual's personality and overall level of psychological health or disturbance. Mental functions include very basic features that do not depend on verbal exchanges, thus they can help clinicians and forensic practitioners to understand the complexity of a given online groomer. The PDM describes nine basic mental functions including the capacity for regulation, attention and learning; capacity for relationships and intimacy; quality of internal experiences; capacity for affective experience, expression and communication; defensive patterns and capacities; capacity to form internal representations; capacity for differentiation and integration; self-observing capacities; and the capacity to construct or use internal standards and ideals (PDM Task Force, 2006, p73). By necessity, some of these categories overlap, but each one highlights an important feature of mental functioning that cannot quite be described by the others. A description of these functions is provided in Table 5.2 below, together with comments on how they might apply to the diagnosis of an individual groomer.

Table 5.2 Cognitive functions according to the PDM and their association with online grooming behaviours (recurrent indicators are shown in bold)

Capacity for regulation, attention and learning	This function underpins fundamental processes that enable human beings to attend and learn from experiences. This includes information processing, executive functioning, memory and overall intelligence. Online groomers tend to be **well-focused and organized**. However, those in the *hyper-sexualized* group may suffer from attention problems or other deficiencies, or may be less able to respond appropriately to stimuli, particularly when they are under stress.
Capacity for relationships and intimacy	Here the depth, range and consistency of an individual's ability to form and maintain emotionally rich and caring relationships is assessed. This capacity tends to be **superficial and need-oriented** amongst online groomers, who may lack real intimacy and empathy for others. The presence of another relationship characterized by intimacy, caring and empathy may be a positive indicator for the prognosis of a treatment. For example, the grooming behaviours may have emerged as a possible regressive (and perhaps reversible) response to some strong emotions such as anger or separation anxiety.
Quality of internal experiences	Here we attempt to understand the extent of confidence and self-regard that characterizes an individual's relationship to others and society per se. Some online groomers show a **vulnerable or unrealistic self-esteem**.

108

Table 5.2 (Continued)

	To that end, they may describe experiencing a sense of vitality only when in contact with a child. In contrast, there may be men that present as psychopathic or organize their internal world around themes of domination and control – here they may have an inflated sense of self-esteem and grandiose sense of self-worth. In our experience, self-esteem tends to be state-dependent, and may, for example, be influenced by a child's reaction to online contact for those men seeking intimacy.
Anhedonia	Deficits in the capacity to feel pleasure and take interest in things. It is rarely observed as a trait amongst online groomers.
Capacity for affective experience, expression and communication	Here the person's ability to experience, comprehend, and express the full range of affect through gestures and words is assessed. Online groomers tend to show non-consistent affective patterns (with the exception of those in the adaptable group) and tend to be under-regulated. There is some need-oriented behaviour and emotional expression, but **they do not have cohesive integrated emotional patterns.** For example, in selected relationships, some online groomers can read the basic intentions of others (such as acceptance or rejection by a child). Further, people in the *intimacy-seeking* and the *adaptable* groups can read specific subtle cues such as feelings of pride, jealousy, shame, partial anger and so on. To that end, rather than presenting as completely deficient when understanding affect, there is a restricted use of emotion for the purpose of sexual abuse. In contrast, there are some people that suffer from higher degrees of affect dysregulation and so may show a reduced ability to mentalize affective experience. Consequently, they can distort the intentions of others, misreading relational cues according to their unrecognized affective states. For example, when feeling sexually aroused, they may interpret a joke by a child as a signal that the young person is sexually excited/interested.
Defensive patterns and capacity	This indicates the way individuals attempt to cope and alter needs, affect and other experiences. Assessing defensive patterns is crucial for clinical and forensic assessment. If primitive defences are extensively deployed (i.e. behaviours that distort experience to help manage stressors, disturbing feelings and thoughts), the more unfavourable the prognosis for successful treatment or resocialization programmes. Psychological defences are often unconscious cognitive strategies used to minimize inner conflict by altering the perception and interpretation of external events or internal motivations.

Online groomers tend to rely on primitive defences such as denial, projection, projective identification, splitting or dissociation. **Denial** involves mentally discounting an act or any of the negative effects of it. For example, refuting the abusive nature by claiming young people's consent to sexual contact with adults. *Adaptable* and *intimacy-seeking* offenders use **projection** of their sexual interest in children, claiming victims purposefully seduce adults. **Projective identification** involves taking disowned thoughts and feelings and mentally 'attaching' them to someone else as their original source. In this way, the projector can feel their own behaviour is simply a response to that of the receiver. For example, desensitizing a child about sexual themes by normalizing sexual conversation, then when the child starts to talk autonomously about sexual topics, attributing seductive behaviour to the child. Thus believing sexual contact with the child is giving the child what they want. **Splitting** involves a psychological demarcation of an 'object' into an all good–all bad dichotomy. Therefore, some online groomers may see a child as 'pure and perfect' others as sexually provocative and 'deserving' of abuse. **Dissociation** implies a disconnection between states of mind, ideas, memories and/or behaviours. It occurs when unbearable thoughts and feelings are quarantined from awareness. Even if unrecognized as dissociated self-states, they alter the individual's normal way of functioning. For example, some online groomers may describe altered states of consciousness when they are online contacting young people. **Displacement** occurs when a consciously disavowed feeling towards an 'object' is unconsciously redirected towards other objects, usually psychologically safer targets. For example, a groomer may feel sexually attracted towards an adult, who they are unable to sexually approach, so displaces their feelings towards a child. Another defence very common amongst online groomers is **rationalization**. This involves devising plausible offence-supportive beliefs to justify sexual offending behaviour.

Capacity to form internal representations
Here the individual's capacity to symbolize affectively meaningful experiences in a mental rather than somatic or behavioural form is assessed. In our experience, some online groomers present an **externally oriented style of thought**, together with a **lack of mentalization** abilities. As a consequence, they will use representations or ideas in a concrete way to convey a desire for action to meet their needs. This function is associated with the

Table 5.2 (Continued)

	capacity for affective experience. To that end, the more an online groomer has challenges with internal representations, the more they tend to use children as an outlet for unrecognized needs or urges.
Capacity for differentiation and integration	This function involves the individual's ability to build logical bridges between internal representations (i.e. to separate fantasy from reality and to connect one's own way of representing the self with past and present experiences). In our experience, groomers tend to show some superficial differentiation, because in almost all cases, the child's needs are not being met. Integration is also a challenge whereby some offenders are **unable to recognize the internal motives and experiences** that lead them to sexually offend online. Useful indicators for treatment may be: the range and depth of internal representations that can be differentiated and integrated without fragmentation; or an excessive polarization in the individual's mental state.
Self-observing capacities	Here we refer to psychological mindedness and the individual's ability to observe their own internal life. It is an extension of the capacity for differentiation and integration, but primarily addresses the ability to reflect on a full range of their own and others' feelings and experiences. We have found that online groomers tend to **lack genuine awareness of their own psychological states and feelings.** For example, they can reflect on moment-to-moment experiences, but not with reference to a longer term sense of self. In addition, people in the *intimacy-seeking* and *adaptable* typological groups can reflect on the child's feelings and experiences, but this tends to be through the lens of meeting their own needs and goals.
Capacity to construct or use internal standards and ideals	This refers to an individual's level of morality. It describes whether moral standards are integrated with a realistic sense of one's capacity in the context of broader social demands. In our experience, this is another crucial function to assess because a **lack of internal moral standards, together with a lack of guilt and shame** may be associated with unsuccessful treatment and resocialization programmes. In contrast, if the individual feels genuine guilt for their offending behaviour, this may be a positive indicator for treatment outcomes.

As Table 5.2 illustrates, understanding the cognitive functioning of online groomers can be critical for accurate assessment and signposting towards an appropriate treatment and/or resocialization programme. In the following section, some examples are presented that show how the assessment of these functions may help develop a deeper understanding of the diverse behaviours of online groomers.

Case examples

The EOGP transcripts of online conversations between two convicted groomers and their victims in Italy were analysed. Using chatlog data in this way, can assist in the assessment of personality traits and cognitive functioning for diagnostic and forensic purposes. These are used to illustrate some of the diagnostic categories identified in this chapter.

The chatlog examples came from covert police surveillance of a cell phone conversation in 2008. A 62-year-old man (who described himself as about 40 years old online) was talking online to a 14-year-old victim. The two people met online during a chat-line session. Here, the online groomer was found to have been sending friendship requests and SMS text messages to young people aged 10 to 16 years old. He was offering cell phone refills in exchange for personal photos. When the covert police surveillance was finished, the groomer was arrested.

The following extracts from the chatlog data are given, together with a commentary in relation to the likely psychopathology involved. The opening exchange of the first online groomer is as follows:

> Online Groomer: Just take advantage, you're talking to a grown-up. Try to be more...you know...open-minded. Why not?...Do you fear you're a little girl?...eheheh, I wish I could help you...eheheh, but it's complicated, we're so far away. But I can help you get rid of your inhibitions, we can play little games...right? This is our first phone call, but if we get more intimate I can help you free yourself from your inhibitions.

This opening exchange suggests that this person shows some psychopathic traits, being manipulative, using seduction, glibness and ingratiation to influence and control the young person. His deceit was evident when he presented as much younger than he was, as was his grandiosity, when he states that he can help the girl mature sexually. With regard to cognitive functioning, his capacity for differentiation and integration seemed poor. Here he confounded the wishes of the girl with his own goals (that the girl should feel free from her 'inhibitions'), which relates to his defence capacities. It is also pertinent to note how quickly he used projective identification to gain control of the young person. For example, by stating that she likely feels too young but that he can help her become more 'open-minded' and 'free from inhibitions'.

Shortly after the opening exchange, the man asked for a picture of the young person and the interaction rapidly escalated as described below:

Online Groomer: How nice of you. Now that I have told you how to take full figure or naked pictures you can get some practice.

Victim: No, no, never.

Online Groomer: I didn't mean you have to send them to me. You can practice. You can take some and then cancel them. It's not that bad. However, you can send me a pic without your clothes on, I've already received some of them. It's the most ordinary thing, it's quite natural. For example, once I asked a girl whether she was willing to send me a picture... she'd taken it and sent it to me right away... eheheh... that was a very nice picture, I must tell, a really nice one. So, you see, I'm not talking about something very unusual.

Victim: No, perhaps you aren't.

Online Groomer: You see, I'm not telling you anything weird, everybody has naughty fantasies, don't you think? So you can try... if you get curious. Now that I have told you how you can do it... you can try just out of curiosity, just to see how you look like when you're naked. You're just the right age to practice with these things, no? At this age you are no longer a baby girl, not yet a teenager and so on... Do you know they want to give driving licenses to 16 year old youth?

Victim: Really?

Online Groomer: Somewhere in the US teenagers get their driving license at 16... you're not as young as you think.

This extract confirmed the manipulative behaviour of the groomer. For example, he was trying to obtain indecent images of the girl by normalizing the behaviour (around taking a naked picture) and trying to minimize any guilt that she may feel. He appeared submissive on the surface when he said that he did not intend for the girl to send the picture to him, but his narrative was underpinned by manipulation to gain her trust. There were also examples of callousness and deceit. For example, it is not true that there are plans in Italian law to lower the driving age to 16. Finally, there was an example of lack of remorse whereby he rationalized his request and used projective identification to psychologically dominate the young person.

At the end of the interaction, he asked the girl to keep their conversation secret. To reinforce this, he scared her by telling her what could happen if someone knew about them. Understanding that this could be a barrier to further conversations in the future, attempts were then made to reassure the girl:

> Online Groomer: Anyway, that thing we talked about, I didn't mean to scare you when I told you that SMS can be stored for five years; one needs a very serious reason to order...you know, it's up to a judge to order they'll be read, do you understand? Police cannot decide on their own...this measure must be authorized by a judge who believes they are evidence in a criminal investigation. Do you understand?

Analysis of these brief chatlogs suggests that this individual was an intimacy-seeking groomer likely to have been driven by paedophilic fantasies and masturbation urges. However, the presence of psychopathic traits (manipulation, deceit, callousness, risk-taking) and changes in cognitive functioning (primitive defences, externally oriented thought) also suggests that he could be particularly dangerous to young people. This groomer is able to identify and exploit vulnerability in a range of ways.

In a further example from the EOGP, another offender was convicted of the possession and distribution of indecent images of children. In this case, the offender persuaded several young people to perform sexual acts and to film this behaviour using their cell phone cameras. The offender was 47 years old and, like the first case example above, would approach young girls online by offering to put credit on their cell phone if they would send him some pictures. Once a girl was approached, he obsessively started to ask her for pictures, as detailed in the chatlog extract below:

> Online Groomer: I'd like a full figure picture of you...kiss (emoticon)...If only you could take a picture of you and one of your friends. [At this point the victim sent a picture]
> Online Groomer: Send a full figure one...you don't answer...you are letting me down.
> [A day later] Online Groomer: I'd like to know why you disappeared without an explanation...don't you want a mobile refill?
> [A day later] Online Groomer: Hello honey...hello honey.

[A day later] Online Groomer: Hello honey.
Victim: Hello.
Online Groomer: Hi, can you send me some pictures.
[The girl does not answer].
[Five days later] Online Groomer: Hello, do you remember me.
[A day later] Online Groomer: How are you there sweetheart?
[A week later] Online Groomer: Hi, some pictures of you?

In the example above, the perseverance of the online groomer is significant. That is, he continued requesting pictures despite repeated periods of non-response from the young person. There is also some evidence of separation insecurity with the fear of being rejected by the victim.

The next example is taken from an SMS communication between the same man and another victim, a 13-year-old girl. The offender presented as being 27 years old. At this point in the conversation, the offender has just received a picture from the girl:

Online Groomer: I like you so much ... send me more pics.
Victim: Do you really mean it or do you say so to every girl my age? You did meet other girls, didn't you? Were they nicer than me?
Online Groomer: I'd like to see more ... Please send another one where you are in underwear and one with your tits as well. I like you so much ... You must be very hot ... The other girls I know are not as beautiful as you ... I wanna see you in underwear.
Victim: Do you really like me?
Online Groomer: You're beautiful ... Think about what you want in return for the other pics.
Victim: You would say that to any other girl!! What do you usually give the others? [At this point the young person sent the pictures].
Online Groomer: I've got them ... Do you want me to show you my ... I don't give anything to other girls ... Now I've got you.
Victim: Of course, unless you find another girl in chat.
Online Groomer: I won't look for any other girl, I swear it ... Now it's up to you.

From the example above, an obsession with pictures is evident. These were obtained through manipulation and deceit – for example, the man said that he would not search for any other girl online. There is also evidence of attention-seeking traits when he asked whether she wanted to receive a picture of his genitalia. Regarding cognitive functioning, here the offender showed minimal moral standards and a superficial, need-oriented capacity for intimacy. After receiving the images from the young person, the offender's grooming behaviour quickly escalated. The next excerpt is the log of an SMS communication recorded shortly after the example above:

> Online Groomer: You are asleep my sweet love? ... I'd like being there with you, I'll cuddle you.
>
> Victim: I'm a little sleepy.
>
> Online Groomer: Can you send me some MMS of your breast... please!!!!:):-):-)
>
> Victim: Yes but only my breast, nothing more, I feel ashamed.
>
> Online Groomer: I'm sure you have a fine ass.
>
> Victim: I don't think so ... it's not so fine.
>
> Online Groomer: Send me the pic and I'll tell you ... have you received my MMS? [He sent her an MMS of male genitalia] How is it?
>
> Victim: Oh ... I don't know ... fine?
>
> Online Groomer: But aren't you going to send me a picture of your pussy?
>
> Victim: No, I don't want ...
>
> Groomer: I THOUGHT YOU TRUSTED ME. THEN PREPARE YOUR-SELF TO SEE YOUR PICTURE ON INTERNET.. YOU'LL REGRET IT!!! [original capital letters].

From this example is a summary of the psychopathological characteristics of hyper-sexualized groomers. The hyper-sexualized groomers tend not to be able to sustain, even for a short time, balanced communication and behaviour. They seem to have little capacity for regulation, differentiation and integration. To that end, they show clear signs of affect dysregulation and are likely to respond immediately to strong emotions by means of action. In this case, the online groomer showed traits such as impulsivity (he sent an MMS depicting genitalia without any request); separation insecurity and suspiciousness (he was sensitive to the victim's refusal to send pictures of her genitalia and felt mistreated by her); and hostility (he directly expressed his anger towards the victim and explicitly threatened her). Alongside this, the individual showed: a reduced capacity for self-regulation with inconsistent emotional patterns; vulnerable self-esteem (as demonstrated by his sense of mistreatment); reduced self-observing capacities; and a number of primitive defences, including splitting. Here, he starts the conversation talking to a 'good girl' and soon after the conversation ends with the girl perceived as 'bad'. Finally, there was evidence of acting out whereby he sent an MMS with genitalia and enacted his anger using verbal aggression.

In our view, these examples of online grooming behaviour demonstrate how critical the assessment of personality traits and personality functioning can be to inform treatment. This is discussed further in the section below.

Implications for treatment

The data and interpretation presented in this chapter have implications for the treatment of online groomers. In fact, the efficacy of treatment programmes for sexual offenders, including child sexual abusers, is likely to depend on the interaction between the specific treatment model and the personality traits and functioning of the offender (Seto & Barbaree, 1999).

In particular, an assessment of psychopathic traits should be required before any treatment begins. This can be conducted using clinical interviews and the Psychopathy Checklist–Revised (PCL-R; Hare, 2003). This assessment would help discriminate between individuals who are able to benefit from evidence-based interventions. That is, with the exception of a few studies (e.g. Salekin, 2002; Skeem, Monahan & Mulvey, 2002), research shows that only a very small group of psychopaths can benefit from treatment programmes (e.g. Gacono, Nieberding, Owen, Rubel & Bodholdt, 2000; Harris & Rice, 2006; Wong & Hare, 2005; Looman, Abracen, Serin & Marquis, 2005; Seto & Barbaree, 1999).

The assessment of psychopathic and other disordered personality traits together with the assessment of mental functions remains crucial for effective treatment planning. This should be accompanied by differential diagnosis for any further clinical disorder that may underpin online grooming behaviours (such as neurocognitive disorders and substance use behaviours). In our view, it is only when individuals are assessed in an accurate diagnostic framework that it is possible to select a treatment programme or a resocialization programme that could work for them.

It is also pertinent to note that although a psychodynamic understanding could be critical for the diagnostic assessment of online groomers, classical psychodynamic therapy is likely to produce unsuccessful or even detrimental results. In particular, for individuals who present with a high number of psychopathic traits. To that end, a risk–need–responsivity (RNR) model should be applied to online groomers' treatment (Andrews & Bonta, 2006; Ogloff & Wood, 2010). This model suggests that treatment should target specific criminogenic needs and dynamic (i.e. changeable) risk factors. In addition, treatment strategies should consider those idiosyncratic charactterististics that may negatively impact on day-to-day management and on the results of the treatment itself (motivation for treatment, cognitive ability, learning style and so on). Furthermore, RNR principles suggest that: (1) high- to moderate-risk individuals should be prioritized for more structured and more intensive treatment; low-risk individuals should be prioritized when they have high criminogenic needs; (2) changeable factors that underpin offending (i.e. criminogenic needs) should be assessed. Other factors that affect psychosocial functioning such as mental health condition, housing stability and educational attainment are important risk and protective factors and should be used to determine the level of need; and (3) outcomes are improved for treatments which are responsive to the risk and needs of individual offenders. The risk–need nexus, plus the degree of protective factors in the person's life, should determine the target behaviours to address in programmes (Andrews & Bonta, 2010).

As has been presented in this chapter, the criminogenic needs of online groomers are often encapsulated in mental functioning where the capacity for differentiation and integration are low and the defences are primitive. Lowering the negative impact of disordered personality traits and improving the quality of general cognitive functioning would require many years of intensive treatment, and even in this case, the probability of a successful outcome might be significantly influenced by a number of external factors such as the individual's response to the offence.

As noted above, in our view, psychodynamic interventions are unlikely to produce effective treatment outcomes for online groomers. Furthermore, if individuals show the interpersonal and affective characteristics of psychopathy, this will disrupt any traditional psychodynamic process. For example, an individual's manipulative style and pathological lying will prevent the development of a genuine therapeutic alliance. In addition, a lack of empathy, callousness and grandiose sense of self-worth will inhibit a genuine motivation to change through therapy (Gacono et al., 2000; Lösel, 1998; McWilliams, 2011).

Arguably, these barriers to positive therapeutic outcomes will also apply to psychodynamic treatment that has been recently developed, such as mentalization-based treatment (MBT; Allen, Fonagy & Bateman, 2008). MBT focuses on increasing the patient's capacity for mentalization – the process by which an individual interprets their actions and those of others as meaningful on the basis of intentional mental states – to stabilize their sense of self and enhance stability and reciprocity in feelings and relationships. In our view, only a limited number of intimacy-seeking online groomers may benefit from this kind of treatment. In all the other cases, cognitive behavioural therapy (CBT) aimed at developing cognitive and behavioural skills such as decision-making processes, controls on violent behaviour and internet behaviour management may be the most helpful way forward (Abracen, Looman & Lengton, 2008; Olver & Wong, 2009). CBT adheres to RNR principles and so addresses dynamic risks and the offender's needs. However, long-term follow-up studies are required to test the impact of CBT interventions with online groomers.

Conclusion

This chapter has proposed that an accurate understanding of online groomers' psychopathology should be based on the assessment of specific personality traits and dimensions of mental functioning. This can improve clinical and forensic practice if diagnostic processes are more able to produce both a description of the symptoms/disordered behaviours and a deeper understanding of the mental processes that generated them. This has been illustrated through the analysis of two case examples from the EOGP. Implications for the treatment of online groomers based on our experience of their personality traits and mental functioning have also been suggested.

We are mindful that a psychopathological understanding of online grooming behaviours cannot be set apart from the context where groomers sexually offend. Information and communication technology has revolutionized our lives. Online technology has transformed our approach to communication and has a significant impact on how we think, feel and relate (Turkle, 2011). In particular, the internet has shaped new relational processes which are very different from those where the other individual is physically present. Today, access to virtual relationships is simpler, totally synchronous and facilitates interaction with complex digital universes (Schimmenti & Caretti, 2010; Schimmenti, Guglielmucci, Barbasio & Granieri, 2012). New technologies certainly have several positive features, as described in other chapters. But there is also the risk that online environments can facilitate the expression of psychopathological conditions (Caretti, 2000; Schimmenti & Caretti, 2010). This applies to online grooming and other criminal behaviours. For example, Suler (2004) argues that the diverse ways in which people communicate and behave online, compared to the real world, are associated with specific factors embedded in the individual's relationship with virtual environments. This includes anonymity, invisibility, asynchronicity, solipsistic introjections, dissociative imagination and minimization of authority. The 'online disinhibition effect' which is the result of an interaction between these factors can facilitate the enactment of fantasies, including those related to paraphilic tendencies. Similar studies that highlight the bearing of 'psychotechnologies' (De Kerckhove, 1995) on behaviour should be included in models of online grooming to provide a comprehensive understanding for practitioners.

Finally, it is important to note that empirical research on the relationship between online grooming behaviours and psychopathological constructs is very limited. We hope that researchers in this field will see this exploratory analysis as a platform for developing new studies on the psychopathology of online grooming.

6
Social Media and Young People

Julie Grove Hills, Antonia Bifulco and Thierry Pham

Introduction

In Chapter 1, data on the prevalence of social media use by young people and the legislative developments that have supported cross-national e-safety efforts were presented and discussed. On the basis of that review and the evidence presented in previous chapters about the behaviour of online groomers, it seems sensible to suggest that effective e-safety interventions will be those that are developed on the basis of two factors: an awareness of the psychological, emotional and social benefits that young people can get from being online; and an evidenced-based understanding of how young people use social media and perceive and negotiate online risks.

To that end, this chapter begins by describing the bearing of social media on psychological friendships and development. It then describes how young people identify and manage online risks by drawing on data from secondary school pupils collected as part of the European Online Grooming Project (EOGP) study described in this book.

Interpersonal aspects of social media

Technology is seen by young people as central to everyday life and forms a vital means of communication with friends (Quayle, Jonsson & Loof, 2012). It is perhaps unsurprising then that amongst normative samples of young people, internet use has been found to be associated with high social competence and extraversion (Anderson, Fagan, Woodnutt & Chamorro-Premuzic, 2012). A study investigating positive words young people associated with going online included 'happy, connected, good, excited, free, entertained, bored, interested, sociable and independent' (Page & Mapstone, 2010).

Adolescents use social networking sites (SNSs) to connect with others, mainly those they already know offline (Reich, Subrahmanyan & Espinoza, 2012). As such, there is evidence that this additional social network contact serves to strengthen some offline friendships (Reich, Subrahmanyan & Espinoza, 2012). For example, in a study with young people about the benefits of social media, Baker and Oswald (2101) reported that Facebook use was positively correlated with both closeness and support received from friends. However at the sub-group level, the direction of this correlation was dependent on the personality characteristics of the young person. For those with *high* levels of shyness, Facebook use was negatively correlated with friendship satisfaction and closeness with friends (online or offline). But for the *mildly* shy, Facebook use was found to predict greater support from friends (Baker & Oswald, 2010). Perhaps this study goes some way to explaining how Mesch and Talmud (2006) found that friendships forged online are perceived as less close and less supportive, with fewer offline activities.

Given SNSs are primarily about relationships, the nature and extent of the association between attachment style and social media has also been examined. Attachment theory was introduced in earlier chapters of this book as a feature of interpersonal style which might make individuals vulnerable to problem relating. Using self-report measures with Indonesian students, Oldmeadow, Quinn and Kowert (2013) found that anxious attachment style (as opposed to the avoidant or secure styles) was highly related to overuse of SNSs. This finding mirrored results with a North American sample but using a different self-report attachment scale. Here, young people with anxious attachment style were more frequent users of Facebook, more likely to use it when they experienced negative emotions and were more concerned by how others viewed them on Facebook (Oldmeadow, Quinn & Kowert, 2013). Given that young people with insecure attachment style are more likely to suffer emotional disorders and to have had an adverse early childhood (Bifulco & Thomas, 2012), their greater use of SNSs may increase their vulnerability to harm online.

As well as risks associated with attachment styles, the extent to which young people's use of online technology can develop into an addiction has also been examined. According to Griffiths (2000), an internet user can be considered addicted according to six criteria:

- salience (the activity becomes the most important in the person's life);
- mood change (subjective experience affected by the activity);

- tolerance (requiring continually higher doses for same effect);
- withdrawal symptoms (negative symptoms associated with reduced use);
- conflict (with those close caused by online activity);
- relapse that results in a return to the addictive behaviour after periods of relative control (Griffiths, 2000).

Studies of young people's internet addiction have found that it can be associated with a number of interpersonal and psychological outcomes. Perhaps unsurprisingly, a Czech study of adolescents found that a higher rate of addictive behaviour was associated with higher rates of initiating friendships online (Smahel, Brown & Blinka, 2012). In addition, an earlier study found that frequent use of the internet for communication can lead to a decline in an individual's offline social circle and an increase in depression and loneliness (Kraut, Patterson, Lundmark, Kiesler, Mukopadhyay & Scherlis, 1998).

This pattern of adverse interpersonal impacts seems to have changed as social networking has become more of a normative behaviour (Smahel, Brown & Blinka, 2012). However, it is possible that young people who prefer online friendships may have more conflict between their online and offline worlds. They may neglect their offline friends, which could feed their tendency to overuse the internet, or they may be searching online for the social support they do not have offline.

Given that online friendships developed on social media sites may be meeting a range of interpersonal and psychological needs for particular groups of young people, this presents a challenge for the development of effective e-safety initiatives. In particular, if there are some young people who believe that providing personal information to strangers or 'virtual friends' is acceptable behaviour (and their online behaviour is meeting other psychological needs), how can young people effectively engage with e-safety messages? In the next section, EOGP findings from focus groups with young people about their online behaviours, attitudes to e-safety and risk-management strategies are described.

EOGP focus groups with young people

Chapter 3 provided the design and sampling strategy for young people's focus groups conducted as part of the EOGP. In the following sections, findings from that research are presented across five themes: the nature and extent of internet use; social networking; awareness of online grooming; online safety; and attitudes towards e-safety campaigns.

Nature and extent of internet use

It is clear from the data in Chapter 4 that some online groomers spend significant periods of time on the internet. It is therefore important to understand how young people spend their time online and whether there are any patterns of use that can be identified by age and gender. This information can be used to target online safety initiatives to particular groups of young people. In the EOGP sample, it was perhaps unsurprising that given the fairly wide age range of the sample examined through focus groups, time spent online was described as being from five minutes to six hours as a maximum. Here, the older group aged 14–16 tended to talk about spending longer online. This is consistent with literature about online/offline friendships in the teenage years and, given homework demands, the use of the internet for schoolwork purposes (Livingston, Olafsson & Staksrud, 2011).

However, with the need to spend significant periods online, some young people in the EOGP in the 14–16 age groups talked about a commitment to going online, sometimes to the detriment of other key daily functions:

> Quite a lot, like from when I get home at about 4.30 until about midnight...sleep is irrelevant. Sleep is irrelevant when it comes to the Internet!
>
> (Girl, 14, UK)

The pattern of time spent online decreased with age, according to the comments of those in their early teenage years. For example, those aged 11–13 tended to spend up to an hour a day during the week but longer at weekends. Interestingly, the Italian young people talked about spending less time online per day than the others in the sample. Here, they also appeared to be spending less time online at weekends in favour of actually going out with friends as opposed to chatting with them online. Thus real face-to-face social interaction appeared to limit online interaction and contrasts with the findings of Smahel and colleagues described above (Smahel, Brown & Blinka, 2012). These cultural differences also point to the need for e-safety materials that are responsive to cultural diversity, and this is discussed further in Chapter 1 and in the final chapter of this book.

When the young people were asked about how they used the internet in the context of the time they spent online, two patterns emerged from the data. First, personal computers (PCs) and personal laptops were used during the week for searches on Google related to homework or for listening to music whilst working. Second, at weekends, young people said that more time was spent social networking and, in the case of the older group, it was conducted from their mobile phones rather than PCs or laptops. Where mobile phones were described as less readily used, this was influenced by the cost of mobile social networking and restrictions on use imposed by parents.

With regard to online gaming, there was a clear gender difference in terms of use. There were no examples from any of the groups of girls using gaming consoles for going online. The boys, however, talked about repeated use of PlayStation, Nintendo or Xbox devices. Again, this information has implications for the development of effective e-safety campaigns about online gaming that will engage young men in particular.

The use of webcams to facilitate online grooming has been described as a key finding emerging from the Child Exploitation and Online Protection Centre (2013). However, the data collected from young people indicated a far more limited use of webcams. This then demonstrates the shifting dynamic of online behaviours, and so presents a challenge for research and e-safety campaigns to remain relevant. When webcams were used by young people in the EOGP, this was to contact family members who were away on holiday, but not to contact friends online. But in some cases, limited use had been informed by awareness of the risks that webcam use can bring:

> Me, I put something on my webcam so no one can see me 'cos there's this girlfriend of mine who got hacked and people were able to see her through the webcam.
>
> (Girl, 13, Belgium)

Finally, the location in which young people go online is described. Here, the implications for safety campaigns are clear, with the earlier Chapter 4 data showing how groomers tended to take interactions with young people to private spaces where possible. In the focus-group discussions with young people, the location of internet use was described as a matter of convenience and expediency. As such, the family sitting-room, dining-room and bedroom were all talked about as common locations. However, the bedroom did seem to be the preferred location. These views were underpinned by the need for privacy and wanting to be away from their parents:

> I like to be somewhere quiet 'cos sometimes my friends send stupid emails and it can be embarrassing if my parents looked.
>
> (Girl, 12, UK)

Yes and somewhere quiet because my sister is a nosey little parker.

(Girl, 11, UK)

It was clear from the focus-group data that the use of Microsoft Network (MSN) had diminished considerably in recent years, whereby the 14–16-year-olds hardly used it at all. At the time EOGP data was collected, Facebook was the SNS of choice used by almost all in the focus groups. Patterns of Facebook use are described in the next section of this chapter.

Social networking: Facebook

In Chapter 4, a number of studies are described that show how online groomers use SNSs to access profile pictures, demographic descriptions and conversations for victim-targeting. To that end, understanding how young people use Facebook can help inform e-safety initiatives. Amongst the EOGP focus-group sample, virtually all of the young people used the site. Where Facebook was not used, it was because the person was not yet old enough to access it. However, even then these young people were clear that the site was definitely going to be accessed in due course:

I don't have Facebook...**yet!** [her emphasis]...so I usually have Google open to do my homework and so I've got YouTube on a lot listening to music when I'm doing my homework.

(Girl, 11, UK)

Adding friends

In earlier sections of this chapter, literature has been presented that shows how online friendships fulfil social and psychological needs in young people. Given the drive to meet those needs, the number of friends young people have on Facebook, and how those friends are established, has a clear bearing on the development of effective e-safety campaigns. Here, key questions for consideration are whether young people know the Facebook friends that they add personally. In addition, how do young people ascertain the real identity of a Facebook friend?

The young people studied discussed having a number of Facebook friends that ranged from 50–1000. Looking across all the focus-group data, around 400 friends tended to be the norm. Irrespective of the actual number of Facebook friends added, what was interesting was the sense of competition to have more friends that underpinned this aspect of Facebook behaviour. For example, some young people added people from a previous school or younger members within their current school to increase their number of friends – even if they did not really know them well or talk to them offline. There were also examples of some young people adding friends that they had not met. Alternatively, adding 'friends of friends' was also discussed. Here, the clear rationale expressed was that even though they were not friends to talk to, adding them would increase their overall total number of Facebook contacts:

> Sometimes I add people I don't know; it's a way to meet people.
>
> (Boy, 16, Belgium)

> Plenty. Some I see around, they're like these smaller kids at school, they bring the number up, but I don't talk to them.
>
> (Girl, 15, Belgium)

Staying with the topic of adding friends, there was an interesting exchange within one of the groups when asked how many of these friends they had met before. This in turn revealed the potential for 'learning' from each other in the possible absence of e-safety awareness or guidance from parents:

> Sometimes I add people I don't know; it's a way to meet people.
> But accepting people you don't know is dangerous.
> Yeah, there are maniacs/perverts out there.
> There could be paedophiles and who knows what else out there.
>
> (Belgium group aged 14–16 years)

Despite the competition driving diverse behaviour when adding friends to Facebook accounts, it was encouraging that some safety messages were getting through. For example, the pressure and competition to have many friends was discussed by one of the older girls as a concern about younger children using the internet. Furthermore, a very recurrent example from the EOGP sample was a form of vetting or screening. Here, the young person checked whether the person making a friend request had mutual friends:

> It [Facebook] is much easier: you can read his wall posts, check on his friends.
>
> (Girl, 13, Italy)

> Q: When you get a friend request [on FB] what do you usually do?
> – I check on his/her wall posts.
> – I check on his friends list!

– I have a look on his profile picture first.
– I check if we have mutual friends.

(Italy focus group)

Profiles and settings

Earlier in Chapter 2, EOGP findings are reported that show how some online groomers *scanned* SNSs to find out information about young people. There are thus important safety implications with regard to how profile pages are set up and the information they contain. When privacy and profile settings were discussed in the focus groups, a range of risky practices were disclosed. Turning first to profile settings, some young people talked about having the profile settings on 'public'. This means that anyone using the internet can access the page and discover personal details about the young person. When the circumstances of these profile-page risk-takers were explored further, two influencing features emerged. First, these young people tended to come from a vocational schooling background and thus lower socio-economic group in both Italy and Belgium. Second, there had been no internet safety-awareness training provided either in their schools or seemingly from their parents.

> I can't remember ... I really don't know if mine is set to public or to private.
>
> (Boy, 13, Italy)

In one Italian school, some of the group said they did not know what to do in terms of privacy settings. In response, one young person set out the instructions for the others to learn.

> You have to customize your privacy settings panel on the prompt 'search for you on Facebook', and you switch if from 'Everyone' to 'Friends only'.
>
> (Girl, 13, Italy)

In direct contrast were the circumstances of the group of young people who talked about having their profile page set to 'private'. Here, these young people said that their profile had been private for as long as they could remember. Directly influencing this behaviour was exposure to either safety-awareness sessions in school, or parents that were very aware of e-safety and were adept users of Facebook themselves.

I was told to [set it to private]...it was the condition before I could
use it.

(Girl, 13, UK)

Despite this encouraging safety behaviour, there were some young people in this group who talked about having good awareness, but who
had not yet put the learning into practice. This reinforces the need for
safety campaigns to highlight the need to implement action and learning immediately and to give instructions on how to change settings for
these initiatives to have maximum impact.

Me, it's public but I think I'm going to change that because I don't
want people I don't know to be able to see my profile.

(Girl, 16, Belgium)

Alongside whether young people keep their Facebook profile settings on
public or private, it is also important to understand what young people think is acceptable profile content and the features influencing this
behaviour. The information listed as acceptable to post on their profiles included their name; gender; birthday; information about their life;
and the name of their home town. In addition, there were also examples of some young people who used profile names such as 'Squiggle'
or 'Jackie's Girl'. Given that some of these profiles are public, and some
online groomers scan and use profile information to target particular
people in the sexual offence process, this is unsettling information.

The type of information young people regarded as not suitable to
post on their profiles was personal addresses and phone numbers.
Encouragingly, young people tended to state categorically that they
would not post such personal details. There were, however, examples
of young people posting a variety of personal pictures, mostly between
friends they knew, but on occasions these images showed the young
people wearing their school uniform. Again, one exchange revealed the
value of safety-awareness training that had been provided in the school
to challenge this risky behaviour:

We're not allowed to send photos with our school uniform.
Aren't we?
Apparently not.
Oops, I did.

(UK group aged 12–14)

The final aspect of Facebook profile behaviour was the practice amongst some young people of having fake single or multiple profiles on the site. In fact, this behaviour was not unusual and there were, for example, some young people that had a different profile for boyfriends or girl-friends. What is very interesting is that young people are developing multiple profiles in response to the safety risk presented online. That is, they posted different information on each profile according to who they expected to view them. There were also examples of some young people with one profile that contained fake information for the same safety reasons:

> I often fake my own information, so that if I'm on the same website as my friends and they need information I always tell them my user name so they know it's me but I will describe myself differently. So I'll say I have black hair, I come from Asia or something like that ... not exactly like that, but I'll fake my settings for my safety.
>
> (Girl, 13, UK)

It is important to note that this behaviour was also unheard of in some of the groups, where participants expressed surprise as to why anyone would want to have more than one profile. However, when they were questioned by the facilitator as to why they thought this behaviour occurred, the suggestions were that it was possibly related to the disinhibition that you can experience when online:

> So that you can change personality ...? You can have two different accounts ... on the computer you can be completely different to like when you're talking to someone in real life.
>
> (Boy, 14, UK)

> I've also got a joke profile ... I made a fake one with my friend ... and it's really surprising how many people accept you ... it's really weird being in a position where you know you're not a real person but some people are so vulnerable that they think you are.
>
> (Girl, 14, UK)

Online groomers

One of the core aims of the EOGP was to make a significant contribution to the development of educational awareness and preventative initiatives aimed at parents, teachers and young people. For safety campaigns to have the most effect, it is important to understand the nature and extent of young people's awareness of grooming. By doing so, safety initiatives can be tailored to address any knowledge gaps or myths identified by this research. In this section, awareness of online grooming per se is described followed by the characteristics young people associated with online groomers. The section concludes with an analysis of how young people talked about responding to inappropriate approaches.

Awareness of grooming

When the young people were asked about whether they had heard of online grooming, in some cases the word 'groomer' was an unfamiliar term. However, when it was established that the groups understood the behaviour,[1] young people provided some broad and specific definitions. An example of a broad definition was 'adults who want to attract young people because they think they're still young themselves'. Specific definitions tended to focus on both the characteristics of the individual, the style of approach and the perceived outcome associated with any encounter:

> It's like when a 50 year old man like pretends to be a 12 year old girl and like says 'oh why don't we meet up and we can talk about this band'...and whatever...and then you meet up and something **terrible** [her emphasis] happens.
>
> (Girl, 12, UK)

With the broad definitions mapped, the next aspect explored in the groups was young people's sense of what type of person would be interested in approaching them online. The range of verbatim responses are organized thematically to aid translation into safety campaigns and materials. Table 6.1 presents this data.

The data presented in Table 6.1 is a stark reminder of the extent of work still needed in awareness raising for e-safety campaigns. The descriptions tended to be stereotypical depictions of old, unattractive or 'sick' people, for example, 'good-looking men don't need to do these things'. Given what is known about how some online groomers can alter their identity so it is desirable to a young person (Seto, 2013; Whittle, Hamilton-Giachritsis, Beech & Collings, 2013), these are risky perceptions. It was however encouraging that some young people provided descriptions that were more accurate:

Table 6.1 Young people's perceptions of groomers' characteristics

Theme	Verbatim data
Age (and presentation)	– Fat and old – They're 20 plus…obviously – This may be very rude but I always imagine them to be like mainly old…something like 50 years old – Old farts, not 70, more like 40 – Creepy old man – staring eyes – Old but lives with their parents – Older than us…and then when hear more about them they're not like you imagine
Unattractive appearance	– Bearded – Bald – Sweaty – Slimy – Someone wearing big thick glasses – Disgusting people – Like those pictures, mug shots, like those people that have gone into prison – Really scary – look scary – Geeks with big old beer guts
Unstable personality	– A sick person – A weirdo – Mentally disturbed – They're crazy – Psychopaths – They must be drunk – They're not right in the head
Relationship	– They're people we don't know – Maybe foreign people who'd ask me out
Sex offenders (generic)	– They are child molesters – They are child profiteers – They're paedophiles – Perverts – Rapists
Accurate (non-stereotypical)	– A man in his thirties who looks for 15 year old girls – Could be a girl though – I always think boys…or men – Adults who want to attract young people because they think they're still young themselves

Source: Webster et al. (2012, p110).

I think anyone…in that, well first of all you think it's like old fat people that just stare at the computer, but then we watched this thing [video in Assembly] where it was actually young people as well.

(UK focus group)

Perceptions about approaches

Identifying how young people think online groomers make their approaches can help address any gaps in e-safety initiatives. The range of verbatim responses are organized thematically for ease of translation into safety campaigns and materials. Table 6.2 presents this data.

The data in Table 6.2 is encouraging as it indicates that some safety messages about the type and style of approach are getting through to young people. The range of responses reflected understanding of how groomers may socialize with young people and the attempt to relate to the young person by wanting to learn more about them.

Table 6.2   Young people's perception of modus operandi

Type	Sub-theme	Verbatim data
Mode	*Computer chat*	– Through a message
	Images	– He would send us pictures/images
Identity Deception	*Age*	– They pass themselves off as a young person, as someone else
		– They'd say they're your age, like, 'I'm your age do you want to come round?'
		– They'd probably try to convince you that they were like you, so they'd probably send you pictures of what they think you'd like…so if he knew you were 12 they'd probably send you a picture of a 12-year old girl.
		– By passing themselves off as someone our age. As far as pictures go, sure, all you have to do is Google 'male 25 years old' and *voila*, you've got loads to choose from.
		– You can tell if it's for real or not because a good-looking guy, let's say it, there aren't so many of them around anymore
	Image	– They could send pictures to pass themselves off as younger than they are, could doctor pictures found on the Internet
		– He could like send us fake pictures anyway, couldn't he?

	Relationship	– If you said 'No' or 'I'll ask my mum', they'd try to convince you to come round and say 'Oh don't tell them, don't worry…it's quite safe'…or something like that
		– Pass themselves off as someone you know
		– And just like trying to be like a friend
		– Yeah, lots of people who've had that sort of experience have said they wouldn't know as it's just like a normal friend
		– If he's way older than me, he could pretend he's a friend of my parents
		– Yes, he might say he's a friend of my father
		– By sending a friend request to a friend of ours e.g. can we meet?
	Intention	– He'll say good things about himself
Socialization	*Generic*	– They'll talk to us and stuff
		– He'd write 'What's up?'
		– Start chatting to you on Facebook and saying 'I saw you in the park and things'
	YP	– They'll ask us about our hobbies
	Interests	– If you share a band say that you like then they might say 'I've got these tickets for two and I was going to take my friend and now she can't come, so would you like to come with me'
		– Or they might when you've said your favourite band, say 'oh come round, she's my favourite too and we could cut our hair or something' (*laughter*)
Information	*Explicit*	– Ask you where you live
seeking	*Implicit*	– He could find our email address on Facebook and use it to add us on MSN as well!
		– They might fake their Facebook profile…like to spend time checking your friends and gathering information and typing your name into Google and that
Outcome	*Meeting*	– Like getting to know you and then eventually meeting up
		– Ask to meet you
		– Write whether we'd like to meet, ask that we trust him
No awareness		– I really can't imagine

Source: Webster et al. (2012, p112).

Young people were also acutely aware of the role that deception can play in these approaches.

Approaches received, appraisal and actions taken

Given the amount of time some online groomers can spend online attempting to approach young people (Whittle et al., 2013b), it is perhaps inevitable that some of the normative young people shared experiences of being approached in an inappropriate way. In fact an approach by some that they judged as 'suspicious' seemed to be an almost expected experience – 'it happens all the time!' The experiences shared by some young people showed that the *identity* and *escalation* features of online grooming, as described in Chapter 4, appeared to be the point when they became aware of a potential risk. Acting 'suspiciously' or not trusting someone seems to refer to persistence by the 'stranger' in attempts at communication, or asking for a phone number.

> Yeah, it was on Facebook, someone added me as a friend and, seeing how he used the photo of someone I knew, I added him as a friend and then he came to talk to me, asking me how old I was and wanting to meet and all. I cut it short because the conversation seemed weird to me because he was asking stuff he should have known already.
>
> (Girl, 16, Belgium)

> Well, once there was this guy who passed himself off as a friend of mine, I didn't know his [my friend's] computer had been hacked. And the guy says meet me at this place, but it seemed strange to me because I'd never been there before. So I said 'yeah' but I never showed up. And the next day I said sorry to my friend for not making it and he said 'what are you talking about?'
>
> (Boy, 13, Belgium)

> Me, once, one of them [and he says 'paedophile'] asked me to do things in front of the webcam. First he passed himself as a 16 year old girl, then he said he was 25, so I reported it to netlog and netlog deleted him.
>
> (Boy, 16, Belgium)

> Me too, he was an old man as well . . . I didn't accept his friend request. I checked on his profile and it was full of very weird photos. They were all very dark and shadowy.
>
> (Girl, 15, Italy)

Yes, he passed himself off as someone that I know and then he asked to turn the webcam on and he had it pointed on his penis. So I immediately blocked him.

(Girl, 15, Belgium)

When young people talked about how they assessed the veracity of an online approach, the type and style of language used by the online groomers was discussed in the focus groups as the key identifying marker of risk. For example, the young people talked about clumsy attempts at shorthand, excessive use of emoticons such as smiley faces and inappropriate use of young people's 'slang' language.

Oh yeah, I can always tell...say if someone is on someone else's account...I can just tell it's not them just because of the way they 'talk'...I know it sounds silly but some people might just put loads of smiley faces on the end or like abbreviations and stuff...I kinda know.

(Girl, 14, UK)

[So by evaluating his language?]...Yes, but also the questions he asks, the slang he'd use.

(Boy, 14, Italy)

How young people responded covered three broad themes. The first was *immediate action* and involved consistent blocking of messages or ignoring inappropriate requests. However, one young person said that when one groomer had been particularly persistent, the only action left to the young person was to close down her Facebook account. Beyond the clear risk of harm these men can present, this Facebook example shows how online grooming can impact on broader aspects of socialization. Second was *risky behaviours* and this encompassed responses such as keeping the phone number of unknown men encountered online who called to meet offline for possible further investigation. The final aspect of a young person's response was the *extent that they disclosed* problematic approaches online.

A common feature across boys' and girls' accounts in the focus groups was the desire to deal with things without involving adults. Boys in particular tended to be more resistant to the idea of telling adults about inappropriate online approaches. This finding is supported by other research with young people that found boys twice as often reported doing nothing about a 'threatening' experience (Davidson, Lorenz &

Martellozo, 2011). In some respect, boys in the EOGP saw themselves as at less risk than girls. These views were influenced by stereotypical perceptions of masculinity and of being 'tough'. That is, boys felt that they could deal with it alone and protect themselves. Girls commented that they would be more likely to tell a friend. In some cases, there was also discussion of mentioning the approach to their parents. However, where there was resistance to telling parents or carers, this was underpinned by a fear that their computer privileges would be removed.

Online safety

Given the number of young people that are using the internet (Livingstone, Haddon, Gorzig & Olafsson, 2011), and the extent of online groomer behaviour, as described in Chapter 4, the importance of young people operating safely online is critical. In 2008, school sample surveys in the United Kingdom revealed quite a high degree of awareness of the existence of risks and dangers on the internet, but this awareness was not always matched by a detailed understanding of the various risks around disclosure issues (Davies, Good & Cranmer, 2009). It is therefore important to understand the extent of young people's awareness about safety issues and the different techniques they may use to manage such risks. This information can then be used to appraise and perhaps refine safety initiatives so that they may have maximum impact. In this section, online safety is described in two discrete, but complementary parts. First the *risk awareness* discussed by young people in the EOGP, second the description and appraisal of *risk-management strategies*.

Risk awareness

When asked the question, 'What does online safety mean to you?', three themes emerged from the group discussions. First was *non-disclosure*, which encompassed the young people not sharing information about their private life to strangers and the sense that people need to be aware of what they say and how they say it. It was striking that young people in the United Kingdom related the need for non-disclosure as helping prevent potential harm from strangers (stranger-danger). One reason for this awareness may be due to the widespread online safety campaigns disseminated in schools, using material provided by the Child Exploitation and Online Prevention Centre.

Yeah, being aware...making sure you don't post pictures of yourself...just staying aware of keeping away from people you don't know.

(Girl, 15, UK)

Don't give out information to people you don't know, don't give information to random people.

(Girl, 15, UK)

Awareness of the stranger-danger concept also seemed to cascade down into attitudes and behaviours around whether it was safe to physically meet with somebody only known online. For example, in one school in the United Kingdom that had welcomed e-safety training, the young people were emphatic that they would never meet an unknown online friend offline under any circumstances. In schools where there had been no safety awareness, some young people (particularly those from the 'vocational' education stream) talked about meeting someone under particular circumstances. For example, if they were attractive.

...if it's a pretty girl.

(Boy 16, Belgium)

If they're not too old, then for sure.

(Girl, 14, Belgium)

Here, the education level of some of the young people with risky attitudes perhaps indicates the requirement for a more targeted safety approach to engage and meet the needs of people with different abilities. This is discussed in the next chapter of this book.

The second theme was about the risks to the *health of their computer and thus the young person*. Here, some young people talked about the need to install antivirus software to prevent computer viruses, getting hacked and/or people taking control of their webcams to spy on them. But some people in this group only talked about viruses in the context of broader risk awareness. In particular, young people in Italy and Belgium had to be prompted by the group facilitator to realize the issue could also be about personal safety online. The final theme was labelled as *no knowledge*, as some young people in the focus groups were unable to articulate any awareness of risk.

Risk-management strategies

Staying safe online for the young people meant having settings set to 'private', not giving out phone numbers or addresses and specifically, not giving out passwords. It appeared that much of the online safety practice had been learnt 'by doing' rather than through explicit advice. This was particularly evident where there had been no awareness training in school. Sources of unstructured learning tended to be from siblings and parents. In some cases, siblings were described as handing down good advice based on their own risky experiences online:

> My sister taught me...before I used it...because some things had happened to her and so she told me to change it.
>
> (Girl, 12, UK)

> I told my sister about a guy who once sent me a friend request. She advised me to block his account and not to answer his emails anymore for he could cause me trouble or steal my passwords.
>
> (Girl, 13, Italy)

In the focus groups where there had been no safety training in school or from parents, it appears that the young people do nothing at all in terms of prevention and had no effective strategies. Across the groups in the United Kingdom, Italy and Belgium, when people gave examples of risk management in all its forms, the unifying theme was that these strategies had been deployed whilst using Facebook, presumably due to the popularity of this SNS, as described earlier in this chapter.

Attitudes to safety-awareness training

When considering the young people's attitudes to safety training, one of the key features that distinguished responses in the focus groups was about the *style or approach of the provider*. For example, whereas in Italy where all training seemed to be welcome, in the United Kingdom, some young people talked about preferring training where they could identify with the individual training provider. This did not necessarily mean the safety trainer needed to be someone of a similar age, but that he or she had characteristics such as liking Facebook. There was a view that some parents who provided advice about social networking were either against it or fearful of it. Young people felt that the key aspect underpinning this fear was that their parents were ignorant or inept at social networking. Where parents and siblings had been more balanced in their approach, the key safety messages seem to have been embedded into consciousness and practice more readily:

> Well because I started the internet when quite young my sister she used to tell me what to do and what not to do...if I hadn't had

that...if I was the older sister and hadn't had that I'd have probably ended up in a lot of trouble. But also because of my parents' professions they're very strict...they say 'oh you can't use this website because we know it's not good'.

(Girl, 12, UK)

When asked about who they think needs safety training, the young people were clear that education programmes need to target younger children. The suggestion here is that the younger children are more vulnerable precisely because of their desire to get online and their competitiveness to have as many friends as possible. This is an important observation and provides a clear message about the need for safety training at an early age:

...internet education doesn't really start until you get like to secondary school and with online stuff it's really very easy to fake your age but people do it...they're doing it pretty young.

(Girl, 15, UK)

...yeah quite...maybe internet education should start when you're six or seven...they're trying to be cool...like they want to be the first person to have over 100 friends...and so they're more competitive then.

(Girl, 15, UK)

The final aspect of the discussion about safety was in the context of putting learning into practice. Here, there was a degree of scepticism, particularly concerning how some sites govern age limits. That is, some young people could be taught about the risk of going on adult sites, but in practice, there was nothing to stop them doing so:

I find it's useless because often on sites they'll ask: 'Are you 18 years old?' You click yes and you're registered anyway even if you're not 18.

(Girl, 13, Belgium)

Recently in the United Kingdom, the government has been working with the online industry to help manage these issues and limit, where possible, some of the risks that young people across Europe described.

Conclusion

The views of secondary school pupils studied in focus groups in three of the partner countries showed a degree of awareness which indicated some potential resilience to harmful experiences. They had some awareness of safety issues and appreciated safety training. However, there was still some naivety and overconfidence about behaviour online. For example, chatting online to 'strangers', keeping telephone numbers for future contact and so on. There were also some stereotypical views of online groomers as old, unattractive, mentally ill and so on, which could make these young people vulnerable to advances from younger socially skilled offenders. Finally, the focus groups demonstrated the power of social mediation in terms of parental controls, sibling advice, peer-group learning and, very specifically, e-safety training in schools. To that end, schools may want to include peer learning as part of their safety-intervention work, and e-safety training clearly needs to start a lot earlier than secondary school level.

With regard to the generalizibility of our work (see Chapter 3 for a summary of generalizibility criteria in qualitative research), the EOGP was in a position to compare findings with those from the Risk-taking Online Behaviour: Empowerment through Research and Training (ROBERT) project (Kolpakova, 2012). The ROBERT study also conducted focus groups across Europe with young people, but selected participants from groups perceived to have a higher risk of online harm. The groups encompassed: looked after young people; people with disabilities; and those from the lesbian, gay, bisexual or transgender community. The themes that emerged were surprisingly similar to the EOGP findings. For example, Kolpakova (2012) reported that technology was central to everyday life whereby having status online was seen as important for a sense of identity and self-worth. The webcam proved vital communication for those with disabilities. It was also seen as a way of offering sexual opportunities.

The young people in the ROBERT study seemed aware of online risks and most restricted the availability of their personal information (Kolpakova, 2012). However, there was a tendency to attribute risk to others rather than themselves. Consequently, the one significant difference between the studies was that in this high-risk group, harmful or exploitative behaviour was also perpetrated online by young people. Strategies to manage this challenge are discussed in the final chapter of this book.

With regard to enhancing online safety, the use of social media as an everyday means of communicating needs to be recognized as a developmental issue by psychologists and educationalists. Here, aspects of socialization, friendship behaviour, sexual exploration and information should be examined. Safety messages for young people need to be conveyed not only in the course of teaching about technology, but also in the sessions about health and social education. Understanding what constitutes friendships and support online and offline requires discussion with young people to increase awareness of those relationships which could be dangerous or are in effect vacuous. For those young people who are shy and lonely, understanding that online friendships cannot replace those offline needs to be understood for the internet to be a place where all young people can safely thrive.

Note

1. Where the word 'groomer' was not understood, the focus-group facilitators used as little explicit prompt as possible to tease out their understanding of what sort of behaviour it refers to. The term 'entice' worked best here.

7
Young Victims Online

Antonia Bifulco and Thierry Pham

In the previous chapter, young people's awareness of online risks and their perception of safety initiatives have been summarized. But for e-safety campaigns to be relevant and evidenced-based, it is important to also understand the experiences of young people that have been victimized online. To that end, this chapter will focus on the characteristics of young victims and discuss how children and young people succumb to grooming advances online. The growing research into victims of online grooming will be outlined and the account of victims given by the groomers in the course of the European Online Grooming Project (EOGP) study provided. From this analysis, a preliminary grouping of types of victim will indicate the profiles of young people who are potential or actual victims as identified from the offenders' interviews. This will be compared with data collected from the parallel Risk-taking Online Behaviour: Empowerment through Research and Training (ROBERT) project (Quayle, Jonsson & Loof, 2012). This study had a specific focus on victims where 27 young victims of online grooming and offline abuse all described their experience. An overarching speculative model of abuse will be presented with discussion of further research needed to identify further those young people most at risk online for preventative interventions.

The scale of the problem

The availability and widespread use of digital technology has transformed the way in which we consider children and young people to be at risk of harm. There are widely acknowledged benefits that internet use provides in terms of schoolwork and information seeking, as well as in leisure through playing games, communicating with peers and the

development and maintenance of friendships through social networking sites (SNSs). There are, however, a range of online risks that children
can be exposed to with the potential for personal harm. Chapter 1 outlined the high usage of the internet amongst children by drawing on
the EU Kids Online Survey (Livingstone & Haddon, 2009). This survey
found the most common risky activity reported by children was that of
communicating online with new people not met face-to-face, affecting
30 per cent of European children aged 9–16. Particular risks have been
identified in relation to use of SNSs, with 38 per cent of 9–12-year-olds
and 77 per cent of 13–16-year-olds having a profile online. However, age
restrictions are only partially effective and younger children are more
likely to have a public profile.

Parental rules for SNS use are also only partly effective, and a quarter of SNS users communicate online with people unconnected to their
daily lives. One fifth of children whose profile is public, display their
address or phone number and younger children are shown not to understand features designed to protect children using SNSs. In terms of
European-wide safety skills online, Italy and Romania are amongst the
lowest, with the United Kingdom slightly above average, but below
Norway and Sweden. Age is clearly an important factor, with different
developmental levels related to different exposure and risk status.

This diverse range of risk-taking behaviours means that some young
people can be at risk for approaches by online groomers. Chapter 4 set
out the key features of online grooming. In the context of this chapter,
the issues to note are the diversity of online groomers' behaviours.
This means that whilst some will hide their identity when approaching young people, others are direct in their requests for sexual talk and
eventual contact (Choo, 2009; Whittle, Hamilton-Giachritsis, Beech &
Collings, 2013 a, b). Identity masking can be reciprocated, with some
victims having reported also hiding their identity online (Quayle,
Jonsson & Loof, 2012). Although the term 'grooming' suggests a process of socialization, data from the EOGP showed that in some cases
approaches were fast, direct and sexually explicit. Therefore, the definition of online sexual offending encompasses not only the viewing, production and/or distribution of indecent images of children, but also the
'online grooming' of children and young people. Here, online grooming involves an interaction and in some cases socialization between an
offender and a child/young person aged 16 years or younger, during
which an offender prepares him/her for sexual abuse (Sexual Offences
Act 2003 – Article 15). Within this definition, sexual abuse can occur
online, offline or in both contexts.

To understand the extent of policy response required, a key question concerns how many young people receive sexual approaches online. In the previous chapter, qualitative data is reported that shows some inappropriate and unwanted approaches. The EU Kids Online reports (Livingstone, Haddon, Gorzig & Olafsson, 2011) show that 15 per cent of 11–16-year-olds say they have seen or received sexual messages on the internet in the last year. The age trend is marked, with 22 per cent of 15–16-year-olds having this experience. In European terms, the rate is highest in Romania (22%), which is substantially higher than in the United Kingdom (12%) and in Italy (4%). Nearly half of those receiving such messages felt upset; this being more common in girls. Meeting 'stranger' online contacts also varied: high rates were found for example in Sweden (54%), Norway (49%) and in Romania (32%), but these were somewhat lower in the United Kingdom (28%) and Italy (27%). Of those meeting in person, 55 per cent said they met one or two strangers initially contacted online, but as many as 23 per cent say they have met five or more people this way. More girls will meet strangers online than boys and parents seem largely unaware of such meetings.

Extensive research undertaken by the National Centre for Missing and Exploited Children by Finkelhor and colleagues in their 'Youth Internet Safety Survey' has examined the prevalence of harmful activity online as well as changes in rates over time in the United States. In looking at online victimization over a five-year follow-up period (2000–2005), they showed a decline in the proportion of youth who received unwanted sexual solicitations, from one in five to one in seven (Wolak, Mitchell & Finkelhor, 2006). The authors attribute this to the youth becoming more cautious about interacting with people online that they did not know offline. Thus they engaged in fewer such interactions. There was also a reduction in chat room visits. However, there was no decline in the proportion who received aggressive sexual solicitations (from 3% to 4%), which are those more likely to result in criminal behaviour. This is where the person soliciting asked to meet in person, or called by telephone or sent the young person mail, gifts or money. There was also no decline in the proportion of youth who received distressing sexual solicitations (5% and 4%). These had the effect of causing upset or fear in the young people.

Finally, a large survey of 1718 young people across the United Kingdom aged 11–16 revealed that 42 per cent had received electronic messages with attachments from strangers, 37 per cent had added a stranger to their instant messaging and 35 per cent added a stranger to their social networking friends group (Davidson, Lorenz, Martellozo & Grove-Hills, 2011). Online risk-taking by young people thus seems fairly common.

Understanding victims: Precursors and consequences of abuse

Child maltreatment in general remains a major public-health and social-welfare problem in high-income countries. Sexual abuse is a particular cause for concern because of the wide range of perpetrators that can be involved (Gilbert, Widom, Browne, Fergusson, Webb & Janson, 2008). True prevalence of any form of sexual abuse is difficult to ascertain given the attendant secrecy, stigma and barriers to both disclosure and approaching services. However, a range of 5 per cent to 30 per cent prevalence is quoted in research studies (Russell, 1984; Finkelhor, Araji, Baron, Browne, Peters & Wyatt, 1986; Radford, Corral, Bradley, Fisher, Bassett, Howat & Collishaw, 2011). This rate is up to ten-fold that reported to services and conviction rates for sexual abuse of children are notoriously low (Davidson & Bifulco, 2010). However, the proportion of sexual abuse that in recent years may have been aided by internet or mobile phone contact and grooming is unknown, which makes research in this area difficult to undertake.

The longer term impacts of all types of sexual abuse are pernicious, including high lifetime prevalence rates of clinical disorders such as depression and anxiety, post-traumatic stress disorder, alcohol or drug abuse, self-harm and suicide behaviours (Bifulco, Brown & Adler, 1991; Gilbert et al., 2008). This is in addition to increased adult vulnerability in terms of inability to make long-term relationships, sexual dysfunction, risky sexual behaviour and attachment difficulties (Noll, Haralson, Butler & Shenk, 2011). The risks for experiencing such abuse include family breakdown, children being 'looked after' in residential care, parental drug and alcohol abuse and child runaway status (Gallagher, 2000). There are also significant gender differences. Whilst twice as many girls experience sexual abuse, boys are over-represented in some at-risk groups, such as those in care. Those sexually abused have a very high rate of re-victimization (seven-fold higher than other groups) with at least a third being re-victimized in a 12-month period (Finkelhor, Ormrod & Turner, 2007).

One aspect of childhood maltreatment that is often underplayed is the resulting psychological dysregulation in adolescent females' sexual behaviour. A study by Noll and colleagues (2011) of 275 maltreated adolescent females and a non-maltreated comparison group found that maltreated females had difficulty regulating emotions, cognitions and behaviours. When this was combined with the propensity to entertain sexual thoughts and engage with sexually explicit material, the likelihood of engaging in risky sexual behaviour increased. Causal analysis was used to show that sexual preoccupation mediates between psychological dysregulation and risky sexual behaviours (Noll et al., 2011). This is important to consider in relation to online behaviour, given the internet is associated with more disinhibiting behaviour in general (Suler, 2004; Whittle et al., 2013).

Sexual abuse related to technology

Whilst there is some evidence that reported incidents of sexual abuse to services is reducing in the United Kingdom (Radford et al., 2011) and in the United States, evidence is also accruing for increases in sexual abuse incidents which are initiated or performed with the use of new technologies (ICAC, 2004). As described earlier, this includes a wide range of technology-related behaviours. For example, internet and mobile phone use for stranger grooming of youngsters for online or offline abusive contact with the child. In addition, the creation and distribution of indecent images of children, often by known adults or peers as a currency in paedophile rings or to aid with the grooming and 'normalizing' or coercive compliance process is increasing (ECPAT, 2012a, b). Thus, the technological elements can involve cameras and web cameras (webcams) and communication through chat rooms, game platforms and mobile phones. The sexual abuse involved can be from strangers (e.g. online grooming to lead to 'travelling' to meet the child for offline abuse), known persons (e.g. adolescent posting of sexually explicit pictures of the victim) or family members (e.g. enacting sexual abuse to be photographed or filmed for subsequent distribution).

Whilst the investigation of sexual abuse involving technology is relatively new, there is evidence of the increasing prevalence from UK, US and cross-European studies (CEOP, 2007; Finkelhor, Mitchell & Wolak, 2000; Livingstone & Haddon, 2009). Adolescents seem to be more frequently victimized (Livingstone, Ólafsson, O'Neill & Donoso, 2012), with girls also more at risk (Mitchell & Wells, 2007; Wells & Mitchell, 2008; Wolak, Finkelhor & Mitchell, 2008). The potential for new categories of children and young people being accessed for sexual abuse is very real because of the high use of the internet. Thus, studies show that one in four youngsters using the internet have unwanted access to explicit pictures; one in five receive a sexual solicitation or approach; one in 17 are threatened or harassed; and one in 33 receive an aggressive sexual solicitation, with most of these occurring whilst the young person is on a computer at home (ICAC, 2004).

Thousands of indecent images of children and young people have been uncovered by police forces, although few of the victims have been identified (ECPAT, 2012 a, b). The argument that this is leading to an escalation of sexual abuse of children and young people through new sources of access has to be taken seriously and requires yet further research.

A review of scientific literature dealing with sexual exploitation of children and youth over the internet identified predictors of unwanted exposure to sexual material online (Ospina, Harstall & Dennett, 2010). The review identified 13 studies between 2003 and 2009 on the sexual exploitation of children and youth over the internet. The two foci were internet-initiated grooming for purposes of sexual abuse and internet-based receipt of sexual images by children and young people. Ospina and colleagues (2010) confirmed that one in five youth had been approached for sexual solicitation purposes online. They also identified a range of risk factors for online sexual solicitation when compared to receiving sexual materials. This showed that risks vary by exploitative category (sexual solicitation or grooming versus unwanted exposure to sexual images). For example, in relation to sexual solicitation or grooming, victims are more likely to be female and over the age of 14. Their pattern of internet use involves using chat rooms; talking to or sending personal information to strangers; engaging in sexual or high-risk behaviours online; having high internet use; and accessing the internet from mobile devices or whilst away from home. In terms of emotional and behavioural problems, there is a range of risk: depressive symptoms and substance abuse; delinquent behaviour; and somatic complaints and insomnia. Regarding past experiences, these include parental conflict, poor emotional bond with carers, prior experience of physical or sexual abuse as well as prior problem internet behaviour with lack of parental controls all identified.

In terms of the second category (unwanted exposure to sexual material online), the risk factors vary somewhat, for example, differences include a higher rate of males and slightly younger adolescents (13–17). There is also some difference identified in internet use, for example, use of file-sharing programmes and frequent use of chat rooms. Both groups engage with strangers online and use of the internet outside the home is, however, common to both groups. As regards emotional and behavioural problems, in the group exposed to sexual material online, being a victim of bullying is also common, but here there is no evidence of somatic complaints or delinquent behaviour. A problem childhood history is also a feature and includes parental conflict and physical or sexual abuse, but not a poor emotional bond with carers or poor parental controls on internet use which feature in the group at risk for sexual grooming online.

Other studies indicate similar family-based risk factors (Quayle, Jonsson & Loof, 2012) which are of the same order as risk factors for offline abuse (Bifulco, Brown & Adler, 1991; Whittle, Hamilton-Giachritsis Beech & Collins, 2013b).

Mitchell and Wells (2007) examined problematic internet experiences with people in mental health care services. Certain harms online were presented as primary health care problems with 'isolative-avoidant' use highlighted. This is where clients chose to have all their social interactions online with little social interaction offline and whose online activity was a factor isolating them from family and friends (Mitchell & Wells, 2007). It also included sexual exploitation victimization. The authors advocate more extensive assessment of problem internet use when treating clients with psychological disorders.

Ybarra and colleagues (2007), in a national US survey of 1588 young people, examined unwanted sexual solicitation as well as harassment online. They found both experiences related to psychosocial problems including substance abuse and having delinquent peers, as well as physical and sexual aggression offline and aggressive behaviour. Both experiences also related to having a poor emotional bond with care-givers and poor caregiver monitoring. They point to the importance of identifying a perpetrator–victim group amongst young people which mental health professionals need to be aware of in treatment.

The psychologically abusive aspects which can accompany grooming and public distribution of abuse images can create feelings of shame and guilt (Palmer & Stacey, 2004). One of the early studies involved 83 Barnardo's cases which showed long-term, chronic psychiatric disorder impacts, including depression and suicide attempts, and preoccupation with shame, guilt and damaged self-esteem (Palmer & Stacey, 2004). The added impact of the photographing of victims was highlighted as a source of distress and disturbance and failure to get closure after the offender is sentenced, given these images remain in circulation. Further research is needed to gauge the extent to which aspects of online grooming parallel the psychologically abusive experiences outlined in child maltreatment literature which include humiliation, emotional blackmail, exploitation and abuse of trust (Bifulco, Moran,

Baines, Bunn & Stanford, 2003). In addition, research is needed to establish the effects of internet-aided sexual abuse in order to inform interventions for victims and appropriate sentencing for offenders. For this, a more detailed exploration of psychologically abusive techniques in the grooming and abuse process needs elucidating, and their impact in terms of psychological damage.

Grooming behaviour online can involve psychological abuse when this involves entrapment, emotional blackmail over apparent complicity and manipulating the child/young person's trust. Similarly, threats to distribute and make public sexually explicit images of the child or images of the abuse can be used to terrorize and blackmail. The psychological impact of these techniques can create additional psychological damage over and above the sexual abuse or near-abuse experiences themselves. This can result in lifelong levels of mistrust and damaged self-concept impacting on future relating ability and attachment.

Other risk factors that are beginning to be examined by research in this area involve the extent to which making friends and attachment style influences online activity and risk of harm. As discussed in the previous chapter, adolescent use of the internet and SNSs relates to issues of identity, belonging and self-esteem (Anderson, Fagan, Woodnutt & Chamorro-Premuzic, 2012; Reich, Subrahmanyan & Espinoza, 2012). In order to better understand issues around shyness, social anxiety, poor relating competence and loneliness, attachment theory is a useful theoretical perspective.

Attachment theory has had a resurgence in recent decades and has been applied to adolescent and adult relationships in relation to well-being and psychological disorder. It is only recently being applied to issues of online behaviour in adolescents and adults (Oldmeadow, Quinn & Kowert, 2013), as described in Chapter 6 in relation to normative adolescent behaviour. However, this approach also has relevance to the development of risk in young people with psychological problems and to difficulties relating to others who access the internet for social interaction. Within adult attachment theory, insecure styles of anxious, avoidant or disorganized are contrasted with secure attachment style. The former have poorer relationships, problematic early childhood experience with carers, lower self-esteem and higher rates of psychological disorder (Bifulco & Thomas, 2012). The associations of these different styles with psychological disorder vary by research study and the measure utilized, but there is increasing evidence for anxious styles (e.g. involving an enmeshed fear of separation or fearful anxiety about rejection) to predict emotional disorder (depression and anxiety) and to relate to early life neglect and problem care. Individuals with anxious attachment styles have difficulty in choosing appropriate relationships and fail to confide and receive good support. This in turn blocks the potentially emotionally regulating effects of good support in stressful situations. The failure to confide in times of need may be due to the fear of being rebuffed or because of an inability to identify a need accurately (Bifulco & Thomas, 2012). There is evidence quoted earlier that in online relationships, those with anxious attachment styles tend to use the internet excessively to maintain a high level of contact, albeit at a distance. Less is documented about those with avoidant styles and their behaviour online. Those with avoidant styles tend to be dismissive of in-person relationships through mistrust or constraints on closeness and tend to avoid interaction with others. However, the outlet for any socializing needs may for some be met by use of the internet to engage in online relationships whereby emotional detachment can be maintained. There is no current evidence of how those with avoidant styles may be at risk from internet use, but given problems in reading social cues and with attunement in interactions, they too may be at risk of not noticing dangers online. This area is one where additional research in relation to cyberharm is urgently needed.

Children's risk behaviour online

Risks of abuse for the children and young people using the internet are in part associated with the widespread, frequent and often unmonitored use of such new technologies. For example, risk-taking behaviour in young people on the internet results in personal information as well as sexually explicit pictures of themselves or their peers being posted, and includes the malicious sending of such pictures by peers in bullying behaviour (CEOP, 2007). For some, the internet is consciously used as a means of selling sex for money and prostitution (Palmer & Stacey, 2004). There are a range of different scenarios whereby children and young people are put at risk of abuse, made more complex by issues of apparent 'complicity' or malevolent intentions towards peers which make the distinction between victims and perpetrators at times blurred.

The issue of apparent 'complicity' in technology-related abuse is complex. Many children and young people are entirely duped by the grooming behaviour of manipulative perpetrators and become entrapped in abuse scenarios quite unwittingly (Lanning, 2005). However, even then, any naïve agreement to be involved in having sexually explicit pictures taken or agreeing to look at adult pornographic pictures can be used

by the perpetrator as evidence of 'compliance' and used to emotionally blackmail the child into secrecy and further compliance (Palmer,
2005). Other young people may have more agency in initiating the
initial contact through use of chat rooms or through posting explicit
images of themselves, but nevertheless become manipulated into meeting and into offline abuse by experienced online abusers against their
volition. Yet other young people may use the internet to sell sex to adults
online, but the likelihood is that many of these young people are already
victims of sexual and other abuse in unmonitored living arrangements,
such as in residential care, hostels or when homeless (Palmer & Stacey,
2004). These young people (often boys) are ultimately equally exploited.
Thus, the apparent 'complicity' is a function of earlier abuse and effective re-victimization. Finally, there may be a group of young perpetrators
who may re-enact their earlier abuse with younger victims using online
technology possibly learned from their own abusive experience. Here,
the boundary between victim and perpetrator becomes blurred, but
is important to an understanding of different longer term effects of
internet-related sexual abuse. Whilst the psychological impact of unwit-
ting 'complicity' is enduring feelings of shame and guilt in the victim
together with a motive for non-disclosure, other impacts might involve
the re-enactment of abuse involving technological means of contact.

Risk factors for online sexual approaches: The EOGP

Research reviews of those at most risk of unwanted exposure to sexual
material online include offline interpersonal victimization, depressive
symptoms, behavioural problems, parental conflicts and a history of
physical or sexual abuse (Ospina, Harstall & Dennett, 2010). Less is
known of specific risk profiles whereby the prior existence of family difficulties, abuse or psychological disorder in a young person may create
additional risk for harm online.

Because the EOGP described in this book focused on interviewing
online groomers, there was no direct research contact with victims. This
is in part because victims are hard to identify amongst children in services since none of the countries involved has a system for recording
whether when sexual abuse was a result of internet grooming. However,
given the online groomers were interviewed about the age, choice of victims, type of grooming approach and victims' response, it was possible
to identify characteristics of victims from this particular offender sample. The demographic profile of the young people targeted by the online
groomers is described in Chapter 4. On the basis of the description of

victims or potential victims given by groomers, a three-fold categorization was devised indicating a group of vulnerable victims, a group of risk
takers and potentially the largest group – that of resilient young people.

Vulnerable victims

The term 'vulnerable' was used specifically to identify those victims
selected by groomers who appeared under-confident, shy and lacking
self-esteem. They could also be described as having internalizing negative characteristics related to emotional disorder. It should be noted that
whereas all victims exhibited vulnerability in its wider meaning in terms
of being prone to interacting with the groomers, the label is used in the
more specific sense described here. These young people are described by
groomers as having a high need for affection. For example, they were
described as lonely:

> I chatted to one girl for half a year. She had problems in her family
> situation. They were all lonely in some way.
>
> (Online groomer, UK)

> Many of the girls were lacking adult contact. They felt safe with me.
> I was there when they needed me, and I always made time. I learned
> about their lives and it was important to them.
>
> (Online groomer, Norway)

In addition, some young people were reported as presenting with low
self-esteem – particularly with concerns about body image, for example:

> She had low self-esteem because she was overweight.
>
> (Online groomer, UK)

There was also some indication of psychological disorder. Here, one victim, when met by the offender offline, was described as showing signs
of scarring from self-harm behaviour. There was also an indication that
these young people were already victims of abuse. Amongst UK online
groomers, one person said that he knew the victim was being abused by
her stepfather. Others stated:

> These were girls who, quote unquote, were already being abused.
> They're aware of it, and they play along.
>
> (Online groomer, Belgium)

Some felt forgotten and lonely at home. Others would talk about how they were being urinated on [by men].

(Online groomer, Norway)

Table 7.1 below presents an overview of vulnerable victims' characteristics as described by offenders in the EOGP.

Risk-taking victims

It was clear from the accounts that not all those young people targeted for online grooming fell into the vulnerable or 'internalizing' category. Some young people were described as being risk takers who wanted sexual adventure and who welcomed the opportunity to interact online. They would, for instance, use explicit sexual screen names and post provocative pictures of themselves. They were seen as extravert and confident and could be described as 'externalizing' in their risk behaviour. Online offenders' views about these young people included statements such as:

My victim was confident, she was happy at home and had lots of friends.

(Online groomer, UK)

As a consequence of this confidence, some of these young people were perceived by the offender as complicit in the online interaction.

The extent of this compliance meant that some of these young people were also reported as asking the groomer for their contact details. For example, one victim was described as instigating the contact because

Table 7.1 The characteristics of EOGP vulnerable victims

Vulnerable victims	Distinguishing themes
High need for attention and affection	• Loneliness
	• Low self-esteem
Difficult relationships with parents and difficult home lives	• Psychological disorder(s)
	• Concurrent sexual abuse
Seeking 'love' on the Internet. Believe they have a true relationship with groomer	• Offender as 'mentor'
	• Self-disclosure and joint problem solving
Resist disclosure because they want to continue the relationship	• Loyalty

Source: Webster et al. (2012, p89).

she asked for his number and for phone sex. In another case, the young person was reported as turning the conversation sexual, which the groomer saw as permission to continue the abuse. Finally, one of the offenders in the sample summed up his perception of compliance as follows:

> There are girls who push you to it in part as well. I want to stress this point, because I've spoken to girls in the past, and I was well aware of their age, and I wasn't after anything, and they're the ones who propositioned me. They had no hang ups about my age and they bragged about that sort of thing. For starters, in the beginning, I met her in a chat room. She knew my age and I knew hers. It was just chatting at first. We then exchanged our MSN hotmail addresses and that's where it started. What happened, in the beginning, on MSN, was that she would get back from school, talk to her friends and what not, and she would then invite you to go on the webcam, and that's where... There's nothing wrong with that initially until she goes off to change. And she comes back wearing a stretch top. I'll never forget it: It was a black top. Then, she began pulling on it until you could see one breast, and then both. What happens then is that you ask for more. I came across certain things... girls who knew how old I was, whom I wasn't asking anything of, and who would strip in front of the webcam and proposition me. I didn't have to do a thing. There are girls who are horny. They're small adults nowadays. They're so convinced they're adults, that in the end, who's the victim?
>
> (Online groomer, Belgium)

However, it is important to note that the apparent confidence online was not matched by behaviour during any offline meetings. This then points to other underlying vulnerabilities that are perhaps being masked in an online environment that can create a sense of anonymity and fantasy (Suler, 2004).

> The girl seemed attractive and popular, outgoing and precocious [online]. I questioned why she was interested in me and found out she was shy, troubled and scarred from self-harm. She was immature and interested in different things to me.
>
> (Online groomer, UK)

> She [the victim] was well developed and womanly and presented as mature but after meeting her I think she had been putting on a

mask. I thought I would have a relationship with her [victim] but after meeting her realized she was immature so it fizzled out.

(Online groomer, UK)

In Chapter 4, a typology of online groomers is presented with 'intimacy-seekers' who felt they had been in a genuine relationship with the victim. These feelings of being in a relationship may also have been experienced by both the risk-taking and vulnerable victims. This sense of 'commitment' to the relationships may therefore explain why in some cases, young people were reported as threatening self-harm or disclosure to another adult if the 'relationship' did not continue. For example, some groomers described developing feelings for the victim and went as far as describing the victim as 'helping sort their lives out'. Intimacy was therefore expressed in a range of ways. In one case, a man said that he wanted to marry his victim when she fell pregnant. There was a further example where one man described how his victim warned him that her parents had found out they had met. Finally, there was the description from one offender of how both he and the victim were happy showing one another attention, how they both felt they had much in common and saw what was a sexual offence developing as a relationship.

Although, sometimes, you became attached to certain girls. You could even fall in love with one. You realize also that these persons are more than just objects. You can have feelings for them.

(Offender, Belgium)

Table 7.2 below presents an overview of risk-taking victims' characteristics as described by offenders in the EOGP.

Model of offender–victim matching

Developing, in parallel, a typology of both online groomers and victims suggests that for at least a proportion of the interaction, some 'matching' was at play between the profiles. For example, the 'intimacy-seeking' groomer is likely to match with the vulnerable victim, since both want a relationship and both mistake the interaction for a real romantic relationship. Here, both offender and victim seem needy in terms of confidence and support, and both desire to continue the interaction over a long period and to make it exclusive. Both will tend to use their own identity and to want to be 'loved for themselves'. In this situation, the victim becomes apparently complicit and may find it

Table 7.2   The characteristics of EOGP risk-taking victims

Risk-taking victims	Distinguishing themes
Young people disinhibited and seeking adventure	• Outgoing • Confident
Young people (and offender) feel they have control	• Complicit and consenting to sexual contact
Less known about family risks, but less confident on meeting than appear online	• Offender re-assessment on meeting • Introverted or immature YP at meeting
Open to blackmail not to disclose because of apparent 'complicity' – own behaviour used as evidence of cooperation	• Non-disclosure of abuse, threats and computer intrusions

Source: Webster et al. (2012, p89).

difficult to disclose even after the abuse comes to light because of their fantasy relationship with the groomer.

On the other hand, the hyper-sexual groomer is likely to interact more readily with the risk-taking young person, given their attraction to the use of sexual screen names and their use of sexual chat. Both seem to want the adventure of an online sexual interaction and are open about wanting sex. However, the apparent complicity of the victim and their apparent precociousness appear to mask a much more fragile and quiet individual who shows much greater inhibition offline than online. It also needs to be considered that in the EOGP, it was the groomer who described the complicity and apparent maturity of these victims – we cannot know to what extent this is a distortion of the reality. Whilst we know little in detail of the psychological state of either groomer or victim, and no psychological or clinical tests were used in this study, a speculative model was developed of the cognitive-emotional characteristics of both. This is presented in Figure 7.1 below.

Investigating victims' circumstances and experiences further

As described earlier in this book, the ROBERT study was undertaken with European Commission funding around the same time as the EOGP. The focus in the ROBERT study was of vulnerable young people who had

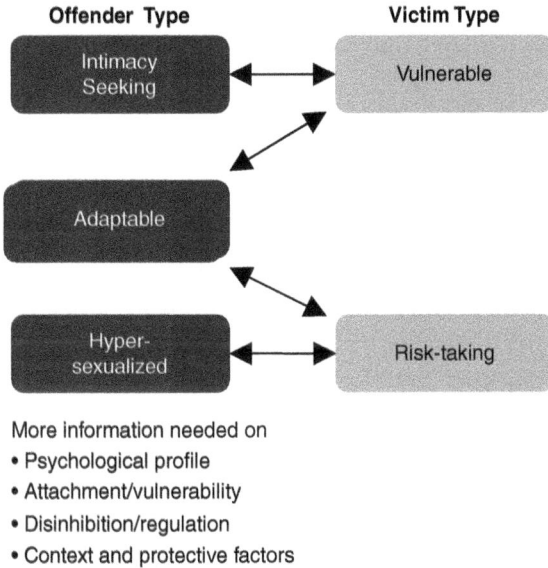

Figure 7.1 Speculative matching of groomer and victim
Source: Webster et al. (2012, p97).

been targeted by online groomers for sexual abuse. A qualitative study, the research involved interviews with 27 young people aged 11–17, all of whom were groomed online for offline sexual abuse and who were referred to the project by professionals treating them (Quayle, Jonsson & Loof, 2012). Participants tended to be female and were selected from six sites across Europe (Sweden, the United Kingdom, Germany, Italy, Denmark and Russia).

The interviews asked young people about their online experience, the abuse and disclosure of the abuse, and their feelings and perceptions of what had happened. The analysis used a grounded theory methodology to develop six themes. These included: 'something missing from my life'; 'being someone who is connected'; 'caught in a web'; 'making choices'; 'others responding'; and 'closing the box and picking up the pieces'. In the description below, aspects of this reported experience are summarized in terms of the vulnerability of the victims to help develop their profiles. These are categorized in terms of (1) victim psychological need, which may have driven young people to engage online; (2) the dangers encountered online, including the abuse itself and; (3) the impacts of the abuse. These are further described below in examples taken from the ROBERT study (Quayle, Jonsson & Loof, 2011):

Victim psychological need
Need for connectedness and security

It was clear that some of the young people in the ROBERT study were lonely and socially anxious, and turned to the internet to fill a gap for intimacy that was missing in their lives. They reported having difficulties relating to others. Some young people sought security and greater autonomy and a degree of avoidance of others. Sexual curiosity was described, which had led them to engage with groomers online. They favoured having a relationship at a distance online where they could test out talking about sexual issues. Here, some people talked about being online as a way of feeling connected, even to the extent of this showing they existed. To that end, being online made the young people feel less shy and less restricted. These findings are in keeping with other research showing links between shyness and Facebook usage (Baker & Oswald, 2010). It also forms a potential link between the few studies beginning to investigate attachment insecurity as a further online risk in victim profiles.

Need for identify: Self-esteem

The issue of identity arose in the ROBERT study, with young people wanting to create a fresh image for themselves without taking their personal history into account. Playing with identities was considered a preoccupation in understanding the self. This is consistent with work by Valkenburg and Peter (2011) which suggests that online communication enhances the controllability of self-presentation and self-disclosure. In turn, this creates a sense of security in their interpersonal interactions (Valkenburg & Peter, 2011). This is enabled through anonymity, asynchronization and accessibility. Again, issues of needs around defining the psychological self and identity are highlighted in potential victims.

Need for belonging

The young people also talked about how meeting people online enhanced their sense of belonging. For those who had recently moved, online links with friends enabled them to maintain these relationships at a distance. However, other research challenges this idea when it suggests that Facebook relationships are actually a form of avoidant coping through less likelihood of facing real-world problems (Anderson et al., 2012). Online relationships that were valued were the ones with the possibility of developing into 'true friendships'. Research supports the view that online contact can strengthen existing relationships offline, although the quality of real-life face-to-face contact was important (Reich, Subrahmanyan & Espinoza, 2012). Thus, a need for belonging is important in adolescents and needs to be considered in relation to potential risk online.

Prior abuse and prior sexual experience offline

In the course of the ROBERT project interviews, it was clear that the young people reported other instances of abuse in the family and by their peers. The young people also described dangers online, including the process by which they became entangled with the groomer who abused them. There is now growing evidence that abused young people present with particular risks in their online behaviour which, in terms of encountering online groomers, may then escalate risk levels and harm.

Dangers online

The young people described how their sexual behaviour online drew them into events that were destructive. Sexual flirting and sexual conversations with strangers were associated with sexual harassment, solicitation or grooming. The process of engagement was described in the ROBERT study as becoming increasingly problematic and entrapping. There was normalization by the young people to start with, although with some suspicions about sexual contact, but this was accompanied by some idealization of the 'relationship' online. Those young people with offline sexual experiences tended to engage more often in online sexual activities, with offline encounters serving to prime those experiences online. The issue of lies, secrets and sometimes payment to keep secrets was raised as a theme.

In terms of being groomed online, the young people talked about how the initial positive engagement turned into something over which they had no control. A form of manipulation took place. Initially, they felt flattered and more independent. They consequently spoke of 'entanglement with technology'. The role of sexual images often predated the relationship with the offender. They felt distress when pictures of themselves were taken by the groomer. Sometimes, these were intimate pictures sent to boyfriends, which then emerged on the internet after the break-up. They felt a loss of control knowing the pictures were out on the internet and regarding whether they would be recognizable. This was sometimes enhanced by threats from the offender.

Psychological impacts of the abuse were also described and encompassed

Loss of control and humiliation

The young people tended to be isolated after meeting the offender, who manipulated them into giving up other friendships. The decision to meet led to loss of control whereby the sexual assault was experienced as aggressive or humiliating. The offline abuse was sometimes repeated and in some cases meant selling sexual activity online to other people. It is perhaps unsurprising that this led to feelings of guilt and in turn silence and resistance to disclose about the abuse. This impact seemed heightened when images were taken of the abuse (Quayle, Loof & Palmer, 2008).

Engaging with services

The young people in the ROBERT study were seen to have made choices during the online relationship. The first was to respond to the sexual contact, and this was done because it was seen as positive. Other choices were around whether to tell others or not, how to maintain control, choosing how to engage and what the disclosure would lead to. Keeping the relationship secret was a way of maintaining a sense of control and protecting the self from the intrusiveness of adults.

Disclosing the sexual abuse was described as an arduous process and rings true when considering other studies in this area (McElveney, Greene & Hogan, 2012). Maintaining control of the disclosure was described as important, but in reality, the disclosure tended to be outside the control of the young person. When the abuse was discovered rather than disclosed, the young people described the event as confusing and frightening. This impact has also been reported in other studies of the victim's experience (Malloy, Brubacher & Lamb, 2011).

Extent of support

The young people in the ROBERT study were all counselled but they did not all feel supported. Some talked about feeling confused and frustrated by the number of different professionals to whom they had to relate their account. Whilst responding well to professionals who were warm and committed to helping them even through the tough times, they were upset by other professionals and particularly by the police. Relating their accounts of abuse was difficult for them. Letting go of these secrets also meant letting go of their sense of control. In addition, dissociation related to trauma meant they found it difficult to relate what had happened to them in a coherent way. They also felt guilt, particularly for abuse incidents repeated over time, and that they may be held responsible in criminal investigations. For many, the involvement of professionals added to the distress and trauma of what had happened to them.

A speculative model

Taking the findings of the EOGP and the ROBERT project together, alongside the victims' profiles shown by Ospina, Harstall and Dennett (2010), this section outlines a speculative model of risk pathways for online abuse in young people. In terms of theoretical psychological approaches, issues around self-regulation, attachment and cognitive-affective processes interact with the socio-ecological factors around the social context of internet availability. In terms of self-regulation, victims appear to exhibit under-regulation or mis-regulation and disinhibition. With regard to attachment patterns, anxious styles associated with fear of separation and rejection and a high need for closeness and intimacy may substitute in online interactions for needs not met in offline contexts. These characteristics are likely to be higher in the 'vulnerable' victims. Cognitive-affective processes around defensive patterns, lack of self-awareness, mentalization skills and denial of danger may be common across the two victim types (vulnerable and risk-taking).

The socio-ecological characteristics regarding the normative social context of internet use in adolescents is common to all young people, but likely to create more risk of harm for those with high-risk psychological and social profiles. In a small proportion, it may lead to internet addiction and may also lead to dangers online. A speculative model is presented in Figure 7.2 below which identifies these factors in terms of predisposing risks, vulnerable profiles, disorder, mechanisms for maintaining dangers and lack of support and disclosure. This is based on the findings of the EOGP and the ROBERT project and is influenced by the research literature on victims. We encourage testing of this model with further high-quality research.

Conclusion

When examining victims of online grooming in the context of the studies described here, it is important to remember that these young

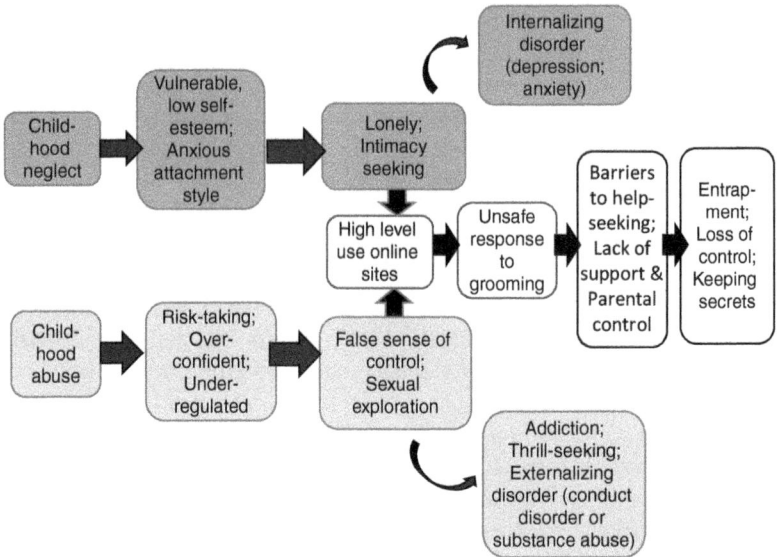

Figure 7.2 Speculative model of victim risk pathways

people are victims of real-life offline sexual abuse in addition to negative experiences in the online exchanges. Therefore, they will have
many of the vulnerabilities and subsequent damaging impacts common to other victims of sexual abuse which can impact negatively
across the whole lifespan. What is specific to online abuse is the far
reach of the offender in gaining access to the children, the victim's
disinhibition and lack of a sense of culpability in engaging online,
and the ease of the victim entrapment during the course of a few
exchanges. Two specific profiles of victims are identified, which have
much in common with risks for online abuse, involving internalizing
or externalizing risk behaviour. A speculative model identifies possible
pathways of risk for these two groups, and indicates both have difficulties in seeking help with subsequent feelings of loss of control and
entrapment.

In order to understand the 'dangerousness' of child sex offenders in
the digital world, it is necessary to also understand the characteristics
of the victims they abuse. It may be only through the potential 'matching' of perpetrator and victim characteristics and the use each makes of
technology that a true understanding of the process of abuse online can

be understood. From this perspective, technological, social and psycho-logical prevention campaigns and interventions need to be established that will help to reduce the likelihood of abuse occurring. One message to come out of the EOGP is that tailoring interventions to the different victim/potential victim profiles may optimize effects. This is discussed further in the next chapter of this book.

8
Implications and Conclusion

Antonia Bifulco, Julia Davidson and Stephen Webster

Introduction

The internet is a fundamental feature of young people's lives and will be for years to come. Engagement with the internet is ubiquitous. As described in Chapter 1, recent high-quality surveys across 25 European countries reveal that approximately 93 per cent of young people aged 6–17 are online regularly. As the move to using mobile online technology overtakes static connections, the nature and extent of online benefits and risks are likely to evolve and increase. The risks on a population basis are relatively low given the widespread usage, not because dangers are uncommon, but because the majority of young people are resilient and capable of fending off harm, for example, sexual approaches made by adults online (Livingstone, Haddon, Görzig & Ólafsson, 2011).

However, there are clearly some young people engaging in risky online behaviours, with approximately 9 per cent (1 in 11) of online teenagers reporting meeting an unknown person offline. This figure rises to one in five in certain European countries, for example Poland, Sweden and the Czech Republic (Livingstone et al., 2011). There is a pressing need to effectively identify the important risk factors and to intervene both in empowering young people to act safely online and offline and also when online grooming for abuse is actually in progress. It will also be critical to inform adults responsible for the care of young people, from parents to professionals, by drawing on all available lessons from work with both young people and sexual offenders, as described in earlier chapters.

This book has presented perspectives about online grooming drawn from groundbreaking research on the European Online Grooming

Project (EOGP) and other scholarly work in the field. This chapter examines the implications of research across three broad areas: online safety campaigns with young people, prevention work with men who have groomed young people online and the implications for policy and legislation. The chapter concludes with a call for closer cross-agency work utilizing a population-based public health approach to reduce risk for young people as well as for an international effort in developing a global legislative framework.

Implications for online safety campaigns

Whilst the initiative involving European Commission Safer Internet Programmes has led to much greater understanding of this area, lack of awareness related to online risk across Europe is still a problem. This involves not only the children or young people involved, but importantly, also their parents. In the large quantitative European surveys it was found that 61 per cent of parents whose child had met an online contact face-to-face were unaware of their actions. In addition, 56 per cent of parents whose child had received nasty or hurtful messages online were unaware that this had occurred (Livingston, Olafsson & Staksrud, 2011; Livingstone et al., 2011).

Access to information and raising awareness is a central focus of the European Commission's Safer Internet Action Plan and this is implemented across Europe through the INSAFE network of national awareness-raising nodes. Thus, a Safer Internet Day is organized by INSAFE each year to promote safer use of online technology and mobile phones. The UK INSAFE network is represented by a consortium of awareness-raising nodes: the South West Grid for Learning (SWGfl), Childnet and the Internet Watch Foundation (IWF). There are now awareness centres belonging to the INSAFE network in 27 European countries. On a broader international scale, centres can also be found in Argentina, Australia and the United States. It is clear that whilst messages are getting through to the general public, these need to be reinforced, repeated and updated in order to help protect children and young people from harm delivered through digital technologies.

Measures to protect children include school-based intervention programmes aiming to educate children, parents and teachers about the dangers posed by sex offenders in cyberspace in order to change online behaviour and access. A variety of initiatives have been developed through the Safer Internet Centres which are focused on the principal issues of safety from risks such as pornography and child abuse images, cyberbullying and the concern over contact with strangers through behaviour on social networking sites and in chat rooms. Amongst these initiatives are hotlines and helplines, teaching and training material for teachers and parents and the establishment of youth panels. The Youth Council (DigiRaad) in the Netherlands is a young advisory group which has proved to be an extremely influential panel of young people aged between 10 and 18 years old that advises the Dutch government about safety for young people. This has yet to be installed more generally across Europe.

Safety for children and young people also has implications for the IT and internet industries. In the United Kingdom, the Child Exploitation and Online Protection Centre (CEOP) works proactively both with industry, for example, in introducing a panic button for children to use online, and with education, in rolling out the Thinkuknow safety-awareness programmes in schools (Davidson, Lorenz, Grove-Hills & Martellozo, 2009). In addition, Childnet UK actively promotes positive and creative ways for young people to use the internet with an emphasis on the three strands of access, awareness, protection and policy. A Safer Internet Day has been run by INSAFE every year since 2007. This event involves thousands of schools in over 70 countries and day-long radio coverage promoting safer use of the internet amongst children.[1]

Austria, France and Germany have developed targeted websites related to safe practices aiming to be user-friendly, offering cartoons and games with safety messages attached, teenager advice and information for parents. One particular initiative in Spain, Navegacion Segura (Safe Navigation), contains games with quizzes to include cyberbullying and grooming warning messages (for more details see Davidson, Grove-Hills, Bifulco, Webster, Gottschalk, Caretti et al., 2010). Childnet actively promotes positive and creative ways for young people to use the internet, with an emphasis on the four strands of access, awareness, protection and policy.

In the United Kingdom, the Thinkuknow Programme, part-funded by the European Commission's Safer Internet Plus Programme, is managed by the CEOP. It is now widely disseminated in schools and concentrates on three key messages: to have fun, to stay in control and to report a problem around dangers online. These three messages perfectly reflect the content of existing safety-awareness initiatives throughout Europe and they have targeted young people, parents and teachers (Davidson, Lorenz, Grove-Hills & Martellozo, 2009). There are a number of other initiatives in the United Kingdom and across Europe, for example, there are hotlines and helplines and teaching and training materials for teachers and parents funded by the European Commission's International Association of Internet Hotlines (INHOPE).

As an example of effective campaigning about bullying online, this has implications for ways of tackling other cyberharm. The Safer Internet Campaign has produced 30-second video clips on cyberbullying, available in all EU languages, and these have been posted on popular internet sites and broadcast on television. The content is aimed at empowering young people in dealing with online dangers. For example, one shows a video clip of a young girl, a victim of cyberbullying, who is assertive and reports the problem to her social networking site. She then further takes control by pressing the 'report abuse' button and finally succeeds in ending the bullying. The clips also provide websites and phone numbers for teenagers to get help and advice for each country. Such interventions and initiatives appear to be having an impact, but these have not yet been developed for vulnerable children and young people or for the practitioners responsible for their care. These are likely to need a different format and focus, with a more specialized understanding of how to reach such young people and how to relay safety messages in a way that can be understood by a young person who may already be inhabiting a dangerous world.

Chapters 6 and 7 described research work with young people conducted as part of the EOGP. From the information provided by both young people and by the online groomers about the young people they targeted, there are a number of implications for the content of online safety campaigns and the way they are delivered by professionals and responsible adults. These are discussed below.

Reviewing the content of safety messages

It is clear that generic campaigns have done a very good job in raising young people's awareness about potential risks online, particularly in the West. This is evidenced by the data reported by Livingstone and colleagues (2011) that shows the majority of young people are resilient to harmful approaches made by adults. However, the EOGP research reported here – alongside studies by Quayle, Jonsson and Loof (2012) and Ospina, Harstall and Dennett (2010) – shows that young people are not a homogeneous group in terms of how they engage with and respond to harmful situations online. In Chapter 7, the diverse risk pathways of young people are described in a speculative model developed for further testing. Here, females aged 14 and above, those with mental health problems, disrupted attachment to parents and prior physical and/or sexual abuse seem at particular risk online. Also, young people with a lesbian, gay, bisexual or transgender (LGBT) orientation can also present a raised risk of online harm. Here, there was evidence that online groomers could sometimes target these boys on the premise of 'educating' or 'mentoring' them about their sexuality (Webster, Davidson, Bifulco, Gottschalk, Caretti, Pham et al., 2010).

There are also cultural connotations to consider when developing effective e-safety materials. In Chapter 1, there is a summary of international policy developments, but whether materials adequately address risk issues that may be underpinned by cultural differences is open to conjecture. Groundbreaking research in the Middle East conducted by Davidson and Martellozzo (2012) indicates that culturally gendered perspectives place restrictions upon young people's usage. Consequently, the focus on internet behaviour in the West has led to a somewhat narrow view which fails to take into account geographical and cultural differences in the context of usage.

Given this knowledge about at-risk groups, there is an increasing responsibility to develop online safety materials that target and are responsive to the particular needs of sub-groups of young people. As discussed below, engaging young people is a critical first step in then empowering them to behave safely online. But successful empowerment is predicated on the development of materials that are relevant and responsive to the lives, circumstances and psychological make-up of these diverse groups.

Tailoring safety messages to risk profiles

The final implication concerns making online safety material more dynamic in its relevance to emerging risks. As the method of connecting online has developed and is likely to further adapt and change (in terms of access, mobility and cost), 'new' online behaviours and risks are likely to be identified. A key area of concern here is the rise of self-taken and distributed indecent images of young people, and related to this, the lack of awareness of the digital footprint in many young people (The Guardian, 2013). The digital footprint is a concept that highlights the permanent nature of online images. This is despite the mistaken belief amongst some young people that an embarrassing image can be 'taken down offline' if they so wish (e.g. by deleting their social networking profile).

The development of mobile applications such as *SnapChat* can add to this false sense of security by implying that any image sent will disappear from the receiver's device in ten seconds. In reality, the receiver can take a quick screen shot of the image and then circulate it to others online. Whilst the majority of young people who circulate private images of themselves online do not intend for them to be viewed by adults or people with a sexual interest in children, this can occur without their knowledge. Research by the IWF (2012) in the United Kingdom found that in an analysis of investigative photographic material over a four-week period, 88 per cent (10,776 out of 12,224 images) of sexual images of young people that appeared on 'parasite porn' websites were in fact originally self-taken.

In addition to self-taken images, the behaviour of young people when playing games online (e.g. PC, X-Box and PS3/4) is increasingly recognized as a risk for harm online. For example, the EOGP study highlighted how some online groomers used online games to befriend and then sexually abuse young people using web cameras, with boys at particular risk. However, online gaming risk seems to receive far less attention than other online behaviours covered in e-safety materials. It is important that developers of e-safety materials consider including more content about self-taken images and online gaming risks in revised safety materials.

Whether e-safety is delivered formally or informally, some young people talked in the EOGP focus groups (Chapter 6) about wanting to be able to relate to the safety provider, whether someone of a similar age, or someone who liked social media platforms. There was suspicion that those providing advice about social networking were fearful or hostile to online contact; a view attributed to the older generation. Young people felt that the key aspect underpinning this fear or hostility was ignorance about social networking. This undermined confidence in the safety information being imparted. Parenting behaviour in relation to IT is clearly having to evolve with the new technologies. As such, there is a need to equip parents with the skills and information to be able to advise their children in an expert manner.

There is a clear message that for e-safety campaigns to be effective, collaboration with young people about their online behaviour is essential, rather than imposing adult-centric campaign messages or interventions. The growth of mobile connections means that caregivers and teachers are unlikely to be physically present to intervene when potentially harmful behaviour is happening. Only through working with young people, engaging, gaining trust and empowering them with relevant knowledge and a suite of effective strategies can there be confidence in the longer term impact of e-safety interventions.

Teachers have a key role to play in the delivery of effective e-safety practice to young people. However, there is no standardized best practice for teachers and other professionals working with young people to draw on. In England and Wales, appraising e-safety teaching has only relatively recently been incorporated into the broader school inspection process (Ofsted, 2012). Whether this goes far enough to appraise whether the style of delivery is effective is open to doubt. Whilst there has been growth in the area of e-safety training provision, the parallel review/regulation of the quality of this provision is not currently available. For example, anybody can set themselves up as an e-safety training provider with no accepted industry standard for good practice. In England and Wales, this may be a strategic priority for the UK Council for Child Internet Safety to consider, as poor instruction within schools may be inadvertently obstructing progress.

Messages to professionals

As described earlier, targeted training and intervention packages for vulnerable children or young people is less developed than for those in normative populations. This is also true for professionals working with vulnerable children and young people. This includes social workers in child protection and family support services and related practitioners such as care workers, youth workers, child psychiatrists and developmental, clinical or educational psychologists. As described earlier, the children and youth considered vulnerable have a range of experiences or characteristics: those neglected or abused; those who have lived with domestic violence or family mental health problems; and those with problematic interpersonal or attachment styles, with their own psychological disorders or learning problems. Many, but not all of these, will already be the focus of child protection, family support or Looked After services. Developing an understanding of models of intervention for online cyberharm and safety for these professionals should be of urgent ongoing concern. Related to the issue of vulnerable young populations, the mechanisms by which such children may become trapped in abusive online contact or the situational constraints on their help-seeking need to be better understood by professionals. These children or young people may have few safe adults to go to for help and may be excluded from school or leisure activities where adult support exists for other young people. They may also have less availability in terms of peer support. Thus, understanding protective or resilience factors in relation to cyberharm also needs further development to aid intervention.

The pressing need for more targeted awareness training for social work professionals was highlighted in a report in the United Kingdom which recounted the experience of some young women that had been the victims of sexual abuse following online grooming (Palmer, 2009). The young women's emotional and psychological vulnerability was reflected in their reasons for not reporting the abuse or seeking help. They reported being 'in love' and having emotional dependency on their online 'boyfriend', perceiving the relationship as a real attachment and not one requiring any outside intervention (Palmer, 2009). These young women provided only minimal information on initial interviews with police and it took as many as 10–12 sessions with the assigned social worker before they were able to talk in detail about their abuse experience. The young women in this report had started to form online relationships with predatory men between the ages of 12 and 14, sometimes years before the relationships came to light.

Online grooming approaches to vulnerable children and young people can cause psychological harm through emotional blackmail, guilt about collusion, distorted attachment to perpetrators, feelings of entrapment online and shame and humiliation due to the widespread nature and permanence of some of the digital evidence of their victimized behaviour. However, even with grooming at a less threatening intensity, this can potentially lead to a distortion of normal developmental processes of sexualization and socialization. Effective interventions therefore need to incorporate expertise in psychological developmental processes as well as in the technology utilized and the likely offender modus operandi. This calls for some high-level expertise in the design and implementation of interventions for high-risk children and young people to counteract harms online.

Work with offenders

Chapter 5 described the psychological disorders associated with sexual offending and speculated on how these may apply to online offenders. In addition, standard diagnostic tools commonly used in both clinical and forensic fields are presented in the context of an assessment of online grooming. This can help to identify some of the cognitive-emotional bases of offender attitudes to their victims and to show some differentiation in types of offender consistent with the model of offending developed in this book. This calls for greater matching of the diagnostic classification with the category of online offender in order to inform psychotherapeutic interventions in both prison and community settings. This argues for a more specialist and integrated approach than the current reliance on the cognitive-behavioural therapy approach used by UK forensic services and prisons.

In his excellent review of internet sexual offenders, Seto (2013) argues that cognitive-behavioural therapies set within the risk–need–responsivity model provide the most effective treatment (Andrews, Bonta & Hoge 1990). Here, the principle of risk determines the degree or intensity of intervention with the offender. This involves the assessment of criminological needs or dynamic (or changeable) risk factors directly related to criminological behaviours. The responsivity principle identifies the relevant type of treatment. In the EOGP, analysis was informed by an initial stakeholder consultation with professionals delivering treatment to online sexual offenders. This showed some support for tailoring programmes according to the different 'types' of online groomer.

The challenge for responsively matching treatment to risk–need levels involves the status of *current* actuarial measures of offender risk and whether these are valid with sexual offenders who operate online, particularly those who operate exclusively online. Offender interviews conducted in the EOGP revealed that there were some men who only offended online. An offline meeting with a young person was never a goal of their offending behaviour. Using current actuarial measures, this type of offender may be incorrectly classified as being at a low risk of recidivism. This is substantiated by a series of studies where Seto, Hanson and Babchishin (2011), Eke, Seto and Williams (2011) and Wakeling, Howard and Barnett (2011) have shown that actuarial instruments failed to predict recidivism in *internet-only* sexual offenders due to the low base rate of recidivism in this sub-group.

The assessment of dynamic risk in online sexual offenders may prove to be a more reliable method of allocating treatment dose and targets. Webb, Craissati and Keen (2007) found that the Stable-2000 dynamic measure was able to identify risky behaviours in the short term, but its longer term prediction of sexual recidivism in online offenders is unknown (Seto, 2013). However, Elliott and Beech (2009) suggest that Stable-2000 may not identify key risk factors for online sexual offenders that may fluctuate over hours, rather than weeks or months. It seems clear that further research, evaluation and measure design is required for practitioners to be confident that assessment instruments accurately reflect the unique static and dynamic risks presented by online sexual offenders.

In addition to the assessment of risk, there is a need to understand how to measure the extent of treatment progress (O'Brien & Webster, 2010). At present, programmes for online offenders such as the Internet Sex Offender Treatment Programme (i-SOTP) use a battery of 12 psychometric tests to assess pre- and post-treatment change. Psychometric testing has been a core part of the sexual offender treatment-assessment model, with a number of tests validated on offline or contact sexual offenders that span overarching areas of risk. These include, for example, interpersonal functioning (Webster, Mann, Thornton & Wakeling, 2007) and offence-supportive beliefs (Mann, Webster, Wakeling & Marshall, 2007). However, there has been little if any research validating these measures with online sexual offenders, particularly those offending exclusively online. Therefore, uncertainty about the efficacy of risk-assessment measures to accurately predict risk in this group requires greater attention being placed on the reliable psychometric assessment of online offenders. To date, there is only one published psychometric test that has been developed and validated on online sexual offenders: the Internet Behaviour and Attitudes Questionnaire (IBAQ) described further below (O'Brien & Webster, 2007).

The IBAQ was developed and piloted on a prison and community sample of 163 men convicted of the collection, distribution and/or development of indecent images of children. It contains 42 items about offenders' online behaviours and 34 items that measure online offenders' attitudes. This instrument has good concurrent, criterion and discriminate validity. The 34 attitude items are organized into two factors. The first factor contains 16 items that measure distorted thinking (e.g. 'The child was often smiling in the child pornography I have looked at, and so I believe that the child is not being harmed'). The second factor contains 18 items and measures online offenders' self-management (e.g. 'I feel more confident on the Internet than I do talking to people in real life'). This instrument needs to be more widely used in the identification and treatment of online offenders involved with indecent image usage. However, since it does not contain any items that would reliably assist practitioners with the assessment and treatment gains of online groomers specifically, there is a pressing need for the development and validation of further similar psychometric-assessment instruments for online groomers. The incorporation of interview, video, case and collateral material also needs to be considered to triangulate measurements and increase the validity of assessments.

In terms of treatment delivery, there is an issue of whether online sexual offenders (including both indecent image users and online groomers) should be in treatment separately or mixed in with offline sexual offenders. Seto (2013) and O'Brien and Webster (2010) provide a brief commentary on the perceived advantages and disadvantages of different treatment allocations. The argument for integrating online and offline sexual offenders in treatment programmes is the belief in the similarity of the characteristics and functioning of the two groups. The argument against integration is the likely barrier to treatment engagement for online offenders when placed in the same group as labelled rapists and child molesters. Ultimately, the optimum composition of treatment groups is an empirical question requiring randomized control trial investigation. Such a study would randomly allocate participants to 'online offender only' or 'mixed offender' treatment conditions (with identical treatment offered to both groups). The study would require an 'at-risk' follow-up period of at least two years (but preferably significantly longer) to develop accurate treatment effectiveness and reconviction data. There is an urgent need for such research to support effective treatment programmes for online sexual offenders.

One specific intervention for internet sexual offenders, i-SOTP, will be described in detail to illustrate the current treatment protocols (Hayes, Archer & Middleton, 2006). This was developed in response to long waiting lists for online offenders (on probation) for 'regular' sexual offender treatment. As discussed by Davidson (2008), the theoretical basis of the programme draws upon several models developed by Quayle and Taylor (2003) with the National Society for the Prevention of Cruelty to Children (NSPCC) and Greater Manchester Probation Service, as well as with Finkelhor's 'multi-factorial' approach (1984) and the good lives model (Ward & Stewart, 2003).

The programme was originally designed to be delivered on an individual basis. In this format, the programme lasts for between 20 and 30 sessions, each of 90-minutes duration. Following a pilot and extensive deliverer feedback, the programme was further developed to be delivered in a group format comprising 35 two-hour sessions, broken into the six modules. Completion of the programme is achieved between four and nine months depending on the choice of format and rate of delivery. Importantly, as Quayle (2007) points out, in delivering the i-SOTP, much emphasis is placed on the style of the therapist, given that successful sexual offender treatment outcomes have been found to be associated with particular therapist behaviours (Marshall, Fernandez, Serran, Mulloy, Thornton, Mann et al., 2003; Marshall, Ward, Mann, Moulden, Fernandez, Serran et al., 2005; Serran, Fernandez, Marshall & Mann, 2003).

The stated specific dynamic risk factors targeted by i-SOTP are listed by Hayes and colleagues (2006) as lack of readiness/motivation for change; intimacy deficits; emotional loneliness; low level of social skills and self-esteem associated with formation of insecure attachments; sexual interest in children; inability to deal with negative affect; sexual preoccupation; and a lack of victim awareness and lack of empathic response. Interestingly, all of these dynamic risk factors are also the treatment targets in the majority of programmes for contact sexual offenders. The programme (or any other, to our knowledge) does not cover important maintenance factors in online offending identified in the EOGP, including online disinhibition, perceived anonymity and online pro-sexual abuse forums.

There is emerging evidence demonstrating the effectiveness of the i-SOTP. Middleton (2009) presents the test results of 264 convicted offenders being supervised across the National Probation Service who attended the programme from 2006 to 2008. The key treatment targets were grouped into two main categories, addressing socio-affective functioning and changing pro-offending attitudes. Offenders were assessed as having positive change post-treatment in 11 of the 12 socio-affective functioning measures. Middleton reports that the change in scores on the pro-offending attitude scales contained within the test battery were also in the desired direction. He further states that 53 per cent of the sample was assessed as having achieved a 'treated profile'. Such a profile was assigned if an offender was indistinguishable in the tests from a non-offending normative sample across a number of key measures that relate to both socio-affective functioning and pro-offending attitudes (Mandeville-Norden & Beech, 2004).

Middleton argues that this emerging data appears to be sufficiently encouraging to justify the continuation of the wide-scale delivery of the treatment programme. He makes the important point that a long-term reconviction study is still required to provide a more pertinent assessment of programme effectiveness as it relates to the overall goal of a reduction in recidivism. However, this programme is clearly an impressive and important step in the attempts to treat online offenders given its scale and research base.

The i-SOTP described above is delivered in the United Kingdom by practitioners for men that have been convicted of online sexual offences against children. However, for interventions to have maximum impact, we would ideally like them to be accessed by people *before* they have committed an online sexual offence. There is a large body of evidence to suggest that sexual offences are rarely impulsive acts that take place randomly or without premeditation. Our own research in the EOGP shows that some online groomers spent considerable time grooming before first contact with a young person was made online with the purpose of sexual abuse. Consequently, there is a window of opportunity for interventions to proactively prevent online (and offline) sexual abuse.

Two intervention programmes for self-referring men will be used to illustrate such programmes. The first programme is the recent Dunkelfeld Prevention Project in Germany (Beier, Neutze, Mundt, Ahlers, Goecker, Konrad et al., 2009) aimed at providing help for individuals unlikely to come to the attention of mental health or criminal justice services. In particular, those men with a sexual interest in children or those who have already committed sexual offences were unlikely to seek help given the stigma associated with their feelings and behaviour. Funded by a range of commercial and media partners, the programme was advertized on mainstream television and radio offering a confidential evaluation. During the media campaign, 1415 men contacted the project between 2005 and 2011. A number of these people had been involved in illegal activity such as accessing indecent images of children or engaging in contact sexual activity with children (Neutze, Seto, Schaefer, Mundt & Beier, 2011). Treatment was offered to 319 of the initial men in contact (others were ineligible due to ongoing legal supervision, inability to access/travel to the treatment site and/or the presence of major mental illness). Outcome data for the programme is now being collected and analysed prior to publication (Seto, 2013).

Alongside the Dunkelfeld Project is the Stop it Now! Programme. Stop It Now! is an innovative programme that aims to prevent child sexual abuse via interventions and advice aimed at potential or actual perpetrators, or their families, friends or relatives. In Europe, the Stop it Now! Programme in the United Kingdom has been run by the Lucy Faithfull Foundation for a decade, and another has run more recently in the Netherlands, by de Waag, in April 2012. Data from the UK Stop it Now! Programme shows that between 2005 and 2009, the programme received 6043 calls (50.5% of all calls received) from adults concerned about their own sexual behaviour. The other 50 per cent of calls received were from family, friends and adults concerned about another adult's behaviour; parents and carers concerned about a young person's sexual behaviour; adults concerned about a child that may have been abused; other professionals; and survivors of sexual abuse (Lucy Faithfull Foundation, 2009).

A key distinction between the United Kingdom and the Netherlands Stop it Now! Programmes is the extent of confidentiality that is assured. This is underpinned by the different child protection legislation in the two countries, discussed in Chapter 1. This is less extensive in the United Kingdom – for example, whilst UK helpline callers are told they will not be asked for their name or other identifiable details, they are also advised that if they provide information about a child in danger of abuse, or being abused, then that information will be passed on to the appropriate agencies. Callers are also advised that the helpline will pass on details of any criminal offence that has been committed (Lucy Faithfull Foundation, 2009). Conversely, in the Netherlands, Stop it Now! caller and treatment seekers are offered full confidentiality, as there is no mandatory reporting legislation in place. Such aspects ideally need to be harmonized in Europe in order to achieve comparable prevention of online sexual abuse.

A European Commission-funded evaluation of Stop it Now! UK and Netherlands was recently delivered by the National Centre for Social Research (Brown, Jago, Kerr, McNaughton Nicholls, Paskell & Webster, 2014) [http://www.stopitnow-evaluation.co.uk/]. The evaluation had four core aims: assessing the implementation of these programmes, focusing on their helpline and email support; identifying the potential impact of the programme for affecting behaviour change amongst offenders and potential offenders; providing an economic analysis of the implementation of Stop it Now!; and setting out a model for developing and implementing Stop it Now! in other European countries. The research found that when reflecting on their contact with the helpline, offenders and potential offenders were able to: recognize their behaviour as risky or problematic; understand that their behaviour was and is dynamic - it can change and be addressed; and importantly, implement techniques and advice on challenging and changing their behaviour. An economic analysis of the helpline involved cost-benefit modelling and showed that the financial benefits of the helpline to the taxpayer outweighed its costs (Brown et al. 2014).

Given the legislative differences underpinning the delivery of the two programmes with regard to offence disclosure, it is hoped that the Brown and colleagues (2014) research may stimulate an evidenced-based discussion in the United Kingdom and across Europe. In particular, it would be helpful to have a debate about the advantages and disadvantages of legislation change to encourage more men with these problematic and harmful thoughts and behaviours to come forward for support before a child is harmed.

Final reflections: National and international challenges

This book was developed at a time of economic austerity within the United Kingdom and across Europe. Since 2008, spending cuts within the United Kingdom have had a bearing on the extent of intervention programmes for young people who have experienced online harm, treatment provision for sexual offenders in custody and the community and on high-quality research investigating the impact of work with young people and sexual offenders. In this climate of limited resources, there is a need for effective information exchange across professionals working with both young people and sexual offenders.

Evidence repeatedly shows that interventions can have important cross-disciplinary and cross-agency benefits, reducing the 'silo' effect in particular professions and agencies. A recent example in the United Kingdom is the response to the long history of sexual offending by the late celebrity Jimmy Savile (Gray & Watt, 2013). Currently, there are five separate enquires relating to this involving historical sexual offending within organizations, care homes, hospitals and other authorities who ignored young people's complaints of abuse; abuse which has been described as 'hidden in plain sight' (Gray & Watt, 2013). What is absent is one enquiry drawing all these separate threads of information and learning together.

The EOGP advocated effectively tackling online grooming by integrating responses within a public health model across a range of professions. This type of model has been selected because of its universality and potential for intervention at different levels of risk and treatment requirement. The components of this model are shown in Figure 8.1 below.

Setting the challenge of online harm as a population-based public health issue compels inter-agency and interdisciplinary working. Various strategic steps have been taken (see Chapter 1), for example, the formation of the UK Council for Child Internet Safety to inform online safety policy responses in the United Kingdom. But there is still work to do to maximize the strategic and operational benefits from committed partnership working. It is only by working in collaboration across disciplines that we can encompass the dangers online that are related to situations, individuals, families and those inherent in the design and use of technology.

However, significant challenges remain. First, the exponential growth in use of mobile technology amongst young people in the developing world, in countries where there is an absence of a strong child protection legislative and policy framework, leaves children particularly vulnerable to online abuse internationally. This, coupled with the absence of empirical evidence to underpin practice in a wider context, is of concern. Recent research in the Middle East also suggests there are key cultural

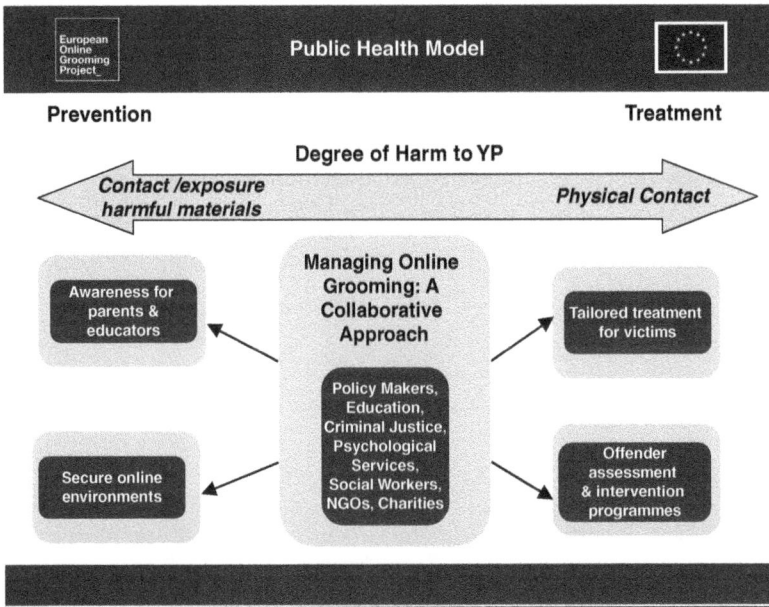

Figure 8.1 Public health approach to tacking online grooming
Source: Webster et al. (2012).

issues which underpin online behaviour by young people, particularly on social networking sites; an aspect rarely considered in the current literature (Davidson & Martellozzo, 2012).

Second, as noted in Chapter 1, the child safety initiatives and law-enforcement initiatives at national level have little impact in the absence of effective legislative frameworks. There is an urgent need for the development of collaborative and effective international frameworks that have a shared definition not only of risk and sexual abuse, but even at the level of what constitutes a *child*. As Kennedy (2013) has argued, the introduction of an internationally unified age of consent and international law courts to address global child abuse (online and offline) seems particularly pertinent in the light of global internet-mediated sexual crimes against children.

We are now at an important stage in trying to both understand and cope with the impacts of technology on everyday life. The benefits are multiple and largely self-evident, but the risks often hidden, misunderstood and of a shifting nature. Those responsible for children and young people, and the online providers, need to find innovative ways of reducing risk. Practitioners need to understand the specific damage done by harm online and the profiles of those who harm online in order to effect positive change in both. We hope this book will help to illuminate the way to help others seek innovative ways of combating such problems whilst still celebrating the benefits that technology brings to our society.

Note

1. Available at: http://www.saferinternet.org/web/guest/safer-internet-day.

References

Abracen, J., Looman, J., & Langton, C. M. (2008). Treatment of sexual offenders with psychopathic traits: Recent research development and clinical implications. *Trauma, Violence, & Abuse: A Review Journal, 9*, 144–166.

Absher, J. R., Vogt, B. A., Clark, D. G., Flowers, D. L., Gorman, D. G., & Keyes, J. W. (2000). Hypersexuality and hemiballism due to subthalamic lesion infarction. *Neuropsychiatry, Neuropsychology, and Behavioral Neurology, 13*, 220–229.

Alexy, E. M., Burgess, A. N., & Baker, T. (2005). Internet offenders: Traders, travellers, and combination trader-travellers. *Journal of Interpersonal Violence, 20*, 804–812.

Allen, J. G., Fonagy, P., & Bateman, A. W. (2008). *Mentalizing in Clinical Practice*. Washington, DC: American Psychiatric Publishing.

American Psychiatric Association (APA) (2013). *DSM-5. Diagnostic and Statistical Manual of Mental Disorders – Fifth Edition*. Arlington, VA: American Psychiatric Association.

Anderson, B., Fagan, P., Woodnutt, T., & Chamorro-Premuzic, T. (2012). Facebook psychology: Popular questions answered by research. *Psychology of Popular Media Culture, 1*, 25–37.

Andrews, D. A., & Bonta, J. (2006). *The Psychology of Criminal Conduct* (4th edition). Newark, NJ: LexisNexis.

Andrews, D. A., & Bonta, J. (2010). Rehabilitating criminal justice policy and practice. *Psychology, Public Policy and Law, 16*, 39–55.

Andrews, D. A., Bonta, J., & Hoge, R. D. (1990). Classification for effective rehabilitation: Rediscovering psychology. *Criminal Justice and Behavior, 17*, 19–52.

Baartz, D. (2008). *Australians the Internet and Technology Enabled Child Abuse: A Statistical Profile*. Canberra: Australian Federal Police.

Babchishin, K. M., Hanson, R. K., & Hermann, C. A. (2011). The characteristics of online sexual offenders: A meta analysis. *Sexual Abuse: A Journal of Research and Treatment, 23*, 92–123.

Baker, I. R., & Oswald, D. I. (2010). Shyness and online social networking services. *Journal of Social and Personal Relationships, 27*, 873–889.

Barker, M., & Morgan. R. (1993). *Sex Offenders: A Framework for the Evaluation of Community-based Treatment*. London: Home Office.

Baron-Cohen, S., Jollife, T., Mortimore, C., & Robertson, M. (1997). Another advanced test of theory of mind: evidence from very high functioning adults with autism or Asperger syndrome. *Journal of Child Psychology and Psychiatry, 38*, 813–822

Baumgartner, S. E., Valkenburg, P. M., & Peter, J. (2010). Unwanted online sexual solicitation and risky sexual online behavior across the lifespan. *Journal of Applied Developmental Psychology, 31*, 439–447.

Beech, A. R., Elliott, I. A., Birgden, A., & Findlater, D. (2008). The internet and child sexual offending: A criminological review. *Aggression and Violent Behaviour, 13, 216–228.*

Beier, K. M., Neutze, J., Mundt, I. A., Ahlers, C. J., Goecker, D., Konrad, A., & Schaefer, G. A. (2009). Encouraging self-identified pedophiles and hebephiles to seek professional help: First results of the Berlin Prevention Project Dunkelfeld (PDD). *Child Abuse & Neglect, 33,* 545–549.

Bellak, L., & Goldsmith, L. A. (1984). *The Broad Scope of Ego Function Assessment.* New York, NY: Wiley.

Berlin, F. S., & Hopkins, J. (1981). Sexual deviation syndromes, *Medical Coyle, G.S. Journal, 14,* 119–125.

Bifulco, A., & Thomas, G. (2012). *Understanding Adult Attachment in Family Relationships: Research, Assessment and Intervention.* London: Routledge.

Bifulco, A., Brown, G. W., & Adler, Z. (1991). Early sexual abuse and clinical depression in adult life. *British Journal of Psychiatry, 159,* 115–122.

Bifulco, A., Moran, P., Baines, R., Bunn, A., & Stanford, K. (2003). Exploring psychological abuse in childhood: Association with other abuse and adult clinical depression. *Bulletin of the Menninger Clinic, 66,* 241–258.

Bourke, M. L., & Hernandez, A. E. (2009). The 'Butner Study' redux: A report of the incidence of hands-on child victimization by child pornography offenders. *Journal of Family Violence, 24,* 183–191.

Bourke, P., Ward, T., & Rose, C. (2012). Expertise and sexual offending: A preliminary empirical model. *Journal of Interpersonal Violence, 27,* 2391–2414.

Bowlby, J. (1988). *A Secure Base: Parent-child Attachment and Healthy Human Development.* New York: Basic Books.

Briggs, P., Simon, W. T., & Simonsen, S. (2011). An exploratory study of Internet-initiated sexual offenses and the chat room sex offender: Has the Internet enabled a new typology of sex offender? *Sexual Abuse: A Journal of Research and Treatment, 23,* 72–91.

Brooks, J. H., & Reddon, J. R. (1996). Serum testosterone in violent and nonviolent young offenders. *Journal of Clinical Psychology, 52,* 475–483.

Brown, A., Jago, N., Kerr, J., McNaughton Nicholls, C., Paskell, C. & Webster, S. (2014). Call to keep Children Safe from Sexual Abuse: A Study of the use and effects of the Stop it Now! UK and Ireland Helpline. Retrieved from: http://www.stopitnow-evaluation.co.uk/publications

Cantor, J. M., Kabani, N., Christensen, B. K., Zipursky, R. B., Barbaree, H. W., Dickey, R., Klassen, P. E., Mikulis, D., Kuban, M. E., Blak, B. A., Hanratty, K. M., & Blanchard, R. (2008). Cerebral white matter deficiencies in pedophillic men. *Journal of Psychiatric Research, 42,* 167–183.

Caretti, V. (2000). Psicodinamica della trance dissociativa da videoterminale. [Psychodynamics of the Video-Terminal Dissociative Trance]. In T. Cantelmi, C. Del Miglio, M. Talli, & A. D'Andrea (Eds.), *La mente in Internet: Psicopatologia delle condotte on line* (pp. 92–110). Padova, IT: Piccin.

Caretti, V., Ciulla, S., & Schimmenti, A. (2012). La diagnosi differenziale nella valutazione della psicopatia e del comportamento violento [Differential diagnosis in the assessment of psychopathy and violent behaviors]. *Rivista Sperimentale di Freniatria, 136,* 139–157.

Carney, F. L. (1977). Out-patient treatment of the aggressive offender. *American Journal of Psychotherapy, 31,* 265–274.

Carr, J. (2004). *Child Abuse, Child Pornography and the Internet.* UK NCH. Retrieved from: http://www.make-it-safe.net/esp/pdf/Child_pornography_internet_Carr2004.pdf

Carr, J., & Hilton, Z. (2010). Protecting children online. In J. Davidson & P. Gottschalk (Eds.), *Internet Child Abuse: Current Research, Policy & Practice* (pp. 52–78). London: Routledge.

Cassidy, J., & Shaver, P. (2008). *Handbook of Attachment. Theory, Research and Clinical Applications* (2nd edition). New York, London: Guilford Press.

Child Exploitation and Online Protection Centre (2007). *Strategic Overview 2006–2007*. London: Child Exploitation and Online Protection Centre.

Child Exploitation and Online Protection Centre. (2010). *Annual Review 2009–2010*. Retrieved from: http://ceop.police.uk/publications/

Child Exploitation and Online Protection Centre. (2013). *Annual Review 2012–2013.* Retrieved from: http://ceop.police.uk/Documents/ceopdocs/AnnualReviewCentrePlan2013.pdf.

Child Exploitation and Online Protection Centre. (20 September 2013). *Children Treated like Slaves to Perform Sexual Acts*. Retrieved from: http://ceop.police. uk/Media-Centre/Press-releases/2013/Children-treated-like-slaves-to-perform-sexual-acts-/

Choo, C. W. (2009). Information use and early warning effectiveness: Perspectives and prospects. *Journal of the American Society for Information Science and Technology, 60,* 1071–1082.

Cierpka, M., Grande, T., Rudolf, G., von der Tann, M., Stasch, M., & the OPD Task Force (2007). The Operationalized Psychodynamic Diagnostics system: Clinical relevance, reliability and validity. *Psychopathology, 40,* 209–220.

Clarkin, J. F., Levy, K. N., Lenzenweger, M. F., & Kernberg, O. F. (2004). The Personality Disorders Institute/Borderline Personality Disorder Research Foundation randomized control trial for borderline personality disorder: Rationale, methods, and patient characteristics. *Journal of Personality Disorders, 18,* 52–72.

Craven, S., Brown, S., & Gilchrist, E. (2006). Sexual grooming of children: Review of literature and theoretical considerations. *Journal of Sexual Aggression, 12,* 287–299.

CWIN Nepal. (2011). *Protecting Children Online in Nepal.* Retrieved from: http://www.cwin.org.np/resources/cwin-publications.

Davidson, J. (2006). Victims speak: Comparing child sexual abusers and their victims accounts of offence circumstance, *Journal of Victims and Offenders, 1,* 159–174.

Davidson, J. (2007). *Current Practice and Research into Internet Sex Offending.* Report prepared on behalf of the Risk Management Authority (Scotland). Retrieved from: http://www.rmascotland.gov.uk/files/7612/7263/5791/Current%20Practice%20and%20Research%20into%20Internet%20Sex%20Offending.pdf.

Davidson, J. (2008). *Child Sexual Abuse: Media Representations and Government Reactions*. New York: Routledge-Cavendish.

Davidson, J., & Bifulco, A. (2010). Investigating police practice in the UK: Achieving best evidence in work with young victims of abuse. *Pakistan Journal of Criminology, 1,* 19–46.

Davidson, J., & Gottschalk, P. (2011). Characteristics of the Internet for criminal child sexual abuse by online groomers. *Criminal Justice Studies: A Critical Journal of Crime, Law and Society, 24,* 23–36.

Davidson, J., Grove-Hills, J., Bifulco, A., Webster, S., Gottschalk, P., Caretti, V., & Pham, T. (2010). *European Online Grooming Project: Literature Review and Legislative Context*. European Commission Safer Internet Plus Programme. Retrieved from: http://www.europeanonlinegroomingproject.com.

Davidson, J., & Hamerton, C. (2015). *International Perspectives on Child Victimisation*. London: Routledge. ISBN 9780415579575.

Davidson, J., Lorenz, M., Grove-Hills, J. & Martellozzo, E. (2009). *Evaluation of CEOP ThinkUKnow Internet Safety Programme and Exploration of Young People's Internet Safety Knowledge*. London: Centre for Abuse and Trauma Studies, Kingston University.

Davidson, J., & Martellozzo, E. (2008). Policing the Internet: Protecting vulnerable children from sex offenders in cyberspace. *Police Investigations Police Practice & Research: An International Journal, 9*, 277–289.

Davidson, J., & Martellozzo, E. (2012). Exploring young people's use of social networking sites and digital media in the internet safety context: A comparison of the UK and Bahrain. *International Journal of Information, Communication & Society, 16*, 1456–1476.

Davies, C., Good, J., & Cranmer, S. (2009). *Increasingly Autonomous: Learners Using Technology in the Context of Their Family Lives and Beyond – 14* Individual Case Studies. Coventry: Becta. Retrieved from: http://www.education.ox. ac.uk/research/lntrg/research/the-learner-and-their-context/

De Kerckhove, D. (1995). *The Skin of Culture: Investigating the New Electronic Reality*. Toronto, ON: Somerville House.

De Masi, F. (2007). The paedophile and his inner world. Theoretical and clinical implications. *International Journal of Psychoanalysis, 88*, 147–165.

Department of Education (2013). *Children and Young People Who Were the Subject of a Child Protection Plan (CPP) by Category of Abuse at 31 March*. London: HMSO.

DeYoung, M. (1982). *Sexual Victimisation of Children*. New York: McFarland.

De Young, M. (1988). The indignant page: Techniques of neutralization in the publications of pedophile organisations. *Child Abuse and Neglect, 12*, 583–591.

De Zulueta, F. (2009). Post traumatic stress disorder and attachment. Possible links with borderline personality disorder. *Advances in Psychiatric Treatment, 15*, 172–180.

Diagnostic and Statistical Manual of Mental Disorders, 5th Edition (2013). American Psychiatric Association, Arlington VA.

Døvik, O. (2008). *Rød knapp skal stanse overgripere (Red button shall stop offenders)*, NRK (Norwegian Broadcasting Corporation). Retrieved from: http://www.nrk. no published 11 August 2008.

Dowdell, E. B., Burgess, A. W., & Flores, J. R. (2011). Online social networking patterns among adolescents, young adults and sexual offenders. *The American Journal of Nursing, 11*, 28–36.

Durkin, K. F., & Bryant, C. D. (1999). Propagandizing pederaty: A thematic analysis of the online exculpatory accounts of unrepentant pedophiles. *Deviant Behavior: An Interdisciplinary Journal, 20*, 103–127.

ECPAT (2012). *Global Monitoring: Status of Action Against Commercial Sexual Exploitation of Children*. Sweden. Retrieved from: http://www.ecpat.net/sites/ default/files/A4A_V2_EU_SWEDEN.pdf.

Eke, A. W., Seto, M. C., & Williams, J. (2011). Examining the criminal history and future offending of child pornography offenders. An extended prospective follow-up study. *Law and Human Behaviour, 35*, 466–478.

Elliott, I. A., & Beech, A. R. (2009). Understanding online child pornography use: Applying sexual offender theory to Internet offenders. *Aggression and Violent Behaviour, 14*, 180–193.

Elliott, I. A., Beech, A. R., Mandeville-Norden, T., & Hayes, E. (2009). Psychological profiles of internet sexual offenders. *Sexual Abuse: A Journal of Research and Treatment, 21*, 76–92.

Elliott, M., Browne, K., & Kilcoyne, J. (1995). Child sexual abuse prevention: What offenders tell us. *Child Abuse and Neglect, 19*, 579–594.

Ellis, A. W., & Young, A. W. (1997). *Human Cognitive Neuropsychology: A Textbook with Readings*. Hove: Psychology Press.

Eynon, R. (2009). *Harnessing Technology: The Learner and Their Context: How Young People use Technologies Outside Formal Education*. Coventry (Becta), UK.

Festinger, L. (1962). Cognitive dissonance. *Scientific American, 207*, 93–107.

Festinger, L., Riecken, H. W., & Schachter, S. (1956). *When Prophecy Fails*. Minneapolis: University of Minnesota Press.

Finkelhor, D. (1984). *Child Sexual Abuse: New Theory and Research*. New York: Free Press.

Finkelhor, D. (2012). Findings from research about online sexual crimes against children and young people in the U.S.and in Europe. *ROBERT Final Conference – Risk Taking Online Behaviour – Young People, Harm and Resilience*, Berlin 23, 24 May. Retrieved from: http://www.childcentre.info/robert/programme.

Finkelhor, D., Araji, S., Baron, L., Browne, A., Peters, S. D., & Wyatt, G. E. (1986). *A Sourcebook on Child Sexual Abuse*. Beverly Hills, CA: Sage Publications.

Finkelhor, D., Kimberly, J., & Wolak, J. (2000). *Online Victimisation: A Report on the Nation's Youth*. Alexandria, Virginia: National Centre for Missing & Exploited Children.

Finkelhor, D., Mitchell, K., & Wolak, J. (2000). *A Report on the Nation's Youth*: Alexandria, Virginia: National Center for Missing and Exploited Children.

Finkelhor, D., Ormrod, R., & Turner, H. (2007). Re-victimization patterns in a national longitudinal sample of children and youth. *Child Abuse and Neglect, 31*, 497–502.

Fonagy, P. (1999). Male perpetrators of violence against women: An attachment theory perspective. *Journal of Applied Psychoanalytic studies, 1*, 1.

Fonagy, P., & Target, M. (1999). Towards understanding violence: The use of the body and the role of the father. In R. Perelberg (Ed.), *Psychoanalytic Understanding of Violence and Suicide* (pp. 53–72). London: Routledge.

Foundation for International Development Research (2009). Retrieved from: http://www.saferinternet.ru.

Freud, S. (1952). *Introductory Lectures on Psycho-Analysis*. 9th Edition. (originally published 1922), London: Allen & Unwin.

Gacono, C., Nieberding, R., Owen, A., Rubel, J., & Bodholdt, R. (2000). Treating conduct disorder, antisocial, and psychopathic personalities. In J. Ashford, B. Sales, & W. Reid (Eds.), *Treating Adult and Juvenile Offenders with Special Needs* (pp. 99–130). Washington, D.C: American Psychological Association.

Gallagher, B. (2000). The extent and nature of known cases of institutional child sex abuse. *British Journal of Social Work, 30*, 795–817.

Gallagher, B., Fraser, C., Christmann, K., & Hodgson, B. (2006). *International and Internet Child Sexual Abuse and Exploitation' Centre of Applied Childhood Studies*. University of Huddersfield, Huddersfield, UK.

Gasser, U., Maclay, C. & Palfrey, J. (2010). Working towards a deeper understanding of digital safety for children and young people in developing nations. Berkman Center Research Publication No. 2010-7; Harvard Public Law Working Paper No. 10-36. Available at SSRN: http://ssrn.com/abstract=1628276.

Gilbert, R., Widom, C. S., Browne, K., Fergusson, D., Webb, E., & Janson, S. (2008). Burden and consequences of child maltreatment in high-income countries. *The Lancet, 373*, 68–81.

Grann, M., Långström, N., Tengström, A., Kullgren, G. (1999). Psychopathy (PCL-R) predicts violent recidivism among criminal offenders with personality disorders in Sweden. *Law and Human Behavior, 23*, 205–217.

Gray, D., & Watt, P. (2013). Giving Victims a Voice: Joint Report into Sexual Allegations Made Against Jimmy Savile. London: NSPCC. Retrieved from: http://www.nspcc.org.uk/news-and-views/our-news/child-protection-news/13-01-11-yewtree-report/yewtree-report-pdf_wdf93652.pdf.

Griffiths, M. (2000). Internet addiction – Time to be taken seriously? *Addiction Research, 8*, 413–418.

Groth, N. A. (1979). *Men who Rape: The Psychology of the Offender*. New York: Plenum.

Grubin, D., & Beech, A. R. (2010). Chemical castration for sex offenders. *British Medical Journal, 340*, c74.

Gudjonsson, G. (1984). The Gudjonsson Blame Attribution Inventory. Personality and Individual Differences, 5, 53–58.

Hall, G. C. N., & Hirschman, R. (1992). Sexual aggression against children: A conceptual perspective of etiology. *Criminal Justice and Behavior, 19*, 8–23.

Hare, R. D. (1998). *Without Conscience: The Disturbing World of Psychopaths Among Us*. New York, NY: Guilford Press.

Hare, R. D. (2003). *Hare's Psychopathy Checklist Revised (PCL-R) – Second Edition. Technical Manual*. Toronto, ON: Multi-Health Systems.

Hare, R. D., & Neumann, C. S. (2008). Psychopathy as a clinical and empirical construct. *Annual Review of Clinical Psychology, 4*, 217–246.

Harkins, L., & Dixon, L. (2010). Sexual offending in groups: An evaluation. *Aggression and Violent Behaviour, 15*, 87–99.

Harris, G. T., & Rice, M. E. (2006). Treatment of psychopathy: A review of empirical findings. In C. Patrick (Ed.), *The Handbook of Psychopathy* (pp. 555–572). New York, NY: Guilford Press.

Hasebrink, U., Livingstone, S., Haddon, L., & Olafsson, K. (2009). *Comparing Children's Online Opportunities and Risks Across Europe: Cross-National Comparisons for EU Kids Online*. London School of Economics and Political Scienice.

Hayes, E., Archer, D., & Middleton, D. (2006). *Internet Sexual Offending Treatment Programme (i-SOTP) Theory Manual*. Unpublished document.

Hayes, S. C., Strosahl, K. D., & Wilson, K. G. (1999). *Acceptance and Commitment Therapy: An experiential approach to behaviour change*. New York: Guilford Press.

Heim, N., & Hursch, C. J. (1979). Castration for sex offenders: Treatment or punishment? A review and critique of recent european literature. *Archives of Sexual Behaviour, 8*, 281–304.

Hijazi-Omari, H., & Ribak, R. (2008). Playing with fire: On the domestication of the mobile phone among Palestinian teenage girls in Israel. *Information, Communication and Society, 11*, 149–166.

Holmes, R. M., & Holmes, S. T. (1996). *Profiling Violent Crimes: An Investigative Tool* (2nd edition). Thousand Oaks, CA: Sage.

Holt, T. J., Blevins, K. R., Burkert, N. (2010). Considering the pedophile subculture online. *Sexual Abuse: A Journal of Research and Treatment, 22*, 3–24.

Hucker, S. J., & Bain, J. (1990). Androgenic hormones and sexual assault, In W. L. Marshall, D. R. Laws, & H. C. Barbaree (Eds.), *Handbook of Sexual Assault* (pp. 93–102). New York: Plenum.

ICAC. (2004). *National Centre for Missing and Exploited Children and Boys and Girls.* Paper presented at the NetSmart presentation.

Internet Watch Foundation. (2005). *Annual Report 2005*. Retrieved from https://www.iwf.org.uk/.

Internet Watch Foundation (2012). *Study of Self-Generated Sexually Explicit Images & Videos Featuring Young People Online*. Retrieved from: https://www.iwf.org.uk/assets/media/resources/IWF%20study%20-%20self%20generated%20content%20online_Sept%202012.pdf.

Jones, L. M., Mitchell, K. J., & Finkelhor, D. (2012). Trends in youth Internet victimizations: Findings from three youth Internet safety surveys, 2000–2010. *Journal of Adolescent Health, 50*, 179–186.

Joyal, C., Black, D., & Dassylva, B. (2007). The neuropsychology and neurology of sexual deviance: A review and pilot study. *Sexual Abuse: A Journal of Research and Treatment, 19*, 155–173.

Kaplan, M. S. (1985). *The Impact of Parolees Perceptions of Confidentiality on the Reporting of Their Urges to Interact Sexually with Children*. Unpublished Doctoral Dissertation, New York University.

Kelly, L. (1988). *Surviving Sexual Violence*. Oxford: Blackwell.

Kennedy, H. (2013). War Child's 2013 Policy Forum – 'War – The Next Generation'. Retrieved from https://www.youtube.com/watch?v=duU8Tv3JZpQ.

Kernberg, O. F. (1984). *Severe Personality Disorders: Psychotherapeutic Strategies*. New Haven, CT: Yale University Press.

Kingston, D. A., Seto, M. C., Ahmed, A. G., Fedoroff, P., Firestone, P., & Bradford, J. M. (2012). The role of central and peripheral hormones in sexual and violent recidivism in sex offenders. *Journal of the American Academy of Psychiatry and the Law, 40*, 476–485.

Kline, P. (1987). Psychoanalysis and crime. In B. J. McGurk, D. M. Thornton, & M. Williams (Eds.), *Applying Psychology to Imprisonment: Theory and Practice*. London: HMSO.

Kolpakova, O. (2012). *Online Behaviour Related to Child Sexual Abuse: Focus Groups Findings*. Sweden: ROBERT project. European Commission.

Kool, R. (2011). Prevention by all means? A legal comparison of the criminalization of online grooming and its enforcement. *Utrecht Law Review, 7*, 46–59.

Kraut, R. E., Patterson, M., Lundmark, V., Kiesler, S., Mukopadhyay, T., & Scherlis, W. (1998). Internet paradox: A social technology that reduces social involvement and psychological wellbeing? *American Psychologist, 53*, 1017–1031.

Krone, T. (2004). A typology of online child pornography offending. *Trends and Issues in Crime and Criminal Justice, 279*, 1–6.

Krueger, R. B., Kaplan, M. S., & First, M. B. (2009). Sexual and other Axis I diagnoses of 60 males arrested for crimes against children involving the Internet. *CNS Spectrums, 14*, 623–631.

Kuhn, T. S. (1970). *The Structure of Scientific Revolutions.* Chicago: Chicago University Press.

Langevin, R. (1990). Sexual anomolies and the brain. In W. L. Marshall, D. R. Laws, & H. E. Barbaree (Eds.), *Handbook of Sexual Assault: Issues, Theories, and Treatment of the Offender* (pp. 103–113). New York: Plenum Press.

Langevin, R., & Lang, L. A. (1990). Substance abuse among sex offenders. *Annals of Sex Research, 3,* 397–424.

Lanning, K. (2005). Compliant child victims: Confronting an uncomfortable reality. In E. Quayle, & M. Taylor (Eds.), *Viewing Child Pornography on the Internet* (pp. 49–60). Dorset: Russell House Publishing.

Lanyon, R. L. (1991). Theories of sex offending. In C. R. Howells (Ed.), *Clinical Approaches to Sex Offenders and their Victims.* Chichester: J. Wiley and Sons.

Lewis, J., Ritchie, J., Ormston, R., & Morrell, G. (2013). Generalising from qualitative research. In J. Ritchie, J. Lewis, C. McNaughton Nicholls, & R. Ormston (Eds.), *Qualitative Research Practice: A Guide for Social Science Researchers and Students* (pp. 347–367) (2nd edition). London: Sage Publications.

Livingstone, S. (2011). Regulating the internet in the interests of children: emerging European and international approaches In: Mansell, Robin and Raboy, Marc (Eds.) *The Handbook of Global Media and Communication Policy.* Wiley-Blackwell, Oxford, UK, 505-524. ISBN 9781405198714.

Livingstone, S., & Haddon, L. (2009). *EU Kids Online: Final Report. EU Kids Online EC Safer Internet Plus Programme Deliverable D6.5.* London School of Economics and Political Science.

Livingstone, S., Haddon, L., Görzig, A., & Ólafsson, K. (2011). *Risks and Safety on the Internet: The Perspective of European Children. EU Kids Online*: London School of Economics, UK. Retrieved from: http://www.lse.ac.uk/media%40lse/research/EUKidsOnline/EU%20Kids%20II%20(2009–11)/EUKidsOnlineIIReports/D4FullFindings.pdf.

Livingstone, S., Olafsson, K., & Staksrud, E. (2011). *Social Networking, Age and Privacy: EU Kids Online*: London School of Economics, UK. Retrieved from: http://eprints.lse.ac.uk/35849/.

Livingstone, S., Ólafsson, K., O'Neill, B., & Donoso, V. (2012). *Towards a Better Internet for Children: Findings and Recommendations from EU Kids Online to Inform the CEO Coalition.* London School of Economics.

Long, M. L., Alison, L. A., & McManus, M. A. (2013). Child pornography and likelihood of contact abuse: A comparison between contact child sexual offenders and non-contact offenders. *Sexual Abuse: A Journal of Research and Treatment, 25,* 370–395.

Looman, J., Abracen, J., Serin, R., & Marquis, P. (2005). Psychopathy, treatment change, and recidivism in high-risk, high-need sexual offenders. *Journal of Interpersonal Violence, 20,* 549–568.

Lösel, F. (1998). Treatment and management of psychopaths. In D. J. Cooke, A. E. Forth, & R. D. Hare (Eds.), *Psychopathy: Theory, Research, and Implications for Society* (pp. 303–355). Dordrecht, NL: Kluwer.

Lucy Faithfull Foundation (2009). Stop it Now! Helpline Report 2005–2009. Retrieved from: http://www.stopitnow-evaluation.co.uk/media/821738/helpline-report-2005-2009.pdf.

Malesky, L. A. (2007). Predatory online behaviour: Modus operandi of convicted sex offenders in identifying potential victims and contacting minors over the Internet. *Journal of Child Sexual Abuse, 16*, 23–32.

Malesky, L. A., & Ennis, L. (2004). Supportive distortions: Analysis of posts on a pedophile internet message board. *Journal of Addictions and Offender Counselling, 24*, 94–100.

Malloy, L. L., Brubacher, S. P., & Lamb, M. E. (2011). Expected consequences of disclosure revealed in investigative interviews with suspected victims of sexual abuse. *Applied Developmental Science, 15*, 8–19.

Mandeville-Norden, R., & Beech, A. R. (2004). Community based treatment of sex offenders. *Journal of Sexual Aggression, 10*, 193–214.

Mann, R. E., Webster, S. D., Blagden, N., Lee, R., & Williams, F. (2012). Sexual offenders understanding of their sexual interests. *Paper presented at the 31st Annual Conference of the Association for the Treatment of Sexual Abusers*, Denver, Colorado.

Mann, R. E., Webster, S. D., Wakeling, H. C., & Marshall, W. L. (2007). The measurement and influence of child sexual abuse supportive beliefs. *Psychology Crime and Law, 13*, 443–458.

Marshall, W. L. (2005). Therapist style in sex offender treatment. Influence of indices of change. *Sexual Abuse: A Journal of Research & Treatment, 17*, 109–116.

Marshall, W. L., Anderson, D., & Fernandez, Y. (1999). *Cognitive Behavioural Treatment of Sexual Offenders*. New York: Wiley.

Marshall, W. L., Fernandez, Y. M., Serran, G. A., Mulloy, R., Thornton, D., Mann, R. E., & Anderson, D. (2003). Process variables in the treatment of sexual offenders: A review of the relevant literature. *Aggression and Violent Behaviour: A Review Journal, 8*, 205–234.

Marshall, W. L., Laws, D. R., & Barbaree, H. E. (Eds.). (1990). *Handbook of Sexual Assault: Issues, Theories and Treatment of the Offender*. New York: Plenum Press.

Marshall, W. L., Ward, T., Mann, R. E., Moulden, H., Fernandez, Y. M., Serran, G., & Marshall, L. E. (2005). Working positively with sexual offenders: Maximizing the effectiveness of treatment. *Journal of Interpersonal Violence, 20*, 1096–1114.

McCarthy, J. A. (2010). Internet sexual activity: A comparison between contact and non-contact child pornography offenders. *Journal of Sexual Aggression, 16*, 181–195.

McCrae, R. R., & Costa, P. T. (1987). Validation of the five-factor model of personality across instruments and observers. *Journal of Personality and Social Psychology, 52*, 81–90.

McElveney, R., Greene, S., & Hogan, D. (2012). Containing the secret of child sexual abuse. *Journal of Interpersonal Violence, 27*, 1155–1175.

McWilliams, N. (2011). *Psychoanalytic Diagnosis* (2nd edition). New York/London: Guilford Press.

Mesch, G., & Talmud, I. (2006). The quality of online and offline relationships, the role of multiplexity and duration. *The Information Society, 22*, 3.

Middleton, D. (2009). Does treatment work with Internet sex offenders? Emerging findings from the Internet sex offender treatment programme (i-SOTP). *Journal of Sexual Aggression, 15*, 5–19.

Middleton, D., Elliott, I. A., Mandeville-Norden, R., & Beech, A. R. (2006). An investigation into the applicability of the Ward and Siegert Pathways Model of child sexual abuse with Internet offenders. *Psychology, Crime & Law, 12,* 589–603.

Miller, L. (1994). Traumatic brain injury and aggression. In M. Hillbrand & N. J. Pallone (Eds.), *The Psychobiology of Aggression: Engines, Measurement, Control* (pp. 91–103). New York, NY: Haworth.

Miller, L. (2000). The predator's brain: Neuropsychodynamics of serial killers. In L. B. Schlesinger (Ed.), *Serial Offenders: Current Thought, Recent Findings, Unusual Syndromes* (pp. 135–166). Boca Raton: CRC Press.

Miller, L. (2012). *Criminal Psychology: Nature, Nurture, Culture.* Springfield, IL: Thomas.

Miller, L. (2013). Sexual offenses against children: Patterns and motives. *Aggression and Violent Behavior, 18,* 506–519.

Mitchell, K. J., Finkelhor, D., & Wolak, J. (2007). Youth Internet users at risk for the most serious online sexual solicitations. *American Journal of Preventive Medicine, 32,* 532–537.

Mitchell, K. J., Finkelhor, D., & Wolak, J. (2010). Conceptualizing juvenile prostitution as child maltreatment: Findings from the National Juvenile Prostitution Study. *Child Maltreatment, 15,* 18–36.

Mitchell, K. J., Jones, L. M., Finkelhor, D., & Wolak, J. (2011). Internet-facilitated commercial sexual exploitation of children: Findings from a nationally representative sample of law enforcement agencies in the United States. *Sexual Abuse: A Journal of Research and Treatment, 23,* 43–71.

Mitchell, K. J., & Wells, M. (2007). Problematic internet experiences: Primary or secondary presenting problems in persons seeking mental health care? *Social Science & Medicine, 65,* 1136–1141.

Mrazek, P. B., & Kemp, C. H. (1981). *Sexually Abused Children and Their Families.* Oxford: Pergamon.

National Society for the Prevention of Cruelty to Children. (2014). The experiences of 11-16 year olds on social networking sites. Retrieved from: http://www.nspcc.org.uk/Inform/resourcesforprofessionals/onlinesafety/11-16-social-networking-sites_wda101495.html.

Neutze, J., Seto, M. C., Schaefer, G. A., Mundt, I. A., & Beier, K. M. (2011). Predictors of child pornography offences and child sexual abuse in a community sample of pedohiles and hebephiles. *Sexual Abuse: A Journal of Research and Treatment, 23,* 212–242.

Noll, J., Haralson, K., Butler, E., & Shenk, C. (2011). Childhood maltreatment, psychological dysregulation, and risky sexual behaviors in female adolescents. *Journal of Paediatric Psychology: Advance Access,* 1–10. Retrieved from: http://www.doi: doi:10.1093/jpepsy/jsr003.

O'Brien, M. D., & Webster, S. D. (2007). The construction and preliminary validation of the Internet Behaviours & Attitudes Questionnaire (IBAQ). *Sexual Abuse: A Journal of Research and Treatment, 19,* 237–256.

O'Brien, M. D., & Webster, S. D. (2010). Assessment and treatment approaches with online sexual offenders. In J. Davidson & P. Gottschalk (Eds.), *Internet Child Abuse: Current Research and Practice.* London: Routledge.

O'Connell, R. (2003). *A typology of cyber sexploitation and online grooming practices. Preston.* England: University of Central Lancashire. Retrieved from: http://www.jisc.ac.uk/uploaded_documents/lis_PaperJPrice.pdf.

Ofcom (2013). *Children and Parents: Media Use and Attitudes Reports.* Retrieved from: http://stakeholders.ofcom.org.uk/binaries/research/media-literacy/october-2013/research07Oct2013.pdf

Ofsted (2012). *Inspecting Esafety: Briefing for Inspectors.* Retrieved from: http://www.e2bn.org/files/Inspecting_esafety.pdf.

Ogloff, J. R. P., & Wood, M. (2010). The treatment of psychopathy: Clinical nihilism or steps in the right direction? In L. Malatesti & J. McMillan (Eds.), *Responsibility and Psychopathy: Interfacing Law, Psychiatry, and Philosophy* (pp. 155–181). Oxford: Oxford University Press.

O'Halloran, E., & Quayle, E. (2010). A content analysis of a 'Boy Love' support forum: Revisiting Durkin and Bryant. *Journal of Sexual Aggression, 16,* 71–85.

Oldmeadow, J., Quinn, S., & Kowert, R. (2013). Attachment style, social skills, and Facebook use amongst adults *Computers in Human Behavior archive, 29,* 1142–1149.

O'Leary, P. J., & Barber, J. (2008). Gender differences in silencing following childhood sexual abuse. *Journal of Child Sexual Abuse, 17,* 133–143.

Olver, M. E., & Wong, S. C. P. (2009). Therapeutic responses of psychopathic sexual offenders: Treatment attrition, therapeutic change, and long-term recidivism. *Journal of Consulting and Clinical Psychology, 77,* 328–336.

Ortmann, J. (1980). The treatment of sexual offenders. Castration and antihormone therapy. *International Journal of Law and Psychiatry, 3,* 443–451.

Ospina, M., Harstall, C., & Dennett, L. (2010). *Sexual Exploitation of Children and Youth.* Alberta: Institute of Health Economics.

Page, K., & Mapstone, M. (2010). How does the web make you feel? Exploring the positive digital native rhetoric. *Journal of marketing and management, 26,* 1345–1366.

Palmer, T. (2005). Behind the screen: Children who are the subjects of abusive images. In E. Quayle & M. Taylor (Eds.), *Viewing Child Pornography on the Internet* (pp. 61–74). Dorset: Russell House Publishing.

Palmer, T. (2009). *Children and Young People Harmed Via the New Technologies – What Works in Practice?* Paper presented at the Child Safety on the Internet: Prevention, Education and Cooperation. Expert Group for Co-operation on Children and Risk Moscow.

Palmer, T., & Stacey, L. (2004). *Just One Click: Sexual Abuse of Children and Young People Through the Internet and Mobile Telephone Technology.* Ilford, UK: Barnardos.

PDM Task Force (2006). *Psychodynamic Diagnostic Manual (PDM).* Silver Spring, MD: Alliance of Psychoanalytic Organizations.

Plan India (2010). *Because I am a Girl – Digital and Urban Frontiers: Girls in a Changing Landscape.* Retrieved from: http://plan-international.org/files/global/publications/campaigns/BIAAG_2010_EN2.pdf.

Prichard, J., Watters, P. A., & Spiranovic, C. (2011). Internet subcultures and pathways to the use of child pornography. *Computer Law and Security Review, 27,* 585–600.

Quayle, E. (2007, April). *Intervention With Internet Offenders.* Paper presented at the Conference of the Australia New Zealand Association for the Treatment of Sexual Abuse.

Quayle, E. (2008). *Child pornography and sexual exploitation of children online*: ECPAT International. Rio de Janeiro, Brazil. Retrieved from: http://www. childcentre.info/public/Thematic_Paper_ICTPsy_ENG.pdf.

Quayle, E. (2009). *Abuse images of children: identifying gaps in our knowledge*. Unpublished paper delivered at the G8 Global Symposium, University of North Carolina, 6–7 April 2009.

Quayle, E., & Taylor, M. (2002). Paedophiles, pornography and the internet: Assessment issues. *British Journal of Social Work, 32*, 863–875.

Quayle, E., & Taylor, M. (2003). Model of problematic internet use in people with a sexual interest in children. *CyberPsychology & Behaviour, 6*, 93–106.

Quayle, E., Allegro, S., Hutton, L., Sheath, M., & Loof, L. (2012). *Online Behaviour Related to Child Sexual Abuse: Creating a Private Space in Which to Offend: Interviews with Online Child Sex Offenders*. Retrieved from: http://www.childcentre. info/robert/public/Interviews_online_offenders.pdf.

Quayle, E., Jonsson, L., & Lööf, L. (2012). *Online Behaviour Related to Child Sexual Abuse: Interviews With Affected Young People*. ROBERT Project (Risktaking Online Behaviour Empowerment Through Research and Training), European Union and Council of the Baltic Sea States.

Quayle, E., Loof, L., & Palmer, T. (2008). *Child Pornography and Sexual Exploitation of Children Online*. Bangkok: ECPAT International.

Rada, R. T., Laws, D. R., & Kellner, R. (1976). Plasma testosterone levels in the rapist. *Journal of Psychosomatic Medicine, 38*, 257–268.

Radford, L., Corral, S., Bradley, C., Fisher, H. L., Bassett, C., Howat, N., & Collishaw, S. (2011). *Child Abuse and Neglect in the UK Today*. London: NSPCC.

Reich, S. M., Subrahmanyan, K., & Espinoza, G. (2012). Friending, IMing and hanging out face-to-face: overlap in adolescents online and offline social contacts. *Devleopmental Psychology, 48*, 356–368.

Rice, M. E., & Harris, G. T. (2003). What we know and don't know about treating sex offenders. In B. J. Winick & J. Q. LaFond (Eds.), *Protecting Society from Sexually Dangerous Offenders: Law, Justice, and Therapy* (pp. 101–117). Washington, DC: American Psychological Association.

Rice, M. E., Harris, G. T., & Cormier, C. A. (1992). An evaluation of a maximum security therapeutic community for psychopaths and other mentally disordered offenders. *Law and Human Behavior, 16*, 399–412.

Ritchie, J., & Lewis, J. (2003). *Qualitative Research Practice: A Guide for Social Science Students and Researchers*. London: Sage.

Robbins, P., & Darlington, R. (2003). The role of the industry and the Internet Watch Foundation. In A. MacVean & P. Spindler (Eds.), *Policing Paedophiles on the Internet* (pp 79–86). John Grieve Centre for Policing and Community Safety. The New Police Bookshop. ISBN 1-90363-912-3.

Russell, D. E. H. (1984). *Sexual Exploitation – Rape, Child Sexual Abuse, and Workplace Harassment* (Vol. 155 of Sage library of social research). Beverly Hills: Sage Publications.

Salekin, R. T. (2002). Psychopathy and therapeutic pessimism. Clinical lore or clinical reality? *Clinical Psychology Review, 22*, 79–112.

Salter, A. (1988). *Treating Child Sex Offenders and Victims: A Practical Guide*. California: Sage.

Schimmenti, A., & Caretti, V. (2010). Psychic retreats or psychic pits? Unbearable states of mind and technological addiction. *Psychoanalytic Psychology, 27,* 115–132.

Schimmenti, A., Craparo, G., Ciulla, S., & Caretti, V. (2013). The mental functioning of the groomer: a psychodynamic perspective. *CRINVE 2013. II International Congress of the Advanced High School of Criminological Sciences,* 236–239.

Schimmenti, A., Guglielmucci, F., Barbasio, C. P., & Granieri, A. (2012). Attachment disorganization and dissociation in virtual worlds: A study on problematic Internet use among players of online role-playing games. *Clinical Neuropsychiatry, 9,* 195–202.

Schulz, A., Bergen, E., Schuhmann, P., Hoyer, J., Santtila, P., & Osterheider, M. (2014). *Prevalence of Online Sexual Solicitation of Children and Adolescents in an International Online Survey of Adult Internet Users.* Manuscript submitted for publication.

Serran, G. A., Fernandez, Y. M., Marshall, W. L., & Mann, R. E. (2003). Process issues in treatment: Application to sexual offender programs. *Professional Psychology: Research and Practice, 34,* 368–374.

Seto, M. C. (2009). *Assessing the Risk Posed by Child Pornography Offenders.* Paper presented at Global Symposium for Examining the Relationship between Online and Offline Offenses and Preventing the Sexual Exploitation of Children, University of North Carolina, 6–7 April.

Seto, M. C., & Barbaree, H. E. (1999). Psychopathy, treatment behavior and sex offender recidivism. *Journal of Interpersonal Violence, 14,* 1235–1248.

Seto, M. C., & Eke, A. (2005). The criminal histories and later offending of child pornography offenders. *Sexual Abuse: A Journal of Research and Treatment, 17*(2), 201–210.

Seto, M. C., Cantor, J. M., & Blanchard, R. (2006). Child pornography offenses are a valid diagnostic indicator of pedophilia. *Journal of Abnormal Psychology, 115,* 610–615.

Seto, M. C., Hanson, R. K., & Babchishin, K. (2011). Contact sexual offending by men arrested of child pornography offences. *Sexual Abuse: A Journal of Research & Treatment, 23,* 124–145.

Seto, M. C., Wood, J. M., Babchishin, K. M., & Flynn, S. (2012). Online solicitation offenders are different from child pornography offenders and lower risk contact sexual offenders. *Law and Human Behavior, 36,* 320–330.

Shedler, J., & Westen, D. (2004). Dimensions of personality pathology: An alternative to the five factor model. *American Journal of Psychiatry, 161,* 1743–1754.

Simon, H. A. (1980). Cognitive science: The newest science of the artificial. *Cognitive Science, 4,* 33–46.

Simon, H. A., & Kaplan, C. A. (1989). Foundations of cognitive science. In M. I. Posner (Ed.), *Foundations of Cognitive Science.* Cambridge, MA: MIT Press.

Skeem, J. L., Monahan, J., & Mulvey, E. P. (2002). Psychopathy, treatment involvement, and subsequent violence among civil psychiatric patients. *Law and Human Behavior, 26,* 577–603.

Smahel, D., Brown, B. B., & Blinka, I. (2012). Association between online friendship and internet addiction among adolescents and emerging adults. *Developmental Psychology, 48,* 238–381.

Soderstrom, H., Sjodin, A. K., Carlstedt, A., & Forsman, A. (2004). Adult psychopathic personality with childhood-onset hyperactivity and conduct disorder:

A central problem constellation in forensic psychiatry. *Psychiatry Research, 121,* 271–280.

Sparks, C. (1982). *The Discovery of Animal Behaviour.* London: Macmillan.

Spencer, L., Ritchie, J., O'Conner, W., Morrell, G., & Ormston, R. (2013). Analysis in practice. In J. Ritchie, J. Lewis, C. McNaughton Nicholls, & R. Ormston (Eds.), *Qualitative Research Practice: A Guide for Social Science Researchers and Students.* (2nd edition). London: Sage Publications.

Spindler, P. (2013). *Key Child Protection Challenges in the Real and Digital Worlds: Implications for Research, Policy & Practice.* Retrieved from: http://www.cats-rp.org.uk/media_and_news.htm.

Sturup, G. K. (1968). Treatment of sexual offenders in Herstedvester Denmark: The rapists. *Acta Psychiatrica Scandinavia Supplement, 204,* 5–62.

Sturup, G. K. (1971). Treatment of the sex offender. Castration: the total treatment. *International Journal of Clinical Psychiatry, 8,* 175–196.

Suler, J. (2004). The online disinhibition effect. *Cyberpsychology and Behavior, 7,* 321–326.

Sullivan, J. (2009). *Professionals Who Sexually Abuse the Children With Whom They Work.* Unpublished Ph.D. Thesis, School of Psychology, University of Birmingham.

Taylor, M., Holland, G., & Quayle, E. (2001). Typology of paedophile picture collections. *The Police Journal, 74,* 97–107.

Teicher, M., Ito, Y., Glod, C. A., Andersen, S. L., Dumont, N., & Ackerman, E. (1997). Preliminary evidence for abnormal cortical development in physically and sexually abused children using EEG coherence and MRI. *Annals of the New York Academy of Science, 821,* 160–175.

The Guardian (2013). *Digital kids: How children are using devices, apps and media in 2013.* Retrieved from: http://www.theguardian.com/technology/2013/oct/31/digital-kids-devices-apps-media.

Turkle, S. (2011). *Alone Together. Why We Expect More From Technology and Less From Each Other.* New York, NY: Basic Books.

United Nations International Telecommunications Unit World Statistics. (2014). http://www.itu.int/en/ITU-D/Statistics/Pages/stat/default.aspx?utm_source=twitterfeed&utm_medium=twitter.

Valkenburg, P. M., & Peter, J. (2011). Online communication among adolescents: An integrated model on its attraction, opportunities and risks. *New Media and Society, 7,* 383–402.

Wakeling, H. C., Howard, P., & Barnett, G. (2011). Comparing the validity of the RM2000 scales and OGRS3 for prediciting recidivism by Internet sexual offenders. *Sexual Abuse: A Journal of Research & Treatment, 23,* 146–168.

War Child. (2013). *Policy Forum War – The Next Generation.* Retrieved from: http://www.youtube.com/watch?v=duU8Tv3JZpQ.

Ward, T., & Hudson, S. M. (1998). A model of the relapse process in sexual offenders. *Journal of Interpersonal Violence, 13,* 700–725.

Ward, T., Hudson, S. M., & Marshall, W. L. (1996). Attachment style in sex offenders: A preliminary study. *Journal of Sex Research, 33,* 17–26.

Ward, T., Hudson, S. M., Marshall, W. L., & Siegert, R. (1995). Attachment style and intimacy deficits in sex offenders: A theoretical framework. *Sexual Abuse: A Journal of Research and Treatment, 7,* 317–335.

Ward, T., & Siegert, R. J. (2002). Toward a comprehensive theory of child sexual abuse: A theory knitting perspective. *Psychology, Crime & Law, 8,* 319–351.

Ward, T., & Stewart, C. (2003). Criminogenic needs and human needs: A theoretical model. *Psychology, Crime and Law, 9,* 125–143.

Webb, L., Craissati, J., & Keen, S. (2007). Characteristics of internet child pornography offenders: A comparison with child molesters. *Sexual Abuse, 19,* 449–465.

Webster, S., Davidson, J., Bifulco, A., Gottschalk, P., Caretti, V., Pham, T., Grove-Hills, J. (2010). *European Online Grooming Project: Scoping Report.* European Commission Safer Internet Plus Programme. Retrieved from: http://www.europeanonlinegroomingproject.com/

Webster, S., Davidson, J., Bifulco, A., Gottschalk, P., Caretti, V., Pham, T., Grove-Hills, J., Turley, C., Tompkins, C., Ciulla, S., Milazzo, V., Schimmenti, A., & Craparo, G. (2012). *Final Report. European Online Grooming Project.* European Commission Safer Internet Plus Programme. Retrieved from: http://www.europeanonlinegroomingproject.com/wp-content/file-uploads/European-Online-Grooming-Project-Final-Report.pdf.

Webster, S. D., & Marshall, W. L. (2004). Generating data with sexual offenders using qualitative material: A paradigm to complement not compete with quantitative methodology. *Journal of Sexual Aggression, 10,* 117–122.

Webster, S. D., Mann, R. E., Thornton, D., & Wakeling, H. C. (2007). Further validation of the Short Self-Esteem Scale with sexual offenders. *Legal and Criminological Psychology, 12,* 207–216.

Weldon, E. V. (1988). *Mother, Madonna, Whore: The Idealisation and Denegration of Motherhood.* London: Free Association Press.

Wells, M., & Mitchell, K. (2008). *How do High Risk Youth Use the Internet? Characteristics & Implications for Prevention. Child Maltreatment, Online First.* Retrieved from: http://cmx.sagepub.com/cgi/rapidpdf/1077559507312962v1.

Whittle, H., Hamilton-Giachritsis, C., Beech, A. R., & Collings, G. (2013a). A review of online grooming: Characteristics and concerns. *Aggression and Violent Behavior, 18,* 62–70.

Whittle, H. C., Hamilton-Giachritsis, C., Beech, A., & Collings, G. (2013b). A review of young people's vulnerabilities to online grooming. *Aggression and Violent Behavior, 18,* 135–146.

Williams, R., Elliott, I. A., & Beech, A. R. (2013). Identifying sexual grooming themes used by internet sex offenders. *Deviant Behavior, 34,* 135–152.

Wolak, J., Finkelhor, D., & Mitchell, K. (2004). Internet-initiated sex crimes against minors: Implications for prevention based on findings from a national study. *Journal of Adolescent Health, 35,* e11–e20.

Wolak, J., Finkelhor, D., & Mitchell, K. (2008). Is talking online to unknown people always risky? Distinguishing online interaction types in a national sample of youth internet users. *CyberPsychology & Behavior, 11,* 340–343.

Wolak, J., Finkelhor, D., & Mitchell, K. (2009). *Trends in Arrests of 'Online Predators'.* Crimes Against Children Research Center, Durham: NH. Retrieved from: http://www.unh.edu/ccrc/pdf/CV194.pdf.

Wolak, J., Finkelhor, D., Mitchell, K. J., & Ybarra, M. L. (2010). Online 'predators' and their victims: Myths, realities, and implications for prevention and treatment. *American Psychologist, 63,* 111–128.

Wolak, J., Mitchell, K., & Finkelhor, D. (2006). *Online Victimisation of Youth – 5 Years Later.* New Hampshire: University of New Hampshire.

Wolf, S. C. (1984). A multi-factor model of deviant sexuality. In T. Morrison, M. Erooga, & R. Beckett (Eds.), *Sexual Offending Against Children.* London: Routledge.

Wong, S., & Hare, R. D. (2005). *Guidelines for a Psychopathy Treatment Program.* Toronto, ON: Multihealth Systems

World Health Organization (WHO) (1992). *International Classification of Diseases and Related Health Problems, Tenth Revision* (ICD-10). Odessa, FL: WHO.

Wortley, R., & Smallbone, S. (Eds.). (2006). *Situational Prevention of Child Sexual Abuse. Crime Prevention Studies.* Monsey, NY: Criminal Justice Press.

Ybarra, M. L., Espelage, D. L., & Mitchell, K. J. (2007). The co-occurrence of internet harassment and unwanted sexual solicitation vicitmisation and perpetration: Associations with psychosocial indicators. *Journal of Adolescent Mental Health, 41,* 31–41.

Young, K. (2005). Profiling online sex offenders, cyber-predators, and pedophiles. *Journal of Behavioural Profiling, 5,* 1–18.

Zasler, N. D. (1994). Sexual dysfunction. In J. M. Silver, S. C. Yudofsy, & R. E. Hales (Eds.), *Neuropsychiatry of Traumatic Brain Injury* (pp. 274–312). Washington, DC: American Psychiatric Press.

Zimbardo, P.G. (1969). The human choice: Individuation, reason, and order vs. deindividuation, impulse, and chaos. In W.J. Arnold & D. Levine (Eds.), *Nebraska Symposium on Motivation* (pp. 237-307). Lincoln: University of Nebraska Press.

Index

Printed and bound by CPI Group (UK) Ltd, Croydon, CR0 4YY